Beyond the Northern Lights

Dedication

This book is dedicated to my wife Mary;
my sons Bill, Ron and Dick;
my daughters Rosanne and Nancy;
and, all lovers of the outdoor life.

Beyond the Northern Lights

A Quest for the Outdoor Life

by W. H. Bell

hancock

house

ISBN 0-88839-432-2

Cataloging in Publication Data
Bell, W. H. (William Harold), 1927–
 Beyond the northern lights

 ISBN 0-88839-432-2

 1. Bell, W. H. (William Harold), 1927- 2. Game wardens--
Northwest Territories--Biography. 3. Forest rangers--
Northwest Territories--Biography. I. Title.
 SK354.B46A3 1998   639.9'092   C98-910500-8

We acknowledge the financial support of the Government of Canada through the
Book Publishing Industry Development Program for our publishing activities.

Editor: Sharon Boglari and Nancy Miller
Production: Nancy Miller and Ingrid Luters
Cover Photo: Courtesy of W. H. Bell

Published simultaneously in Canada and the United States by

HANCOCK HOUSE PUBLISHERS LTD.
19313 Zero Avenue, Surrey, B.C. V4P 1M7
(604) 538-1114 Fax (604) 538-2262

HANCOCK HOUSE PUBLISHERS
1431 Harrison Avenue, Blaine, WA 98230
(604) 538-1114 Fax (604) 538-2262
Web Site: www.hancockhouse.com *email:* sales@hancockhouse.com

Contents

Preface

*B*eyond the Northern Lights is a story about the attractions of an outdoor life and how they formed the driving force for my youthful ambitions, culminating in a career as a guardian of the forests and its animal inhabitants. It is also a tribute to things that no longer exist except in my memory—the Calgary of my youth and a simpler, more innocent time.

I know there are many people who would be delighted to engage in pursuits similar to those I describe—traveling secluded byways far from the stress of urban overcrowding, coping with climate at a primordial level, confronting nature in the raw—but who can only partake of such experiences vicariously through the medium of the printed word. I hope they will find pleasure in these pages.

The events related here are based on personal experience. The participants are real people, identified by their actual names when they could be dredged from my memory, although I have twice deliberately neglected to provide surnames to avoid causing anguish or embarrassment to the persons involved or to their families.

The Greenhorn

There I was, upside down, flying through the unfriendly sky and gazing in dismay at the dark earth below, its threatening contours cloaked in deep shadows. Above me, the dull gray firmament was just beginning to brighten, heralding the dawn of a bitter cold day. The controls of my craft seemed clumsy and ineffective. I twisted them this way and that, but all in vain—nothing functioned properly.

No, this is not a story about World War I "dogfights." Such tales often start with a pilot dramatically exclaiming: "There I was, upside down..." as he commences another improbable yarn about his harrowing escapades. I did have some involvement with dogfights, though—sled dogfights—and, at the time this narrative begins, I certainly was upside down and hurtling through the air.

Had there been any eyewitnesses around that day in 1952 to observe the involuntary acrobatics of their local game warden, peals of laughter would have rent the brittle winter sky. That warden was me, the newly appointed (and very inexperienced) guardian of 40,000 square miles of remote wilderness in the Mackenzie District of Canada's Northwest Territories. My home base was the small settlement of Fort Resolution on the south shore of Great Slave Lake. I had a lot to learn.

Earlier that morning I had decided to check the condition of my patrol boat, a cabin cruiser hauled out of the lake for the duration of the winter at a convenient location about two miles from the village. The round trip would be a suitable distance for my dog team's first outing of the season. Not yet fully acquainted with their strength, and desiring to exercise each member of the team equally, I harnessed all five dogs to the empty sled. Little did I know.

There was a stout rope attached to the sled, which I had sufficient foresight to tie to a sturdy wooden post embedded in the frozen ground near the dog compound. This prevented the dogs from traveling away with the equipment before I was ready to go with them. Perhaps I should have anticipated some future excitement after putting the first two dogs in harness. Eager for a run and straining hard against the traces, they were able to bounce the heavy sled off the ground with every lunge they made. I finished hooking up the five dogs and silently congratulated myself on the ease with which I—a complete novice—had accomplished the task. Then I stood on the rear of the sled, grabbed the upright handlebars with one hand and, with the other, slipped the knot on the restraining anchor rope. Away we went at breakneck speed!

In front of the warden station lay the road to the local airstrip. A snowplow had, on several occasions, cleared accumulations of snow from it, leaving a high snowbank on one side. The dogs hurled themselves over that obstacle at full throttle. The sled followed, only to be projected up the slope of the snowbank and launched into space like a rocket on a trip to the moon. Somewhere on the way to orbital altitude it turned over, with me standing on the rear, maintaining a death grip on the handlebars. There I was, upside down...

Time stood still as I hung suspended in mid-flight, momentarily defying gravity. My breath formed a smoky wreath, flecks of ice dispersing gently in the frosty air. It was twenty degrees below zero. The absence of atmospheric detail gave an illusory sense of tranquility. I looked down to see my feet planted firmly on the rear boards—but, strangely, the sky was beneath the sled. Above me, the snow-covered earth moved with surrealistic slowness by my head. Something was definitely wrong here.

Suddenly I crashed to the ground and the sled was torn from my grasp. I tumbled over once or twice before my forward momentum was completely expended. Then I slowly raised my head and peered about. Time had resumed its inexorable pace. The anchor rope was slithering rapidly by me like a jet-propelled snake. I lunged desperately at it but couldn't wrap my heavy gauntlets securely around it. I had to grab that length of hemp or lose the team. It sizzled through my mitts until the knot at the trailing end fetched up against my hands. Then I was able to hold tight. The rope moved relentlessly on, dragging my prone form along with it, hauling me over the frozen crust on my chest. My shouts of "whoa" just made the perverse dogs—and the rope— move faster. Finally, I couldn't hang on any longer and had to relinquish my grip.

Regaining my composure, I stood up to watch the team disappearing in the distance, with the now upright sled bumping along at a great rate, swaying from side to side, and the anchor rope trailing out behind. I shook myself carefully, one appendage at a time, assuring that all my bones were still intact. The collapsing snow crusts and my thick parka had cushioned the fall. Sob! My brand-new parka—tailor-made by a local seamstress at great expense! The front of it was torn completely away as a result of that brief excursion over the sandpaper-like snow crystals.

Fortunately, I was just a short distance from home, rather than many miles out in the bush. At least I would not have to walk for several days seeking safe haven, freezing and hungry, all my means of sustenance gone with the sled. It was a lesson well-learned for later occasions when I would be far from assistance. But, oh, the ignominy of it all!

Plodding along in the wake of the wayward animals, I wondered what a city boy like me was doing up here in the frozen North instead of having a soft job in a warmer climate. As the shock of the spill dissipated, the explanation became clear—I was here because my goal had always been to pursue a career in the Great Outdoors.

The Future Foreshadowed

One Christmas when I was a youngster, an aunt presented me with a book which gave me my direction in life. The book was titled *Snowshoes and Sledges*, by Kirk Munroe. According to the dust jacket: "Any adventurous-minded boy will thrill to this strange and exciting tale of the frozen North." How true! It was a marvelous story of the Yukon River country, full of adventure and exploration, trappers and traders, wolves and moose, danger and excitement—an enthralling tale for an imaginative youngster. The story took place mostly in winter and it kindled in me a strong desire to live and work in the "great white wilderness."

My aunt certainly knew about my predilection for the outdoors. She never heard me talk about anything else (except for flying, and she'd previously given me a book on that subject). It seemed that I was destined for an outdoor life. A solitary child by nature, I delighted in roaming the vacant landscape near our Calgary home, where neighboring fields were still in a primitive state. Wild flowers grew there in profusion—buffalo beans and bluebells and brown-eyed susans. The occasional clumps of trees and bushes harbored robins, orioles and yellow warblers. Meadow larks voiced melodic serenades from atop old fence posts, and swallows dashed erratically through the air in pursuit of insects. I would lie back in the tall grass, hidden away from the world, watching phantasmagorial cloud forms parade by in the summer sky, while listening to the avian assembly singing their sweet songs just for me.

A few small ravines penetrated a nearby hillside. Saskatoon and chokecherry bushes grew in the sheltered folds, nurtured by moisture and sunshine. There were small groves of aspens, their leaves quivering in the slightest breeze. In this milieu a boy could do many exciting things: discover strange new lands, explore secret trails and treasure caves, construct native huts and hideaways. My imagination was unlimited—I was the monarch of a great outdoor kingdom.

Later, living near the confluence of the Bow and Elbow Rivers—a locality of historical fame because the Royal Northwest Mounted Police had constructed Fort Calgary on the western side of the junction in 1875—a new world opened for me. While the Elbow River flowed placidly through an urban setting, the larger Bow River, with its wooded banks, backwaters and stagnant pools, and swift main stream, was much more attractive. Convolutions of the dark cold surface waters presented fascinating ever-changing patterns. The river marge was covered with brush and trees—in some places for hundreds of feet back from the water's edge. I was ecstatic about the opportunities for exploration.

Unfortunately, I reckoned without the restriction imposed by my parents: "Don't go near the river," emphatically stated. Often, though—on the trip between school and home—I made a detour to the Bow River, ignoring my conscience. Once there, I would become engrossed in the pleasant surroundings and lose all track of time. When I finally did return home, it was usually to find that the rest of my family had already finished supper. The script would then read something like this:

Mother to son: "Where have you been all this time?"

Son, contritely (after a short pause while several alternate stories were considered): "At the river." Then, following on quickly, "I would have been home sooner but I lost track of the time." Nothing but the truth—I hoped that the wages of sin might thereby be reduced.

Mother, a rising inflection in her voice: "Young man, how many times have you been told not to go near the river?" An unanswerable question—I'd lost count.

As punishment for my disobedience I was sometimes sent to bed without supper, and a few times with a licking to boot. On weekends, free of school, I would tell my mother that I was going to a friend's house. I would start out with every intention of doing so. Somewhere along the way though, I would usually hear the call of the river—a call that I could never ignore.

There were many ways to occupy one's time in that enchanting environment of woods and water. In the first days of summer, I chased fish trapped in shallow pools left behind by the retreat of the spring freshet from the flooded backwaters. As the river level receded further, exposing gravel bars, I became a "rock hound," collecting stones and breaking them open with a hammer "borrowed" from my father's toolbox, marveling at the complex internal structures and colors of some of the specimens.

I built a tree hut overlooking the river where I could abide quietly, watching the currents and listening to bird song. Sometimes I sought out nests to collect an egg or two. Egg collecting was an honorable hobby then, for educational purposes, but rightly frowned on today for conservation reasons. With the press of "people pollution" (overpopulation, the root cause of all of the world's environmental problems) whole species might be decimated if such collecting were to come into vogue again.

Skinny-dipping was also part of the fun. I used the backwater pools; they were much warmer and safer than the main channel whose dangerous waters were still frigid with the chill of their glacial origins. Sometimes I lashed pieces of driftwood together to form a raft and paddled around in the quiescent shallows. Fortunately, I had sense enough not to take such flimsy craft out into the main stream of the river.

Once, while cruising the river bank, a bright red canoe came drifting down on the current, torn from its moorings somewhere upstream by the spring freshet. A daring swim out into the current rescued the craft, and I subsequently spent several glorious days in the backwashes playing voyageur. Somehow an account of the acquisition leaked out to the local constabulary, resulting in the appearance of a police officer one day just as I landed for the start of the next (imaginary) portage. There was some questioning, a consequent mild reprimand for not reporting the incident promptly, and confiscation of what had seemed like legitimate marine salvage.

I joined the Boy Scouts the year after World War II began. I wanted to go on their overnight hikes, and to participate in the annual Jamboree, an event when most of the Scout troops in the city camped out together for several days on the wooded Pearce property in East Calgary. During the Jamboree there were competitions in various aspects of woodcraft such as firemaking and tracking, not to mention the nocturnal contests in tent-collapsing and similar mischief.

I rejoiced in a three-day camping trip up the Elbow River, beyond the army rifle range on the Sarcee Indian Reserve, during an Easter vacation. There were still patches of snow lying on the south bank of the river where the sun's warmth had yet to penetrate, and a skim of ice remained on stretches of quiet water. What fun we had in spite of miserable weather, learning woods lore and improvising bridges across the stream (and drying out by a roaring fire after falling into the frigid waters). For me, the climax of that trip came after our return home when I was publicly commended by the scoutmaster for camping like an expert, being the only member of the troop to set up a campsite that remained dry during a night of cold rain. The scoutmaster himself had been swamped out. His remarks reinforced my belief that I was meant to pursue an outdoor life.

Reading and rereading *Snowshoes and Sledges* led me to seek out other books about the North, not an easy chore in the days when there were no local community libraries. Then I discovered that Calgary had a public library that I could access by taking a lengthy streetcar trip across town. Tickets cost money and my parents could ill afford them, so I had to generate some income of my own. I scavenged back alleys for discarded metal—plumbing materials, bed frames, old car batteries—which I could sell to a local scrap dealer. Iron or steel was worth one cent per pound; lead from batteries brought ten cents a pound. I collected old newspapers from door to door, selling them for a penny a pound to a local florist for use in wrapping bouquets. Less desirable stratagems included lawn-mowing, sidewalk-shoveling and baby-sitting. The going rate for each of these chores was about twenty-five cents per occasion, no matter how much time was involved.

At the library I found more exciting tales, such as Arthur Heming's *Drama of the Forests*, enhanced by striking illustrations. There were books by R. M. Ballantyne, a fur trader with the Hudson's Bay Company in the mid-nineteenth century, about the remote Labrador wilderness. There were the dramatic tales of Jack London and, not to be forgotten, the entertaining story poems of the Bard of the Yukon, Robert Service. These books expanded my vocabulary with intriguing vernacular, like "jumping-off place" and "land of little sticks" (a descriptive designation for the Barren Grounds of the Northwest Territories), and amplified my desire for a future life in the "Northwoods."

Eventually, with earnings from my various enterprises and from work in a grocery store after school, I was able to purchase my first bicycle. It had the advantage of being more convenient than the streetcar for the journey to the library. It was an old wreck for which I paid some unscrupulous individual the sum of seven hard-earned dollars. Talk about taking advantage of a naive youngster—I certainly learned a lesson about high-risk financial ventures on that day. A cursory examination of the bike suggested that it was in reasonable condition but, after a short period of ownership, I discovered that everything on it was badly worn. In fact, even before getting the bicycle home for the first time, I suffered both a blowout and the indignity of completing the last few blocks of the trip on foot. The inner tubes, peeking through the rotting tires in a few spots, continued to undergo frequent blowouts. New tires were almost unobtainable because of the war. Still, armed with a patching kit and youthful enthusiasm, I used to take that clanking collection of worn-out parts on the round trip to the library nearly every weekend to learn more about life with *Snowshoes and Sledges*.

New Horizons

Before the end of World War II, Canada was a much less crowded country than it is today. Calgary had a population of 80,000 people. (Today it is about 800,000.) Adjacent rural areas hadn't yet transmogrified into suburbia. There were no shopping malls, grocery stores had free delivery and doctors made house calls. Housewives hung their weekly laundry on backyard clotheslines, a numbing experience in winter when long johns and petticoats froze into stiff slabs, difficult to collapse into laundry baskets. The mailman completed his rounds twice a day on weekdays and once on Saturdays. Local letters posted on one day were always delivered on the next working day.

There were no commercial jet aircraft, those modern-age sardine cans with wings. The usual method of getting to some distant destination was by train or bus. Paved highways were few and far between. There was no television; radio was the latest medium of communication, and a new receiver in its varnished wood case was given pride of place in family living rooms. Not everyone had the luxury of a telephone.

Private motor vehicles weren't considered a necessity because streetcar service was nearly always to be found within a reasonable distance of one's home. There was no dirty brown cloud of particulate and gaseous automotive emissions hovering over the city, as there is today. Indeed, the Calgary Natural Gas Company, which supplied heating and cooking fuel for most of the city, used to maintain large billboards exclaiming: "Look up. The cleanest skies in the world are above you!" No more—not for many years.

Soon after I began to ride Calgary's streetcars, I discovered that the network of rails could be useful for more than just going back and forth to the library. It could be a magic carpet, transporting a prospective vagabond to a variety of jumping-off spots on the outer fringes of the city for a promenade into rural surrounding. Then one could spend the day enjoying a space that was seldom invaded by the noises of civilization—no city hustle and bustle, no sputtering cars or rattling trucks, no roaring aircraft overhead. Here, for all the days of my youth, I found my Utopia hiking out on the local prairies. It wasn't necessary to have a specific goal in mind. Just being out there, anywhere out there, was sufficient. Nature itself was the justification and the reward.

Each season had its own delights, but spring was possibly the best time of all. Spring was the fresh smell of Earth renewed, that sweet scent almost forgotten through the long winter months; it was bright blades of new grass pushing their way through the withered remains of last year's kin; it was nascent flower buds reaching for the sunlight, soon to flaunt the fragile beauty of their blossoms as they danced to Aeolian tunes; it was a frenzy of bird song filling the air as multitudes of winged exiles returned from more southerly climes. I can't help waxing lyrical. Nature's springtime reawakening really moved me, and still does. Perhaps only a child of the prairies can understand the feeling.

As ecstatic as I felt about the arrival of spring, it did have its drawbacks. It was the worst time for concentrating on schoolwork, beginning when—in Swinburne's words—"the hounds of spring are on winter's traces." The snow had all but disappeared and the crocus buds were pushing out of the cool earth in response to the strengthening rays of the sun. I admit to playing truant on a few occasions then, to ramble around the outskirts of the city. There was just no way to avoid it; it was the only antidote for spring fever.

No School Today

I should have gone to school today
But the wind was blowing free;
The fragrance of Spring was in the air
And the country called to me.

A butterfly flitted across my path,
Robins sang from a budding tree,

16

Prairie grass on the hillside waved
And the country called to me.

Nature was in the ascendent;
My schoolward steps were slow.
The countryside was calling to me,
So what could I do but go?

My favorite destination was reached by boarding a rickety old streetcar, a travel-worn outcast of the transit system no longer used in the downtown area, for a journey to the Ogden Loop at the far southeastern tip of Calgary. From that point, the most interesting hike was to Sugarloaf Hill alongside the Bow River. In summer, the leafy poplars along the river bank offered cool shade to a weary hiker. Some trees held the huge jumbled-stick nests of magpies, those talented rogues of the bird world. They were consummate experts in the art of silent flight, gliding gracefully across the sunlit sky with their white feathers flashing in stark contrast to the iridescent dark portions of their plumage.

Multitudes of songsters had their homes in thick bushes or tall grass, hiding their eggs and hatchlings away from the sight of the predatory magpies. Ducks paddled contentedly in tranquil stretches of water, a scattering of ducklings trailing behind the parents. Handsomely decorated shore birds skipped about on the gravel bars, sometimes voicing shrill complaints about any trespass into their domain. If a watcher was both quietly patient and lucky, a sandhill crane might suddenly drop out of the sky to wade in the marshy shallows, looking for a light lunch of insects or small frogs.

A family of bank beavers was in residence at Sugarloaf, as evidenced by the unmistakable tooth marks on freshly cut poplars and warning splashes in the evening dusk. Porcupines, too, were in the area, the sign of their presence being trees with the bark gnawed away at some distance above the ground. Other wildlife—small mammals of several varieties—could be heard, and perhaps seen by a discerning eye, rustling about in the underbrush.

It was at Sugarloaf where I first discovered that some animals that don't normally take to water will do so if the occasion demands. I was spending a weekend bivouacked beside the river. Sitting quietly by my campfire in the evening, I heard "tlot, tlot" in the distance (just as Bess did when her lover rode up to meet her—and his doom—in Alfred Noyes' poem "The Highwayman"). Soon it began to sound like the thundering hooves of a horse, approaching nearer and nearer at great speed. (Did this portend a ghostly rendezvous?) I was about to dodge behind a tree when into the clearing where I was camped dashed...a rabbit! The animal was closely pursued by a large brown collie. Without hesitation, the rabbit plunged into the river and swan rapidly out to a nearby island. The dog saw me and retreated back toward the farm from whence he had come. Since dogs are quite light on their feet, even when galloping along at a great rate, I could only assume that the loud hoof-beat clatter originated with the rabbit. The volume of sound generated by the wee beastie's paws smashing frantically against the ground surprised me as much as its swimming ability.

Other attractive destinations were readily accessible by hiking from various locations along the streetcar lines. There were shady wooded regions along the gently flowing Elbow River southwest of Calgary. In the high hills of the Shouldice area, on the way to Bowness, there were groves of aspen trees interspersed with sunlit meadows and fields of wild flowers, and a crystal clear spring of sweet water flowing down a long gully. To the north, one could trek to Nose Hill or Nose Creek. The latter place was one of my favorite spots for a skating excursion in winter, especially if the ice had formed smoothly in the absence of wind and snow with no subsequent overflow to roughen the surface. Then one could glide swiftly for miles, oblivious to everything but the weather, the world hemmed out by the high creek banks.

On some of the streetcar trips I would take my Cooey .22-caliber rifle (bought secondhand for five dollars) for "plinking" gophers and predatory birds. The provincial government paid bounties on these animals; one cent for each gopher tail and two cents for each pair of crow or magpie legs. The flying thieves preyed on the eggs of game birds such as prairie chickens and pheasants, and the gophers foraged on farm crops, hence the perceived justification for the bounties. Usually I garnered the gopher tails by snaring their owners, or by pouring water down the burrows to force the animals out to face a club. These were cheaper methods than expending a bullet, but shooting provided greater sport. It all sounds cruel now, but perspectives were different then.

Astounding as it may seem today, I could not only walk the streets of Calgary carrying my rifle and wearing a hunting knife at my belt, but I could also board the streetcars with these items openly displayed without engendering a second glance from fellow passengers. Perhaps their nonchalant attitude was one of the last vestiges of the frontier spirit. Out of courtesy, I would first ask the conductor if he objected to my coming on board with my rifle, and would point out that I had removed the bolt (part of the firing mechanism) from the gun so that it was absolutely safe. There was never a refusal.

My bounty hunting days for birds came to an end one day when I took a quick shot at a small shore bird running along the edge of a prairie pothole. It was, I think, mostly a reflex action, but the bullet hit and killed a spotted sandpiper. As I examined the beautiful bird, I thought to myself what a waste I had caused. I swore that I would never deliberately kill another winged creature just for the sport of it.

Rural Rambling

In the earliest days of spring, with winter reluctantly yielding to the new season, water from the melting snow ran into depressions in the frozen prairie earth, forming shallow ponds which were covered by a skim of rubber ice during the frigid nights. These frangible surfaces were so tough and flexible that one could walk on them without breaking through...sometimes. Waves would form in the ice sheet, rising and falling in crests and troughs as one's weight was transferred from foot to foot. Then, inevitably, cracks would suddenly bolt out in all directions like jagged streaks of frozen lightning, signaling that the breaking point of the ice had been reached.

The boisterous winds of March quickly absorbed the remnants of winter moisture, except for a few bedraggled patches of snow sulking away in sun-sheltered spots and the meltwater filling the deeper potholes. The previous summer's lush prairie grass lay shriveled and sere, wind-dried and combustible, sometimes ignited by human carelessness into fast-moving fronts of orange flame, blackening acres of pasture land. Thin columns of smoke from smoldering cow pies wafted skyward for hours after the grass had finished burning.

The thawing earth liberated the gophers from their winter dens. Those cheeky rodents were everywhere, basking in the heat of the sun or industriously scooping out new burrows. When an interloper invaded their domain, a high-pitched warning whistle from an alert sentry made the gophers scurry for the sanctuary of their dens. After an appropriate cautionary interval, a few bold individuals would emerge into the daylight, heads bobbing up and down and tails flicking erratically, looking to see if previous activities could safely be resumed.

Crocuses pushed their fuzzy buds up from the ground ahead of their leaves, sometimes rising into the cool air even before all the winter snow had disappeared. Their flowers—mauve petals surrounding yellow stamens—were a certain sign of spring. So too were the pussy willow blossoms, the soft fur of their pollen-tinged flowers providing a gray border around the prairie ponds. There followed—in the progression assigned to them by nature—asters and avens, bluebells and buffalo beans, crowfoot and camomile, all the way through the floral alphabet past stonecrops and shooting stars to violets and Venus' slippers. Soon wild flowers shimmered in polychromatic splendor everywhere, on the hillsides and in the coulees, resplendent against the ashen green background of sagebrush and the less-somber greens of the short grasses—a delight to the eye of the prairie nomad.

With trees budding anew, songbirds returned from the south, giving voice to courtship songs and territorial clamor. In the open spaces, meadow larks were among the most prominent members of this avian chorus; finches and thrushes and warblers preferred to sing from the leafy recesses of shrubs or trees. In the marshes, balancing lightly on slender bulrushes, the red-winged blackbirds were the more vocal inhabitants. Mysterious drumming sounds reverberated across distant pastures, a signal that grouse were also acclaiming the season of renewal. Farmers' fields, being cultivated in preparation for spring sowing, were besieged by myriad gulls seeking a meal of grubs and worms, their raucous cries the antithesis of sweet melody.

If the farmers ploughed their lands in late spring when the ground was dry, then a wind out of the northwest might pick up quantities of fine soil and carry it along, to be deposited far away. The roiling black clouds could be seen for miles, almost like the outpourings of a volcanic blast or the suffocating simoons of the Arabian Desert. The light of the sun would be blocked, bringing twilight at midday. To be caught out in a dust storm meant grit-stung cheeks, soil-packed ears and red-rimmed eyes; the grains would even infiltrate one's mouth, to be ground between the teeth like wheat between millstones. Breathing could be difficult. The wise hiker sought shelter from the fury of the wind—even just a depression in the ground—where he could put his jacket over his head and tie his handkerchief over his mouth to filter the dust from the air before it got to his lungs. Fortunately, such dirt-laden storms were infrequent and of short duration.

❖

Spring passed imperceptibly into summer. Hawks soared high in the sky, extracting flight energy from thermals, now and then folding their wings to dive sharply in pursuit of a meal: a field mouse or a young gopher. Grasshoppers leaped and soared in the heat of the day, their wing beats making a strange clacking sound. It was said that grasshoppers could spit tobacco juice, a claim easily verified by capturing one in the hand and observing the disgusting discharge deposited there. Butterflies, flitting from one radiant flower to the next, left only a powdery substance from their wings when held in cupped hands.

The polliwogs that filled the sloughs turned into frogs, their noisy croaking a not-unwelcome chorus even though it could intrude upon the serenity of the countryside at all hours of the day and night. Multitudes of gossamer-winged dragonflies flew above the water, feeding on mosquitoes and other insects—now hovering motionless except for rhythmically beating wings, now darting swiftly away. Some believed that dragonflies, with their long slender bodies, could stitch one's lips together. This was a much less likely hazard than stepping inadvertently into a fresh, juicy cow pie, its pungent aroma thenceforth clinging to one like a shadow. Infrequently, a jackrabbit (or prairie hare), might startle a wanderer by exploding suddenly from the grass, hopping rapidly away with mighty bounds of fifteen feet or more.

Summer heat made distant objects dance and shimmer, obscuring details. By the time the sun reached its zenith, rising currents of hot air had generated towering banks of fluffy white cumulus clouds. Sometimes, as the day wore on, these friendly clouds changed character, turning dark and ominous. A tension arose in the air, the prelude to a late afternoon thunderstorm. Gusty winds in the vanguard of the storm made intricate, ever-changing patterns in the swirling grass. Then thunder claps echoed from the hillsides, while fierce lightning streaked from cloud to ground. Here was a genuine hazard for anyone in an exposed position on the prairie. (Several hundred people are hit by lightning every year in North America and nearly half of them die.)

Huge raindrops pounded the ground, throwing up spurts of dust and water, running together first into rivulets and then into erosive torrents. After an interval of intense precipitation, the downpour eased to a network of scattered drops, finally ceasing altogether. A brilliant rainbow appeared against an indigo sky, one end seemingly within a short walking distance from the observer. The fabled pot of gold lay buried under the other, far-away end. After the rainbow faded away, the air was vibrant—cooler and more invigorating. The heat haze was gone; the horizon stood clear in the distance. Birds trilled the "all clear" signal, and gophers gave a sharp little whistle as they re-emerged from their burrows.

Sometimes the storm clouds contained hail, a most unwelcome form of precipitation because of the crop damage it could cause, and also another possible hazard to one's health. For small hail stones, pea- or marble-sized, a jacket pulled over one's head offered sufficient protection from the stinging particles. If the hail stones were larger, let the hiker beware; there was no place to hide on the bald-headed prairie. Once, an unusually severe storm hurled down spheres of ice the size of golf balls and just as dangerous. Vehicles sustained sheet metal damage and cracked windshields. A local farmer had a dozen pigs killed by the missiles. It was no time to be out rambling.

Summer storms, feeding on the energy of the sun, were usually confined to the daytime. Summer nights were clear and warm. One could lie out on a hillside, watching the moon rise in the darkling sky, looking for shooting stars, or gazing at the splendor of the Milky Way. Perhaps it was just such a majestic scene that inspired an anonymous poet to pen the profound lines:

I?
Why?

What was out there in the incomprehensible depths of space? Even Buck Rogers and Flash Gordon didn't know for sure. Away from the city lights, when the moon was new and the sky at its

23

darkest, I thought that there were uncountably many stars shining down on me. When I was older, it was a surprise to learn that of the myriad distant suns in the heavens, only about 2,000 were sufficiently bright to be visible to the naked eye. (And it was an even bigger surprise to learn that the Milky Way, with its hundred billion stars, was only one of a hundred billion similar galaxies.)

All too soon, it was autumn's turn on stage. The fall weather was an invigorating release from summer lethargy. Trees assumed their fall colors, a change from summer's solid curtains of green. Shortly, they would show only bare bones. The birds flew south, taking their music with them. The clamoring columns of geese were the last to go.

Most of the sounds now came from the wind, whispering gently through sheltering groves or howling vigorously over exposed hills and up the coulees. Leaves scurried across open fields in response to the vagaries of the turbulent air, pausing awhile to savor one spot of ground before skipping hurriedly along to the next stop. Tumbleweeds abandoned their earthly roots and rolled across the prairies, tossing out the seeds of the next generation as they traveled along. Sometime in October, there would be a few brief flurries of snow, precursors of icy blizzards yet to come.

❖

The arrival of winter chill and reduced hours of daylight restricted hiking activities, but it was still a delightful time to walk over the windswept prairies, marveling at the variety of ivory forms sculpted by the wind and the terrain in the hard-packed snow. Winter activities could be carried on at night if the sky was clear, because of the starlight reflected from the snow. Rarely, illumination was provided by the Northern Lights. (Calgary is well south of the auroral zone, so the prairie skies see only an occasional appearance of that spectacular phenomenon.)

Best of all was the bright light of a full moon, allowing one to see for some distance without difficulty, with shadows helping to delineate ground contours and obstacles. If it was very cold, the snow crystals sparkled like fireflies. Hiking in such conditions was quite romantic. But clouds could quickly scurry in to hide the moon and turn the countryside into a flat dull plain. Then, with no visual clues to indicate dips and rises in the surface, depth perception was lost and walking without an occasional stumble was difficult.

Moon Shadows

The moon
cast deep shadows
on the silver snow;
until,
obscured by some
gray cloud,
its bright beam faded
and the world disappeared.

During the day, when the air was crisp and clear, the Rocky Mountains southwest of Calgary could be seen looming far up in the sky, just beyond what appeared to be a short stretch of snow-covered prairie. It seemed that it should be possible to hike to them in a matter of hours instead of days. Too bad the streetcar line didn't run a little closer to those glistening, distant towers!

Fur Trader

Before getting a real job in the "Northwoods," I first had to graduate from high school. I attended Crescent Heights Collegiate Institute—a fine-sounding name for an ordinary school—located on the North Hill in Calgary. During my second year there I started getting fidgety. This was wartime and the armed forces would soon be after my body, if not my soul. I wasn't worried so much about the prospect of going to war as I was about the regimented military discipline. It wasn't compatible with my free-spirited temperament. I found it difficult to do any serious studying and became lackadaisical about class assignments. In my first year I had relieved the tedium by being ill occasionally—or so the school officials believed—in order to seek a cure out on the prairie. When I was caught forging my mother's signature to the obligatory note explaining my absence, I had to desist temporarily. But now I took up truancy in a serious way. This time, though, I was more circumspect about explaining my absences. My devious mind worked out a scheme. After the first legitimate illness of the term, I discarded the note written by my mother and substituted one of my own. From then on all the notes in my school file appeared in the same handwriting—mine.

"Oh, what a tangled web we weave, When first we practice to deceive!" Walter Scott knew whereof he spoke. There were a few close calls when I was subjected to some probing questions by my homeroom teacher, who had her suspicions about me, but I survived the interrogations. Eventually, though, as Mother always told me, the truth will out. In late January she received a letter from the school principal advising that her son would receive no credit for that school year if he was absent for just three more days. I reformed immediately.

At the beginning of my third year in high school, the principal called me into his lair and said that a major office supply company was looking for a young man to learn the business from the ground up. If I was interested, he would recommend me. I had mixed feelings about this; it seemed to me that the principal was involved in a slight conflict of interest. His offer of an endorsement was very suspicious. However, after some thought, I accepted the proposal.

For the first week on the new job I watched my schoolmates returning to their studies and thought how lucky I was. During the second week I wasn't quite so certain. In the third week I resigned and returned to school. I've been thankful ever since because, first, I would have missed the outdoor employment opportunities that came my way and, second, when the desire arose in me for some higher learning, it wasn't necessary for me to finish high school first. However, rather than going back with a late start to the heavy schedule of the Grade Twelve matriculation course, I elected to attend school only in the mornings for each of the succeeding two years. The afternoons were spent laboring at Whitburn's Nursery, a block of greenhouses in southwest Calgary, where I earned enough money (at twenty-five cents an hour) to purchase my own clothes and sundry other items. All things considered, it was a satisfactory arrangement.

❖

The pursuit of persons of the opposite gender, also known as chasing girls, distracted me occasionally during my years at high school. Eventually I found one attractive companion—Mary, my future wife—who had compatible interests, engaging willingly in hikes, fishing trips and similar outdoor activities. Mary lived in the country nearly three miles beyond the streetcar line, so I got a lot of exercise walking her home from school or from an evening movie, or just walking out for a visit. Out and back represented a trek of six miles, usually every day and sometimes twice a day. In a year, that represented a lot of shoe leather.

Weather didn't matter either. Come rain, sleet, snow or sunshine, I trudged happily back and forth. Thunderstorms caused me a little more concern, especially after one night when the highly charged atmosphere made the barbed wire fences on either side of the road light up with the eerie blue glow of Saint Elmo's

27

fire, and crackling sounds filled the air. The image of that electrical surcharge remains vivid in my memory and I understand why sailors of long ago were struck with superstitious dread when this natural phenomenon occurred in the rigging of their ships.

"Where was my car?" you might ask, being conditioned to the fact that almost everyone over the age of sixteen now has a car. In those days—considerations of gas rationing aside—many families, let alone students, could not afford such a luxury. My parents never owned a vehicle of any description and I was thirty-five years old before I owned one myself.

The war ended during my final year at high school. Everything was going along smoothly. I wasn't skipping school anymore (except for French class) and I was working hard at the nursery. The prospect of military service was no longer a concern. I had no thought of continuing my education at a higher level; aside from a lack of funds, I was not acquainted with anyone who had been to university and so was ignorant of the possibilities.

As the end of the school term approached, an advertisement appeared in the local paper. It read: "Wanted. Adventurous young men to join the Hudson's Bay Company Fur Trade Division for an interesting career in Northern Canada." Here was a good starting point for a life in the bush. Needless to say, my application was submitted immediately, even though I had misgivings about leaving Mary. After a series of interviews, I joined the "Honourable Company" of historical fame as an apprentice clerk (pronounced "clark" in the old English tradition) in the fur trade. Now I would really begin living the saga of *Snowshoes and Sledges*.

In an interview with the HBC's Athabasca section manager, Bruce F. Clark, I had been told that I was assigned to the Upper Hay River post in northern Alberta. The trip there required a three-day journey in a horse-drawn wagon after leaving the railroad. However, just prior to my departure, word came that I would go instead to the Sturgeon Lake post to fill the position left vacant when a clerk had departed without notice. This latter post, on the eastern approach to the Alaska Highway between the towns of High Prairie and Grande Prairie, was much more accessible.

The Alaska Highway, constructed with great difficulty through muskeg and mountains from Dawson Creek in British Columbia to Fairbanks in Alaska, was born out of wartime expediency. The link running by Sturgeon Lake—also called a highway, with more optimism than accuracy—was then still in a primitive state, with no gravel surface. It was composed entirely of gumbo, a soil type that becomes extremely sticky when wet. Consequently, the road was impassable when rain-soaked or during spring breakup when the frost was leaving the ground.

My new destination was somewhat of a disappointment, not being in the "land beyond," although in the end it turned out to be all for the best. As events unfolded, I found that I missed my sweetheart back home much more than I had anticipated. No possibility of marriage existed for a lowly HBC clerk. For one thing, there were no married quarters available (except those of the post manager). For another, a clerk's wage was only seventy-five dollars per month, minus various taxes, and minus twenty-five dollars for board and room. In less than a year I had resigned, thankful that I could return home with minimal inconvenience.

My journey to Sturgeon Lake began with a train trip to Edmonton where I got a final briefing at the HBC district office and then boarded the Northern Alberta Railway for the tour along the south shore of Lesser Slave Lake to High Prairie. There I had to wait over a day until I found a freight truck heading west. The truck I connected with bore some trade goods consigned to the Sturgeon Lake post, so the post manager, Dick Howell, was anticipating our arrival. After we unloaded the freight, Dick introduced me to his wife Lorna and gave me a tour of the establishment. The HBC property occupied a portion of a Cree Indian reservation, between the highway and the shore of Sturgeon Lake. It encompassed several acres of cleared land on which were situated a general store fronted by a gas pump, a goods warehouse, a residence and a utility shed containing a gasoline-powered generator and banks of storage batteries for the supply of lighting current to all the buildings.

This location on reserve land enabled me to make acquaintances among the Indians and to learn something of their traditions, their hunting and trapping procedures, and their language. It was necessary for me to attain at least a minimal comprehension of Cree since many of the older Natives spoke no English. They found my unskilled attempts with their language to be very entertaining. Cree grammar seems convoluted to an English-speaking person, but the pronunciation is easy. Unfortunately, I have forgotten most of the vocabulary.

One of my language mentors was a gruff old Native who had once been a tribal chief. The HBC had, at some time in the past, given him a magnificent black felt hat with a broad brim which he unfailingly wore whenever he came to the store. Perhaps there had been some other largesse as well, since he gave the impression of a continuing commitment to the company. He spent nearly every available minute in the store, lounging against a display counter and puffing away on a disreputable old pipe. He claimed his mission was to be a custodian of sorts, to keep an eye on the "young fellers." He suggested that some of them might be tempted to remove part of the store's inventory if not kept under surveillance. When I was having difficulty understanding a customer, the old chief would listen for a while as I struggled with the language. Then, in a rather disdainful and impatient manner, he would remove the pipe from his mouth and toss out a few words of interpretation.

During the summer, much of the work at the post was no different from any grocery store clerking job except that I was learning the bookkeeping system and the methods for ordering stock. Mike, the other clerk at the store, had been there for a year or more and knew the ropes. I was surprised to learn, from a newspaper item a few years ago, that Mike subsequently became a business mogul of some repute and was chairman of the board of several large companies. But, at the time I knew him, Mike was sowing his wild oats. He knew where to get booze and he had a couple of local girlfriends.

Mike and I were friendly enough but had few interests in common except our work. He liked the wild life and I preferred the wildlife. My spare time was spent roaming the countryside—much as I had done on the prairies—observing birds and animals, or visiting with the Natives in their homes, picking up more of the Cree language and learning about life on the reserve. For the most part, their existence differed little from that of some Calgarians during the Depression: it was primarily a tussle to keep a family fed and clothed, with few added frills. Neighborly get-togethers, usually small country-style dance parties, provided occasional inexpensive entertainment.

I was invited to attend several such dances. They were congenial affairs, held in the crowded quarters of a log cabin with the music provided by a local fiddler, or even just by an old hand-cranked phonograph and some scratchy cowboy records. The big social event of the season was the marriage of lovely Mary Ghostkeeper to the son of Bill Desjarlais. Bill and his wife were friendly people, the latter being especially helpful in acquainting me with reserve "doings." Mary had an older unmarried sister, bashful but capable Nora Ghostkeeper, whom I admired for her intelligence. I wrote jokingly to Mary, my wife-to-be in Calgary, that Nora might supplant her in my affections if our separation caused me to become too lonely.

Several Natives at Sturgeon Lake had served in the Canadian army during World War II. After demobilization, three of them had banded together in a partnership for farming and trapping. They worked long and hard, with a good understanding of resource management. They amalgamated their allotted portions of land and farmed them in rotation, with alternating crops, to avoid depleting the soil nutrients. They also rotated their trapping areas from winter to winter so that no animals would get trapped out of existence on any one trap line. Trapping was an honorable profession then and the only way for many people in the North to earn a meager living.

These trapper-farmers definitely didn't fit the white man's generalization of "lazy" Indians. Neither did most of the other Natives on the reserve when allowances were made for differing

31

circumstances and cultures. One old Native claimed that it is white men who are lazy—instead of satisfying their needs by hunting animals and gathering plants, white men just go to the store and buy them. Implicit in that statement is the perception that white men haven't had to spend years acquiring survival skills which, of course, is not necessarily true. Only the skills are different. In any case, I hope that I have long since learned not to make criticisms based on racial generalizations, but to judge the people with whom I come in contact on the basis of their personal attributes.

In late autumn the Natives would begin preparations for the trapping season. For most trappers, the first step involved requesting credit from the post manager. The value obtained depended on past performance—how much fur was usually garnered over a winter and how promptly the previous debt had been paid off. With the new credit, the necessary items would be obtained to sustain the trapper and his family on their trap line until just before Christmas, when most of the Natives returned to the settlement for the holiday season.

Credit negotiations concluded, the trapper would order ammunition, traps and tobacco. Then his wife, who had been hovering in the background, would hold a whispered consultation with her husband before stepping up to the counter to acquire some groceries. Her requirements usually included tea, canned fruits, sacks of flour and sugar, a case or two of lard, tins of jam and butter, packages of yeast and condiments, a big slab of bacon, candles, and a coil of brass snare wire (for catching squirrels and rabbits). If there was any credit left over, she would pick out some dry goods for making clothes for her family. Purchasing over, the wife would shove all of the goods into a gunny sack and carry them out of the store.

Upon the trapper's return to the settlement—two or three months later—now having some furs to trade, he would enter into another negotiating session with the post manager. The latter, first checking that the skins had been properly cleaned and stretched, would carefully examine the pelts for prime condition, shaking them out to fluff up the fur and blowing the guard hairs aside to look at the finer hairs beneath. Then he would advise the amount that he was willing to pay, based on condition and size, and on the HBC tariff for furs in effect at the time. Invariably, the trapper accepted the offer because it was a fair one. Then his first responsibility was to pay off his existing debt. The balance of his earnings would usually be spent on more supplies and some presents for his children.

I no longer remember most of the prices paid for fur at that time. Some coarse long-haired furs, such as wolf and coyote, were not in favor so their value was relatively low. In fact, the province paid a bounty on wolves which was greater than the value of the hide. Fox and lynx fur paid reasonably well, but it was the pelts of mink, otter, beaver, muskrat and marten which were much sought after and commanded high prices. I do recall exactly what we were paying for prime weasel (or ermine)—two to three dollars—because I trapped a few of those myself.

For squirrels, we were paying seventy-five cents each. This was much better than the prewar price of ten cents, but less than the previous season (1945–1946) when they had been worth a record one dollar each. One of our customers, a white trapper, had traded 3,000 squirrel pelts, plus much other fur, to a total value of about $6,000. Compare this to my annual wage of $900 or, more meaningful, to the $1,800 salary which the post manager received. That trapper was the exception though. The average fur return for the Native trappers from the reserve put them about on the same financial level as the clerk who served them in the store.

Rough Stuff

I encountered an unpleasant situation shortly after my arrival at the Sturgeon Lake post. One Sunday afternoon, as I was wandering through an isolated meadow, I came upon an Indian male swinging a woman around by her braids and throwing her to the ground. When she got up, he repeated the process, with a few slaps and punches thrown in for good measure. There was also a great deal of concomitant shouting and screaming. The man was intoxicated but I was uncertain about the woman's condition. I made my presence known and attempted to intervene in the dispute. Surprisingly, both the participants turned on me and belligerently told me, in so many words—some in Cree and some in very plain English—to buzz off. I did leave, but I wasn't comfortable with my decision. Telling Dick Howell about it, he advised me to ignore it, saying it was a frequent event.

Sometimes such affairs had drastic conclusions. Just prior to the incident which I had observed, a local woman had disappeared. Relatives advised the Mounties in Grande Prairie, who came to the reserve and eventually found the woman's body with the aid of tracking dogs. The husband remorsefully admitted to beating her to death. He had been intoxicated at the time, so liquor was the real culprit. Apparently a bootlegger made occasional trips through the region, selling or trading his wares, and a rash of problems always followed in his wake. The police were trying to provide the bootlegger with an extensive holiday in jail, but were unable to collect firm evidence against him.

Inebriated people were troublesome, the white people often more so than the Natives. Mike and I were out in a rowboat one day, fishing for pickerel. He had a bottle of whiskey from which he frequently imbibed. I didn't join him; I'd tried liquor before and didn't care for it. After a while, the sky darkened and a storm roared in with pelting rain. The wind lashed the water into short-crested waves and blew their foaming tops right into the boat. It

34

was my first experience with the squall-whipped seas that can quickly arise on any lake of reasonable size. It would be hard to find a better description of the resulting chaos than that provided by Joaquin Miller in his poem "Columbus," about that intrepid voyager's first Atlantic crossing. The worried mate says:

This mad sea shows his teeth tonight.
He curls his lip, he lies in wait,
With lifted teeth, as if to bite!

Columbus said, "Sail on, sail on," whereas I said, "Let's get the heck back to shore." I started rowing in that direction and suggested to my mate that a little bailing might be in order as a considerable amount of water was now sloshing around in the bottom of the boat.

Until then, I hadn't realized that Mike was becoming very intoxicated. In fact, he was "half seas over," to use an old expression. Now he stood up in the boat and started waving his arms about, howling loudly into the face of the wind. He appeared to be enjoying the storm immensely, ignoring the fact that he was threatening us with an upset, perhaps taking us both into the dark waters of the lake. What would Columbus have done?

I shouted at Mike to remain seated—to no avail. He tried walking toward me and stumbled over some gear. I held my breath as he came crashing down. Fortunately, he fell into the bottom of the boat and not over the side. He continued to rave and thrash his arms about, but he couldn't raise himself high enough to unbalance the boat so we finally made it safely back to shore. I never went fishing with him again.

Some months after my arrival at Sturgeon Lake, the Howells were transferred to another location and a new man, Gene Martin, arrived to take over as post manager. He was younger than Dick, and a little less congenial, but his more businesslike approach to post affairs provided me with better training.

In the early winter of that year, section manager Bruce Clark came on an inspection trip and, in a discussion with him about my future with "The Bay," I expressed my desire to get married in the reasonably near future. He reminded me of the company policy that a clerk couldn't get married until he had achieved the status of post manager and had a post of his own to look after. In the usual course of events, this involved at least two years mastering all aspects of the retail trade, followed by a term at the company-run fur school in Montreal learning the niceties of grading furs. Then the clerk returned to the bush to engage in fur buying under a post manager's supervision, and to acquire some skill in estimating the amount of debt allowed to accrue to a particular trapper. The complete process usually took eight to ten years. It could be even more protracted if there was no vacancy at the post manager level.

I made my position clear to Mr. Clark by tendering my resignation. The normal training period was much too long to fit in with my plans for the future. He urged me not to make a hasty decision. He said he was impressed with the speed at which I had learned the store's operation, and he was confident enough in my ability to send me to the school at Montreal after my first year's employment. Following that, I would be given the chance to achieve a managership at the earliest opportunity. When I thanked him for his consideration but indicated my continuing determination to leave, Mr. Clark then offered me a trip home for the Christmas holidays to reconsider my options. I said that I would welcome the trip but did not expect to change my mind upon my return. He accepted the gamble, and wished me well before his departure on the remaining portion of his travels. I enjoyed the holiday immensely, but the reunion with Mary only confirmed my resolve to resign.

The return trip from my holiday had its complications. This time I traveled by bus from Edmonton instead of by train. The bus broke down some miles before reaching the small town of Slave Lake. The weather was bitterly cold and many passengers, myself included, were not dressed for frosty hikes. After an hour or so of foot stomping, a large truck came along that was capable of towing the bus to Slave Lake. On arrival there, the local mechanic was unable to get the vehicle running again. The bus driver telephoned his company in Edmonton and learned that a spare bus could not be sent to the rescue until the following day. The village hotel had only a few rooms—the *raison d'être* for the typical country hotel being the beer parlor, not rooms—so most of us passengers spent the night sitting in the lobby, sleepily nodding our heads and dozing off from time to time.

The replacement bus appeared on schedule the next day and hauled us the remaining distance to High Prairie. Here, as on my first trip, I had to wheedle a lift with a westbound vehicle. I managed to locate a truck leaving just after supper with only the driver and one other person going along, so there was room for me up front. We had gone but a few miles along the highway when the engine sputtered to a stop, apparently starved for fuel. In the darkness and the cold, the driver fumbled at the gas line plumbing with a crescent wrench and half-frozen hands. Foolish me, with only my oxfords and thin socks between bare feet and the icy road, occupied the time by stomping up and down in an attempt to maintain some circulation in my feet.

After the driver had worked for twenty minutes, the engine roared to life and off we went. But even before the truck heater began generating hot air, the engine sputtered again and stopped. Obviously, there was water in the fuel tank and it was turning to ice in the fuel line or the carburetor, causing a blockage. The driver had no de-icing agent with him, a dismal indictment of his lack of foresight but, standing there in my street shoes, I was in no position to complain. So it was up with the truck's hood and out with the crescent wrench again to repeat the whole annoying process of removing and replacing the fuel line.

This scenario was replayed over and over again. I was becoming concerned about the possibility of losing a few toes to frostbite. No other traffic had yet appeared in either direction from which to seek assistance, an indication of just how inappropriate it was to call that road a highway. Finally, after the engine had been restarted for the umpteenth time, with the truck rolling along once more, a gleam of light suddenly appeared through the bush. Tracks could be seen veering off the road, leading toward the source of the illumination. We drove in and found a small building, where we were welcomed by two operators of a telephone repeater station. This was one of twenty-three such stations belonging to the Northwest Communications System, a voice transmission line constructed by the U.S. army between 1942 and 1943 from Edmonton to the town of Snag in the Yukon.

We warmed up thoroughly, drank our fill of coffee and, best of all, obtained some methyl hydrate which we could pour in the gas tank to prevent further freezing of the fuel line. Thus equipped, we made it to the HBC post without further ado. The driver dropped me off there and continued on his way. It was the middle of the night. I had not been in a bed for nearly forty-eight hours. I went quietly to my room and slept soundly until late the following afternoon.

I might have slept even longer except for Gene Martin's intercession. I came back to consciousness to find him shaking me vigorously by the shoulder. As I sat up and rubbed the sleep from my eyes he complained that there had been an emergency situation during my absence and he thought that I might be able to explain it. Apparently, shortly after my departure, a strange aroma had begun to permeate the store premises. Soon the place reeked to high heaven. The source of the stench was uncertain— it seemed to come from everywhere. The odor was so offensive that Gene was certain it had deterred some customers from entering the store. I ruefully admitted that I might have some knowledge of the circumstances.

It so happened that, prior to leaving on my Christmas trip, I had decided to run a short trap line for weasels. The old chief had given me some advice about suitable baits. I found a small tin can, dumped in a dozen sardines and added some asafoetida and some oil of anise. Then it was only necessary to allow the mixture to become thoroughly rotten in order for the fragrance to be most appealing to some fur-bearing animals. The chief assured me that, even after the vile stuff froze on the pan of a trap, it would still produce an ample emanation of attractive smells. I never thought about how obnoxious it might be to humans, although I did have to hold my nose when adding the asafoetida.

The contents of the can certainly wouldn't ripen if left out-doors—much too cold. So I tucked it nicely out of sight under the large wood stove that was fired up early every morning to heat the store. The can fitted neatly into the cupped hollow of one of the supporting legs where a casual glance beneath the stove was unlikely to reveal its presence. The bait container was put in place a couple of days before the commencement of my trip. At the time of my departure, the concoction had not yet started to ferment sufficiently to attract attention and, in the excitement of leaving, I completely forgot about it.

After I left, the mellowing process began in all of its fetid glory. Gene asked the clerk if he was inflicted with an intestinal problem, but that inquiry lead to a dead end, so to speak. Then it was decided that a mouse or some other small mammal must have died in the store, but a casual inspection revealed nothing. Soon the stench was so pervasive that there was no hope of local-izing the source by nose alone. No one thought to search under the stove. The oversight was understandable; the stove was usu-ally glowing red hot from the heat generated by the burning wood in its interior. Even the old chief was unable to find the bait, his sense of smell having long ago been overwhelmed by the foul tobacco he smoked. After my return, he claimed he knew it was my bait that created the stink, but he didn't tell anyone for fear of getting me in trouble. I thanked him for his consideration by buy-ing him a pack of cigarettes.

Finally, after three days of frantic searching under dry goods counters, behind all of the shelved groceries, and even into the recesses of the building's attic, Gene decided to examine the stove and its surroundings before lighting the fire in the morning. *Voila*! There was the nasty business hiding under a stove leg. The can of moldering corruption was tossed out into the snow behind the store, from where I eventually recovered it. The stench grad-ually faded away and business returned to normal. Had Bruce Clark been in attendance during this period, it is reasonably cer-tain that he would have withdrawn his previous offer to me. As a footnote to the affair, I might add that the bait was effective. I used it to trap several weasels on the HBC grounds.

After apologizing to Gene for the bait episode, I learned that a new clerk had arrived to take the place of Mike, who had gone back to civilization to begin working his way to the top of the heap. I submitted my resignation, effective three months hence in the spring.

Before leaving Sturgeon Lake, I purchased a pair of wonderfully beaded moosehide jackets which had been commissioned from Mrs. Desjarlais by an American military person and never paid for. Fortuitously, one was a man's jacket just my size and the other was a lady's jacket just right for Mary. The pair cost me thirty-five dollars, almost one month's take-home pay for a lowly HBC clerk, but properly valued then at several times that amount.

Soon the big day arrived when I loaded my few belongings on a truck headed for High Prairie and points south. I was homeward bound. My romance with *Snowshoes and Sledges* would have to be deferred for the time being.

Thrills and Chills

In Calgary once again, I found work as a warehouse clerk. The job offered sufficient security to consider marriage. I was wearing out a lot of shoe leather trekking back and forth to Mary's residence, and matrimony would help to alleviate that problem, so we set a date for an autumn wedding.

On one occasion, while awaiting the great day, we took advantage of a weekend excursion fare on the railroad to travel from Calgary to Banff, where a winter carnival was underway. After scrutinizing the attractions there we decided to try hitch-hiking home to Calgary. Out on the highway, car after car passed us by. Then, just as we were becoming discouraged about the prospects for a ride, a huge black limousine squealed to a stop. The rear door opened and a gruff voice ordered, "Get in." The rearward-facing jump seats were folded down for us to sit on, we climbed in and pulled the door closed, and the limousine roared away toward Calgary.

We looked around. Facing us in the rear seat were three large swarthy gentlemen in black suits. In the driver's seat there was another large swarthy gentleman in a black suit. The speedometer on the dashboard read eighty-five miles per hour. The speed limit was sixty miles per hour and even that was a bit much for the twisty old road. Yet another man in a black suit, not a muscular type like the others but heavyset and swarthy, occupied the front passenger position. Nobody said anything for a while. I thought to myself, "My God, we're in the middle of a Hollywood gangster movie." I was certain that I could see the bulges under their arms made by guns in shoulder holsters. What had we gotten into?

Soon the front-seat passenger began some small talk and it was immediately apparent that he was the boss. There was no mistaking it. Every time he made a remark that was even remotely humorous, all of the other black suits would roar with laugh-

41

ter. It was "Yes, Bull! Ho, ho, ho!" or "Great, Bull, great!" Obviously, the boss went by the name of Bull and his henchmen were anxious to keep on his good side.

Apprehensive as we were all the way to Calgary, not only because of the electrifying ambience but because we had never traveled that road at such high speed, nothing untoward happened. Everyone was most polite from the time we entered the vehicle until we debarked in downtown Calgary. After getting over the thrill of the trip we discovered, from a worldly wise acquaintance, that we had been taken for a ride, so to speak, by one of North America's big-time gamblers, Bull Montana. All's well that ends well. We learned to be a little more circumspect about future hitchhiking occasions.

❖

Mary and I were married on October 18, 1947, and honeymooned in Banff among the first snow flurries of the approaching winter. On our return, we set up house in a little three-roomed shack poised on the edge of the lofty east bank of the Canadian Pacific Railway irrigation canal (otherwise known as "the ditch"), on the eastern outskirts of Calgary. It was actually a converted chicken house, about twelve feet wide and thirty feet long. We had no electricity or water and, worse, no indoor plumbing, which was sorely missed on the occasions when I had to bare my bottom to the wintry blasts of air rising up through the circular hole in the wooden seat of our outhouse. Instead of three rooms and a bath, we had three rooms and a path. Mary, having been raised under similar circumstances, was used to coping with such deprivations.

Situated high above the land to the west, we had a superb scenic view overlooking the Bow River and the city of Calgary, and ranging to the distant Rocky Mountains. It was this elevated location which was responsible for the lack of water; the cost of a deep drilled well was far beyond our limited resources. For cooking and drinking, I carried water in buckets from a well about a quarter of a mile away. For laundry purposes, we caught rain runoff from the roof in wooden barrels, or melted snow in winter, and heated it in buckets on the stove. Mary did the laundry manually, using a galvanized metal washtub and a corrugated scrub board, wringing the wet clothes by hand. To bathe, we utilized that same washtub, slopping water all over the floor in the process. We used a gasoline-fired lamp for illumination. I liked that lamp for one reason—when it was turned off at night there was time to find one's way to bed before its light was completely extinguished.

Winter was tough in that uninsulated shack. I banked earth up high around the foundations on the outside of the building in an attempt to eliminate drafts of cold air, but without much success. The exterior walls probably lacked a layer of building paper under the siding. A southeast wind, with snow on the ground, always resulted in a small snowdrift appearing in the living room. It began several inches tall on the inside of the exterior wall and extended for three feet or so toward the middle of the room. A similar situation prevailed in the bedroom, when a nor'wester would cause the curtains covering some shelves to flap like a flag blowing in a breeze. The formation of a snowdrift there was only precluded by our location on the brow of the ditch bank, with no level fields to the west.

In addition to the cookstove in the kitchen, we had a small coal-burning heater in the living room. Neither of these devices allowed a fire to be banked sufficiently at night to retain any warmth for more than a few hours. As a consequence, in very cold weather, the water bucket acquired a thick layer of ice overnight, and other freezable items also congealed. Mary would jump out of bed in the morning, light a fire in the kitchen stove, then dive back into bed until the stove was throwing off enough heat to start thawing the place out. She got this job because it was a crucial one requiring much experience. (Ho, ho, ho! Yes, Bull.)

The windows, during winter, were always covered with a thick layer of ice on the inside. All the moisture in the air—from the steaming water in the stove's copper reservoir, from the boiling kettle and coffee pot simmering on the back of the stove top, even from the stew pot and the Saturday night bath water—ended up precipitating out of the cold air layer adjacent to the windows and freezing into intriguing Jack Frost patterns on the window panes. Ice as thick as one inch would gradually accumulate on each pane. A very thin layer of it would thaw and evaporate during the heat of the day, only to be redeposited during the cold night—with interest added from the day's activities.

Our "mansion" was much like my abode of early childhood, around which my first recollections revolve. I was three years old. My parents were living in "reduced circumstances." In fact, we were on relief—the term used for welfare during the Great Depression. In return for a subsistence allowance, my father toiled with pick and shovel on a road-building project. We resided in a little shack which lacked amenities like electricity and running water. We depended on a kitchen stove for heat, supplemented by a small coal-burning heater, and had a coal-oil lamp to provide illumination. The shack was relatively isolated in an expanse of ashen green pastureland, with the towering form of Nose Hill rising up behind. This area was then well beyond the northern edge of Calgary's residential districts, but is today overwhelmed by urban growth. Eventually my parents' circumstances improved and we moved into the city, where I soon became accustomed to all of the comforts offered there (especially the indoor plumbing).

So now it was *déjà vu*. But we were young, and cheerfully coped with our relatively primitive lifestyle. There were compensations for the deprivations and hardships. In addition to savoring the great westward view, we could observe pheasants and ducks poking about in adjacent stubble fields after the harvest. Playful crows roosted in nearby trees along the ditch bank. And, lying in bed at night, we were often entertained by the ghostly swishing of the wings of geese as flocks flew very low over our rooftop on their way to rest on the Bow River.

❖

Almost a year after our wedding Mary was expecting our first child. I was about to begin a more remunerative job as a laborer at the Imperial Oil refinery in East Calgary. With these events on the horizon, a short holiday seemed in order while the opportunity presented itself.

44

We traveled by bus to Waterton National Park in southern Alberta, and stayed for a few days at the big chalet there. Room rates were very reasonable because the tourist season was over and the resort was almost closed down. Delightful autumn weather prevailed, permitting some brisk scenic strolls. We almost came to grief during one off-trail excursion when we failed to see a sign advising of blasting operations for a new road. A loud explosion, followed by small rock fragments raining down on the bushes around us, caused us to beat a hasty retreat. If the blast had been delayed for a few more minutes, we would have been in a region where large chunks of rock were falling, and would have been lucky to escape injury.

The best adventure of the trip, one that Mary was unable to participate in because of her "delicate" condition, was an energetic hike up the slopes on the east side of Waterton Lake to a small glacial reservoir called Crypt Lake. A local fishing guide ferried me across the Bosporus Narrows to the east shore of Waterton Lake at seven o'clock one morning, where I climbed up to a ridge-top trail leading to Hell Roaring Creek. A strong crosswind howling over the ridge tried to blow me off the path.

Arriving at the impressive Hell Roaring Falls, I found they consisted of a series of chutes where the water dashed down a steep decline in several short stages, alternating in direction. At each change in course, the forceful jet had carved out a cavern in the solid rock, like a bowl standing on edge. The water plummeted downward from one bowl to the next on its turbulent drop to the lake. Traveling upward over a steep trail with many switchbacks, I next came to Twin Falls, much higher and spaced farther apart than the cascades of Hell Roaring Falls, but just as striking. For a while thereafter the trail traversed timbered slopes. Then it opened out again so that off to the east I could see an even more spectacular waterfall, with the stream proceeding over a cliff and dropping far down onto the valley floor below.

A further struggle, ever upward along the switchbacks, led to the most magnificent view of all. I came around a curve in the trail to see a great brown wall of rock some distance ahead. This sheer face was the mountainside above which, in a cirque—a crater-like depression carved out of the mountaintop by glacial action in some remote ice age—lay Crypt Lake, unseen at this juncture. The lake was fed by melting glacial snows on the surrounding peaks. The exit for the lake water was a huge hole right through the mountainside below the rim of the crater. The departing stream spurted through the opening in a shower of spray before attaching itself to the rock wall to tumble hundreds of feet down into the valley bottom. It was difficult to tear myself away from this powerful scene to continue upward.

Quite suddenly, the trail ended at a rock face. There, fastened into the cliff, was a short steel ladder, perhaps eight feet high. After climbing the ladder, I found myself at the entrance to a small tunnel which had to be traversed in a crouch. Once I was through the tunnel, the trail reappeared in the form of a slender ledge, so narrow that some considerate person had fastened a steel cable into the rock wall for use as a handrail. I easily negotiated a distance of several yards with the aid of the cable, to a point where a proper path appeared once again, leading up and over the crater rim.

The view from the rim revealed a magnificent aqueous jewel—an elegant tarn occupying the southern portion of the amphitheater formed by the depression in the mountaintop. To the east and south, the crater walls were molded from snowy crags and talus slopes. On the north side, the ground sloped gently down to the lakeshore, a pleasant alpine meadow ablaze with late-blooming wild flowers. Exquisite floral patterns were everywhere, cascading the transcendent hues from the Master's palette across the landscape—recalling the wise counsel offered by an ancient Persian philosopher:

> If of thy worldly goods thou art bereft,
> And two loaves of bread alone to thee are left,
> Sell one, and with the dole
> Buy hyacinths to feed the soul.

Here was soul food aplenty—truly nourishing, and free as well. The beautiful clusters were so abundant that it was impossible to avoid crushing some with every step. In this attractive setting I had to force myself to return to reality.

I ate my lunch and headed back down the trail in a frantic rush. I didn't want to be marooned for the night on the wrong side of Waterton Lake. By seven o'clock, the appointed time for my return ferry trip, I was only nearing the mouth of Hell Roaring Creek and still had the ridge trail north along the lake shore to negotiate. The strong blustery wind had arisen again, adding to the difficulty, and daylight was fading fast. When I finally reached the rendezvous point, the guide's small boat was nowhere in sight. Then, just as I began cursing fate, I heard the sound of an outboard motor and my water taxi appeared out of the gloom. Happily for me, the guide had decided to give one last look at nightfall.

Home again from our all-too-brief holiday, it was time for me to join the labor gang at the Imperial Oil refinery, toiling at the many kinds of dirty jobs to be found around a refinery. This was definitely not the clean outdoor life I longed for. Ditch digging assignments usually came as a welcome relief—at least they were out in the fresh air, and dirt was the cleanest thing around.

On one memorable occasion, the foreman sent me off to assist a member of the refinery's engineering staff who was doing some land survey work—measuring distances, angles and elevations. The engineer was very helpful, responding patiently to my many questions about the work we were doing. I was with him for three full days, and a new world opened for me.

I learned that there was a strong demand for surveyor's assistants (called rodmen and chainmen), but that old bugbear—previous experience—was usually required. The engineer suggested that some additional studies relating to surveying might be acceptable in lieu of experience, so I signed up for a surveying course with a well-known correspondence school. The course was supposed to take about three years to complete, but I studied diligently and churned through the lessons at a rapid pace, hoping to cut the completion time in half. Had I worked half as hard at high school, my teachers there would have been overcome with amazement. But these new studies had the advantage of being interesting and goal-oriented.

Meanwhile, the year was drawing to a close. On New Year's Eve, Mary insisted that she would like to go out to a dance, but finally reconsidered. It was just as well because, in the early morning hours of New Year's Day, she unexpectedly found herself in hospital, delivered of a baby boy we named William Thomas.

In the summer of that year—even though I was far from completing the correspondence course—I contacted a Calgary surveyor who was seeking someone to work in the field (meaning away from the office) as a chainman, as well as to help draft survey plots in the office. He tested me on my surveying knowledge and drafting skills and I passed muster. However, he was reluctant to hire me because he felt that the wage being offered was insufficient to support a married person. I responded that I was willing to take the gamble provided that, if he observed sufficient progress in my surveying capabilities, he would increase my salary after the first six months. He agreed, so I was back to interesting work in the outdoors.

Chains and Challenges

The surveyor in whose employ I now found myself was Bob McCutcheon, Dominion and Alberta Land Surveyor. Bob had several crews—each consisting of an instrumentman and two chainmen—working on different projects throughout the province. The instrumentman was the crew chief, responsible for tactics in the field. He used the transit (theodolite) and the level to measure angles and elevations. Chainmen measured distances over the ground using a steel measuring tape. The task was called chaining because the original standard measuring device—consisting of a series of short steel rods linked by chainlike loops, with a total overall length of exactly sixty-six feet—was designated as one chain. Chainmen also acted as rodmen when required, holding up a calibrated rod used to establish elevations. Everyone in the crew pitched in on the heavy work, such as chopping a line through trees and brush.

I was assigned as a chainman to accompany an instrumentman named Jerry on short undertakings in the field, usually oil well location surveys in Alberta's oil fields. This work broke me in gently and permitted frequent returns home. It was only now (at the age of twenty-two) that I first learned to drive a car properly. I practiced on the survey sites, away from public thoroughfares. My first venture into actual traffic came about one Friday evening as we returned to Calgary. Jerry drove to the street where he lived, hopped out of the vehicle and said, "Take it away!" All my protestations that I really didn't know how to drive yet were to no avail; he just grabbed his suitcase and left. Since our office was closed for the weekend, I cautiously drove out of the city to my ditch-bank home. Then, on Monday morning, I cautiously drove back into Calgary again.

Bob was rightly incensed when he learned what had taken place, expressly pointing out the insurance implications arising from the fact that I had no driver's licence. The lack was quickly rectified. I went to the Motor Bureau office, filled out an application form, handed over the requisite amount of cash, and received a licence right on the spot (no driving test being required at that time). Jerry's unusual behavior was explained when I returned to the office and found that he had just tendered his resignation. Apparently he was unhappy in his work.

Next, I was teamed with an instrumentman engaged on longer-term projects such as road and powerline surveys. We were nearly always billeted in small towns or villages that had a single hotel. These, for the most part, did not have today's amenities. The government of the day only permitted beer parlors in hotels so, the beer parlor being the prime revenue producer, a minimal hotel was built around it. Usually the rooms were on the second floor. They contained no luxuries such as bathtubs and toilets. One of each of these facilities was shared among all the residents, with first-come, first-served being the rule. The toilet was sometimes just a glorified outhouse, with a long chute down to a ground-level pit. Electrical power was generally available but it was often supplied by a gas-driven generator of insufficient capacity and poor quality, so a permanent flickering brownout was maintained during the evening, to become a blackout at eleven o'clock when the beer parlor and the generator were shut down for the night.

While the accommodations didn't inspire rave reviews, the locales of the small towns, with vacant property abounding, made it easy for me to get in some hands-on practice with the transit in the evenings when I was not studying my correspondence course. It wasn't all work though. Often I found time to examine the attractions of nearby prairie meadows or marshes. Once I found a family of mallard ducks which had taken up residence in a grain field with an old trail running across it. An extensive series of ruts in the trail was filled with water, providing the family with private swimming pools. As I walked over the trail, the ducklings paddled furiously along from beginning to end of a rut. There they would leave the water and race across the intervening dirt to the beginning of the next rut, their small feathered rumps wobbling comically from side to side. Occasionally, in their haste, their bodies would get ahead of their feet, tumbling the little creatures onto their beaks. The performance was repeated until there were no more pools left to negotiate. At the end of the last rut, the ducklings dashed off in all directions into the cover of the tall stalks of grain.

On the muddy shore of a marsh I was sometimes privy to another comical sight—the rapid zigging and zagging of what looked like small white balls of fluffy wool running about on toothpick legs. These were killdeer young, able to scamper around soon after their release from imprisoning egg shells. Less amusing but equally fascinating, I once observed a coyote stalking stealthily along the edge of a pond. A plover, afraid for its chicks, repeatedly swooped at it, uttering frantic cries. The coyote, concentrating on the hunt, completely ignored the antics of the distraught bird. Suddenly, as if released by a spring, it pounced on some prey. As the beast trotted away I could see—not feathers—but a small tail hanging out of the corner of its mouth. Obviously, a rodent of some description was about to form a meal for the coyote or its pups.

Another time, on dry pasture land, I caught a movement out of the corner of my eye. A small golf ball-sized sphere of cow manure was rolling slowly through the short grass. Closer inspection revealed that the ball was being manipulated by two beetles. One at the rear had its shoulder to the wheel, metaphorically speaking, heaving for all it was worth. The other was climbing up the front of the ball, helping to overbalance it. Proceeding in this fashion, the miniature manure pile was moving along at a steady pace, only occasionally slowing a bit as it had to be maneuvered around an unyielding stalk of grass. A distance of several paces had been negotiated by the time I left the scene. Later, I learned that these were called dung beetles or tumble bugs, a common insect. The ball of manure was being taken to their nest, a hole in the ground, where beetle eggs would be laid in it. The heat from the decomposing dung incubates the eggs.

Some areas of southern Alberta were antelope country. It was great fun to lie quietly in the grass as a herd of these animals, their curiosity excited by the colored ribbons attached to survey markers waving in the breeze, cautiously approached to get a bet-

51

ter look. The antelope would spread out in an arc, each wanting a clear view of the object. The animals were wary, but unable to resist moving closer, tugged by their inquisitive nature. Finally, a vagrant breath of wind would carry the human scent to them. In unison, the herd would wheel swiftly about, running away in great, graceful bounds, their white-haired rumps quickly disappearing into the distant landscape.

❖

As I moved around the province on various jobs, I met many people with interesting experiences to relate. In the oil fields at Leduc and Redwater, I learned about seismic exploration and drilling techniques. In the Leduc field, one of the early wells went "wild," the crude oil and natural gas breaking away from the well casing and spurting up uncontrollably around the drilling rig. Gas was also bubbling up in the surrounding fields. The oil company that owned the well wanted the farmer, who owned the land on which the well was situated, to leave the property for his own safety, since any small spark might trigger a raging inferno. Vehicles were kept at a safe distance and aircraft were prohibited from flying overhead.

The farmer refused all entreaties to move until, one day, he went out to do his daily business in his outhouse. He closed the privy door, pulled down his pants, sat down on the seat, took his tobacco pouch from his shirt pocket and rolled himself a cigarette. Meanwhile, an explosive mixture of natural gas collected in the confines of the outhouse. When the farmer lit his cigarette, the resulting explosion had just sufficient power to blow out the building's walls and drop him neatly into the hole beneath the seat. Perhaps neatly is the wrong word! After the farmer got cleaned up it was discovered that his only injury was singed eyebrows (and hurt pride). Needless to say, he was suddenly anxious to comply with the oil company's request.

On another occasion, I met a geologist who had just come from examining a farm property in which his company had some interest. The farmer told the geologist that the rock outcrops around the place were precisely one million and three years old. Since the dating of rocks is not such an exact science, the geologist asked the farmer how he had arrived at that figure. The latter replied, "Well, three years ago, there was another geologist fellow around here and he told me...." Do I really need to complete the quote? Actually, I believe this was an old joke, well known among the geological fraternity, which my acquaintance took delight in relating to all newcomers.

At the end of the first three months of my employment Bob gave me a raise because he was pleased with my progress. It was most welcome, though unexpected because of our original agreement. Another raise followed after a further three months. A good thing, too, because our second son, Ronald Arthur, came along the following spring. At the time of Mary's confinement I flew back to Calgary from the job site near Edmonton. This was my first ride in an airplane, a Douglas DC-3, the workhorse of the airways for years.

Shortly thereafter Bob agreed I was ready to assume the mantle of instrumentman and crew chief. I was moving up in the world. Soon my chainmen and I were engaging in major projects all around the province. We surveyed oil well locations, transmission lines, a major portion of the Calgary-to-Banff gas pipeline, highways, railroad rights-of-way and housing subdivisions. The responsibility for evaluating the technical problems involved in the projects made the work even more interesting, although it also required me to spend most of my evenings doing calculations of various kinds.

In order to maximize my time at home with my family, I made a deal with Bob to work as much overtime in the field as circumstances, and daylight, permitted in return for a corresponding amount of time off when we returned to Calgary. Bob was happy with this arrangement because it reduced his expenditures for maintaining us in the field. Once or twice we even finished a job with the aid of our vehicle headlights to avoid the necessity of returning to the site for less than an hour the following morning. Then we headed for home, driving through the night, saving the expense of an additional day on the hotel bill.

Beginning in 1872, much of the Canadian prairies was surveyed into mile-square sections of land, with interposed road allowances one chain wide. Each section contained 640 acres; thirty-six sections, six to a side, comprised a township. To compensate for the convergence of the meridians of longitude as they come closer together in the north, while maintaining approximately square townships, a correction was made every thirty-six miles, resulting in a jog in the north-south section lines. Boundary markers, normally in the form of iron posts, were placed at every section corner, centered in the middle of four large pits excavated in the prairie soil. Posts were also placed at quarter-section corners, halfway between the section corners. The original settlers could easily establish their property lines with some degree of accuracy by reference to the pits, even if the marker itself was missing. However, once the settlers started tilling their fields, the pits soon filled up with wind-blown dust, effectively eradicating them. Only the corner fence post remained as an obvious, but approximate, guide.

When a new survey is contemplated, the original boundary lines in the area must be confirmed to establish a basis from which to begin. If the boundary markers are not clearly visible on the ground, an educated guess about their probable locations is made, deriving clues from fence lines, soil indentations and other evidence. Usually the markers are buried, and an excavation is required to uncover them. This can be very difficult in parts of the country where strong winds blow extraordinarily large amounts of soil off the farmers' fields. The dirt particles drop back to the ground along the fence lines, their passage impeded by piles of tumble weeds stacked there by previous winds. Over time, large drifts accumulate. More than once I commenced digging at a conjectured marker location and, perhaps four or five feet down, came across the top of an old fence post. Then the line had to be determined from other more accessible markers.

On one occasion, when trying to re-establish a section line across the Bow River east of Calgary, I discovered an error of more than one hundred feet in a distance of half a mile. This is a horrendous error, most unusual in the work of the early surveyors, so it was not their results but mine that were first called into question. A difficulty existed in that the distance could not be measured directly with a chain—because of the wide river—but only by a procedure called triangulation. After repeating the measurement three times, each time with the same outcome, both Bob and the Land Titles Office were convinced of the accuracy of my measurements and accepted the results. Somewhere in that area the early surveyors must have made another, compensating, error or their mistake would have been obvious at least by the time the next correction line was reached. I left it to the Land Titles Office to worry about that problem.

Another time, I was surveying some extensive—and expensive—industrial real estate in East Calgary and succeeded in finding all the old survey markers. Then I noticed some new survey stakes which didn't correspond with the correct layout of the property. I investigated at the Land Titles Office and discovered that an Alberta land surveyor had filed a plan of a recently completed survey on which he swore under oath (a standard procedure) that he could find no evidence of the original markers. Thus, he had re-established the corner posts to his own satisfaction. However, they were all in error by a distance of about eight feet! Since the man was still working in the area, I approached him to help resolve any problems he had in locating the corners. Unfortunately, he was a crusty old gent who turned the volume down on his hearing aid every time I attempted to engage him in conversation. My plan was filed with the Land Titles Office where the conflict between it and the earlier one was investigated. Eventually, the elderly surveyor was charged with unprofessional work and his licence was suspended for a period of six months.

A difficult conundrum was presented by another project involving the complex intersection of a number of property lines and road curves, and included the complication of the Canadian Pacific Railway irrigation canal crossing through the middle of the survey area. I derived much satisfaction from conceiving a solution to the geometrically intricate problem. It all came down to doing some of the layout work in the middle of the irrigation ditch, not possible when it was filled with water in summer but perfectly feasible on the solid ice cover in the middle of winter. So that's when I did the job.

Vehicular Vaudeville

A set of company "wheels" was one of the perquisites that came with the position of crew chief. In my case it was a surplus Jeep from World War II. It was capable of going almost anywhere, no matter how rugged the terrain. And on icy snow-bound highways or rain-slick backcountry roads, when other vehicles were being rendered *hors de combat* by sliding into ditches or stalling in drifts or mudholes, I could put the transmission into four-wheel drive and keep on truckin'. I rescued many a stranded motorist along the way by towing them to solid ground. I was beginning to think that the Jeep was invincible until the right combination of circumstances disproved the thought.

One such instance occurred at the commencement of a survey for a natural gas pipeline from Calgary to Banff. Rain had been pouring down for several days and so the first obstacle we encountered on our first day of field work was a flooded backwash near the Elbow River. A foot or so of water covered some ground which, I assumed from external appearances, was normally quite high and dry. I asked a chainman to drive the Jeep through this area to a point further along our survey line.

After splashing over about twenty feet of the soggy terrain, the vehicle slowed to a stop. I knew it wasn't because of a damp ignition system because all the electrical appurtenances on the Jeep had been waterproofed. Besides, I could hear the motor roaring and see a rooster-tail of spray being thrown up from the tires. The driver, unable to move forward, put the transmission into reverse and tried backing up, to no avail. Then he scrambled out, shouting excitedly, "It's sinking!" Sure enough, the water was climbing up the side of the cab. Just as I was about to get excited myself, the downward progression of the vehicle stopped.

I waded in and found that the water beside the Jeep was two feet deep and rising. The floorboards inside the cab were covered by about six inches of water. I used a piece of wood to feel around in the black mucky water and could find nothing substantial under any of the wheels. Since I was already soaking wet from the rain, I ducked down until my shoulders were immersed and began probing with my hands. I felt a large old tree trunk. Who knows for how many years its waterlogged bulk had lain there? The Jeep was high-centered on it. At least it had saved the vehicle from sinking irretrievably into the ooze.

Now the recovery chore began. We gathered all the driftwood lying around and jammed it into the muck underneath the vehicle, trying to build a base from which to jack the Jeep up off the central log. Placing the jack properly under the axle required taking a deep breath and ducking below the surface of the water. As soon as we started jacking, the wooden base was pushed further into the mud, with the Jeep refusing to be elevated even a fraction of an inch. So we alternately crammed more wood under the wheels and continued the jacking process. After hours at this thankless task, the Jeep gradually rose up out of the murky water. Then, having used up the available driftwood, we cut down some live trees and built a corduroy road back to the water's edge. Finally I was able to climb into the driver's seat and start the engine. Holding my breath, I depressed the throttle and let out the clutch. With a tremendous roar and a great splashing of liquid mud, the vehicle went bouncing backward to firm ground. Total elapsed time from the start of the recovery operation until its completion was seven hours!

The next case of an immobilized vehicle happened on the same pipeline survey. Now it was winter and we were billeted on a ranch near the Morley Indian Reserve. The daytime temperature was thirty-below. The pipeline route lay across a large stubble field, wide open to the strong local winds so that the field was swept clear of snow except for an inch or two retained by the remnants of the grain stalks. Once again I requested a chainman to drive out some distance ahead along the survey line. I saw him start off, then I turned away momentarily to make a calculation in my notebook. When I looked up again to monitor his progress, the Jeep was nowhere in sight. It had disappeared in the middle of a large open field!

While I was trying to decide if this was another case for Sherlock Holmes, the chainman's head came into view, floating ethereally above the frozen ground. Soon his whole body was visible, but there was no sign of the vehicle. I walked out to meet him and the mystery was solved. In the summertime, there was a clearly evident erosion channel running across the field. Now, it was filled to the brim with soft, powdery snow, indistinguishable from the rest of the field except for the lack of stubble protruding through the surface of the snow. The Jeep had dropped in at right angles to the axis of the channel at a spot where the bottom was barely wider than the Jeep was long. The momentum of the vehicle had allowed it to get nicely centered over the trap before it sank down in the soft snow, coming to rest with its front and rear bumpers just clear of the channel sides. The sides consisted of solidly frozen clay. The top of the Jeep's cab was slightly below ground level, hence not observable from a distance. Now what to do?

We began by digging the snow away from the vicinity of the vehicle to provide some working room. We had to get the Jeep faced around until it was parallel to the channel axis. We thought that, by jacking it up repeatedly, and pushing it sideways to tumble it off the jack, we could get it pointing in the right direction. On the first attempt, we discovered that the fit of the Jeep between the channel walls was too tight for such shenanigans. We picked away at the frozen ground at the ends of the vehicle, being extremely careful that the pick didn't bounce off the frozen earth into the radiator. Eventually we made minimal, but sufficient, concavities in the channel sides. Soon we had jacked and pushed enough to get the Jeep facing along the channel.

Now we had to make a ramp up out of the depths of the defile, back into the field. We packed snow down by jumping on it. We found a derelict fence line, its posts lying on the ground and apparently no longer of much use to the rancher. Dragging the posts back to the scene of operations, we built a corduroy ramp on top of the snow base. Finally, I climbed into the Jeep and drove it back to freedom. Total elapsed time on this occasion was another seven hours.

❖

A few days after retrieving the Jeep from the erosion channel, the spell of very cold weather was broken by a Chinook. The balmy breath of this fabled wind began in the middle of the day, while we were out on the job. I had previously experienced Chinooks every winter at Calgary and was impressed there by the increase in temperature over the span of a few hours. Here though, right at the base of the mountains, where compression heated the air as it poured down off the heights, the increase was really spectacular. I swear that my upwind ear was in air at thirty degrees above zero while my downwind ear was still experiencing the thirty-below stuff. Perhaps the hoary old story of a settler caught out in a Chinook might have a grain of truth to it after all. No doubt you've heard it before. The settler was observed lashing his team to greater effort as they sped homeward with his sleigh. The front runners were slipping over the smooth frozen snow but the back ones were kicking up a cloud of dust as they dragged along on bare ground. Such is the power of a genuine Chinook!

As spring arrived and the pipeline survey advanced along the ground, we encountered a long steep hill leading from the high country down to the river flats near a mountain pass. We had to negotiate the hill twice a day, once up and once down. It was so steep that the lowest gear in the four-wheel-drive transfer case, known as "bull" low, had to be used in both directions. The chainmen always chose to walk rather than take the scary ride in the Jeep. I had no choice in the matter. One day, about halfway down the hill, the clutch broke. Jeep brakes, not great at the best of times, were quite ineffective for holding the vehicle on steep grades, so I had a thrilling ride to the bottom of the hill. We managed to get a tow back to Calgary, where repairs were made.

All good things must come to an end, though. The motor in the Jeep was getting pretty tired. Eventually it was traded in on a Ford half-ton truck with a winch on the front. The Ford was much more comfortable to ride in. It was also harder to push through mud and snow than was the Jeep but, with the winch available, pulling it out of awkward spots was easy. If there was no tree within reach of the long winch cable, we had only to drive a few of our surveyors' standard iron posts into the ground ahead and hook the cable over them. If that didn't provide sufficient purchase, in sandy soil for example, we dug a hole some distance ahead of the vehicle and buried a bundle of bars with the cable attached. Then, after it had served its purpose, the bundle could be retrieved by positioning the front end of the truck directly over it, and winching it straight up from the ground.

❖

One day we were driving along a gravel highway (most of the highways were gravel then), following in the wake of a new model Ford car. Even under a layer of road dust, we could see its finish sparkling brightly in the sunlight. Suddenly an old tin lizzie roared out of a side road without stopping, smashed into the side of the car and pushed it off the highway into the adjacent ditch. The driver of the lizzie was a young farm lad who wasn't old enough to qualify for a driver's licence.

The owner of the automobile climbed out and carefully examined the damage. "I just bought this car a few days ago," he wailed. The door was somewhat bashed in but, fortunately, there were no injuries to the occupants. I offered to try hauling the vehicle out of the ditch, but the owner preferred to get a tow truck from the service station in a little town which we could see nearby. I didn't press the issue because the car was sitting in quite a precarious position on the sloping side of the ditch.

The tow truck arrived at the scene in response to our summons and its driver casually examined the situation. "Nothing to it," he said. He hooked a tow chain to the front bumper of the car, jumped into his truck and slammed the shift lever into gear. Then he revved the motor, let out the clutch and...roared backward into the car with great force, putting both vehicles well into the ditch! Liquid spurted from the front of the car. The owner nearly had heart failure. He now had a badly damaged hood and radiator to go along with the bashed-in door. The tow truck driver jumped out of his cab, his face as white as a sheet, and held up two fingers separated by a small fraction of an inch. "Reverse and forward gears are only this far apart," he shouted hysterically. In the end, we pulled them both out of the ditch.

Wildcat Well

One of the most memorable survey projects in which I took part involved a wildcat, or exploratory, oil well drilling site in the sparsely inhabited country north of Athabasca Landing in Alberta. Seismic crews had been through the area and the geological data they acquired suggested the possible occurrence of oil and gas in the subsurface rock structures. Now the oil company who held the lease on the land wanted to drill a hole and check it out. First, though, a survey was required to accurately position the well site on the ground.

The area was very remote, with no means of outside contact, so the oil company required Bob to be present in case any problems arose. An oil company representative and his technician were to accompany us. Thus a party of six—the above-mentioned three plus my two chainmen and me—arrived one summer morning at the small town of Athabasca Landing on the Athabasca River. This place, before the building of the railroad to Waterways (near Fort McMurray farther down the river), was the jumping-off point on the water route into the northern regions of Canada. We boarded a cable ferry, powered by the river current, for the short trip to the north bank. We were traveling in a winch-equipped oil company vehicle, packing our camping gear along with the necessary surveying equipment.

Once across the river, we headed out on a rough trail through the bush (the usual colloquialism for the trees and shrubs of the northern forest). There was no proper road in the region, only a track pushed through by some homesteaders trying to hack a living out of the wilderness and by the seismic survey crews. The route was marked by a succession of deep mudholes through swampy willow-populated terrain. Our driver's heavy foot on the throttle bounced the truck through some of the mudholes, but others required the use of the winch. Now we discovered just how well the trail had been used by seismic crews. No bushes remained within a winch-cable length of any bad hole. All the willows which might once have been within reach had been torn out of the ground during previous vehicle extrication attempts! We had to resort to burying a bundle of iron bars for use as a "deadman" to hold against the pull of the winch cable.

By the end of the day we had arrived at Calling Lake, about thirty-five miles from the river. At one time a small commercial fishing camp had been established there, and several decrepit log cabins remained among the groves of poplar trees. We cleaned two of them as well as we could—throwing out the mouse nests and other accumulated debris—and bedded down for the night.

The next morning my two chainmen and the oil company technician, who were in one cabin by themselves, had a story to tell about a nocturnal visitor. In the middle of the night there had come a soft rattling at the door. One of the chainmen woke up and quietly roused the others. The rattling continued intermittently, interspersed with scratching and snuffling sounds. What was the source of the strange noises? The chainman found his flashlight, warily left his sleeping bag, and threw the rickety cabin door open. The flashlight beam illuminated a startled wolf—so the chainman claimed—poised with a paw in the air immediately in front of the door. The wolf reacted first and sped off. The chainman, his adrenalin level suddenly increased, almost ran through the back wall of the cabin. After recovering his composure, he closed the door and fastened it as tightly as possible—tightly is used loosely here, since the door was falling off its hinges. The occupants of the cabin spent much of the remainder of the night worrying about other unfamiliar sounds. My own opinion upon hearing the story was that the visitor had been a coyote rooting around after the mice whose tenancy of the buildings had been rudely terminated by our arrival.

After an early breakfast cooked over an open fire, we headed north again. The trail was much better now, with fewer marshy areas. We eventually arrived at a spot where a large bulldozer was parked. It belonged to the oil company and had been used for pushing some of the seismic lines through the bush. At this point we knew we had to head in a westerly direction for a few miles, with no suitable trail for the truck, only a primitive 'dozer track. We stowed our gear aboard the bulldozer as best we could, carefully cushioning the transit to protect it from harm. Then the oil company man started the machine up and away he went for a kidney-jolting ride over the rough terrain. The rest of us walked along in his wake.

The bush started to change from deciduous trees to coniferous types, some of substantial size. By noon we found ourselves on the fringe of a broad region of deadfall. This was a section of forest through which, at some time in the past, a fire had swept, killing all the trees. Then the dead roots gradually decayed. The trunks, battered by wind and winter snows, began falling over, stacking themselves up in a jumble, like some monster game of pick-up-sticks. Stiff gray branches, devoid of bark, stuck out from the tangled trunks like quills on a porcupine. In some places, young poplar saplings poked up through the corpse of the old forest.

A cursory examination indicated that we would have to park the bulldozer and penetrate the mess on foot, packing our gear on our backs. I had the doubtful privilege of carrying the transit, an instrument which was vital to our enterprise, so I had to be careful not to damage it. I took it out of its protective wooden case and fastened it onto a tripod. In this normal operational configuration, I could carry the instrument over my shoulder. As if it wasn't enough of a burden, I also had to don a packsack containing a share of the camping gear.

Before starting off through the deadfall we turned back into the unburnt forest and searched out an old cut line. This slash through the trees, partly obscured by new growth but with some of the old stumps still in evidence, marked a section line laid down during the original survey many years before. It led us to four pits and an iron bar. The bar was stamped with code numbers which told us exactly where we were. The proposed well site lay in a southwesterly direction.

Our plan was to follow an extension of the section line through the deadfall by using compass bearings. We were hopeful that the fire-ravaged region would be limited in scope. Little did we know! How much easier it would be today, with aerial photographic coverage of the whole area, to predetermine the nature of the terrain and ground cover. Today, too, one could make use of a small hand-held satellite navigation system to find the location of any point on the earth's surface with an accuracy of a few feet—a marvel of modern technology.

Finally underway into the arboreal chaos, my companions at first thought it was a great lark to be clambering over, under and around the long tangled tree trunks with their protruding branches. But they weren't carrying the transit. I had to be constantly on the alert to avoid smashing the instrument against a trunk or spearing it on a branch. Soon the clutter became so thick that we could only clamber on top of the trunks, painstakingly trying to maintain both balance and footing on the slippery surfaces, sometimes six feet off the ground. For minutes on end, we were unable to touch a boot to the dusty soil.

This was far and away the worst deadfall I ever encountered. It was useless to maintain the fiction of following a compass course; we just tried to keep the sun in the correct position ahead of us. As evening approached, we optimistically estimated that we had covered a distance of two miles over the ground, but certainly not in a direct beeline. We were all exhausted and, worse, hadn't found any fresh water along the way. All we had was the water remaining in our canteens. We made the best of a dry camp and turned in early, sleeping under the stars. I doubt that the chainmen even gave a thought to wolves as everyone quickly fell asleep.

The next morning we continued our struggle through the deadfall, our muscles complaining from the uncommon exertions of the previous day. At noon, we stopped for a rest and a dry lunch, nibbling on whatever food we had that was palatable under the circumstances before reluctantly resuming the journey. Late in the afternoon, to our utter amazement, we stumbled over another set of pits along the old survey line. We couldn't have had any better luck after all of our tribulations. Now we not only knew our exact position again, about one mile east of the projected well site, but we had a reference point from which to commence our survey. To add to our joy, the tangle of fallen trees

Left: The author on a jaunt across the prairie *ca* 1945.

Bottom left: Mary doing the cooking chores on a hike.

Bottom right: Winter wonderland.

HBC Post at Sturgeon Lake.

Mary and Nora Ghostkeeper on Mary's wedding day.

The author with black wolf hides.

The author with some weasel pelts from his own trapline.

Mary in the doorway of the ex-chicken-shack abode.

Spectacular falls on the Crypt
Lake trail.

Crypt Lake looking east from
the crater rim.

Bill and Ron camping out with Dad.

Ron and Bill swimming in the CPR Irrigation Ditch below the ex-chicken-shack home.

Surveying oil well sites in the Redwater oil field.

Nechako dam site showing the diversion tunnel taking the river away from its original bed.

Billy McNeil and 4x4 on the Pine Lake trail.

Warden cabin at Pine Lake in Wood Buffalo National Park.

Buffalo bull contesting the right-of-way on the Pine Lake trail.

The MB *Buffalo* at Rocher River.

Beaver aircraft on the Slave River at Fort Smith, N.W.T.

The wharf at Fort Resolution. In the foreground a Native family is seen leaving for their bush camp.

Bill, Ron and Grandma Bell at Pinsky's store.

Warden's house and school in background; Ron, Bill and friends in foreground.

George Pinsky and friends.

Bombardier delivering a case of canned peaches to Bill, Dick and Ron.

The author's dog team on the south shore of Great Slave Lake.

Spider, a great leader.

Fort Resolution airstrip in winter. The aircraft was chartered to the Girl Guide Commissioner for the N.W.T., inspecting Mary's group of Brownies and Guides.

Crack-up of a Cessna on Great Slave Lake.

Above: Ron and Bill at Native summer camp with caribou-hide tepee.

Left: Bill, Ron and Grandma Bell at the Post Office-cum-Court House.

Picnicking on the "beach" at Fort Resolution.

Jolly with the author aboard—not a comfortable ride.

Starving elk at Boundary Cabin hay pile.

Dusty II.

Indian trappers with beaver pelts.

Boundary Cabin after the first winter snowfall.

had thinned out considerably. We staggered westerly for a short distance and, yet more good fortune, found a small stream of fresh water, where we set up camp. It had taken us nearly two days to hike about three miles through that dreadful burn.

On the following morning we surveyed the well site without difficulty and then headed back to the bulldozer. Now, though, free of the constraint of trying to follow a section line, we were able to find a way around the *terre brulé* or burnt land. A leafy, green parkland of deciduous trees existed just to the west of that terrible wasteland. After a trek of several miles of fairly easy going we were back at our starting point of three days before.

On our retreat from the well site we mapped a route over which the oil company could easily make a road for hauling in their drilling rig. This they planned to do during the following winter, when the swampy ground would be frozen solid. I later heard that the drilling went ahead on schedule. There was a moment of excitement when a bear was discovered hibernating on the site. One of the roughnecks (the customary label for members of the drilling crew) crawled into the bear's den and despatched the animal with a small ax. A foolhardy exploit, to be sure, but with a bear rug for his reward. As for the oil company, after the drilling was completed, all they had to show for it was a dry hole and a big tax deduction.

Surveying had its hazards and its rugged working conditions: clambering over deadfall, felling trees, fording streams, climbing cliffs and encountering wild animals. It also had its lighter moments. My co-workers provided some of them.

One of the first chainmen assigned to my crew was a strapping young fellow just out of school but, despite his physique, not in the best physical condition. He was also not used to the routine of rising unassisted after a night of slumber. He missed his mother's wake-up call. Every morning I had to act as a surrogate parent and beat loudly on his hotel room door to rouse him or he would never have made it to the breakfast table.

The job we were on required a great expenditure of energy. We were working in deep snow at low temperatures, coping with snowshoes on our feet all day long, and cutting a line through fairly large trees using only axes (there were no chain saws then). We were all very tired by day's end, but this particular chainman was so exhausted that, after supper, he would retire directly to his room and go to bed. I wasn't aware of this because I was nearly always busy with my paperwork until quite late. One evening, about nine o'clock, I had finished working on my field notes a little earlier than usual and thought that I would invite him out to the hotel cafeteria for a cup of coffee. Knocking on his door brought no response, so I assumed that he was out of his room. The other chainman wasn't around either, so I went for coffee by myself.

Shortly after I returned to my room a rap came at the door. I opened it to find the young fellow standing there, rubbing his eyes, obviously not completely conscious. "Ready to go?" he queried sleepily. "I've just come back," was my response. "You've been for breakfast already?" he asked. Then the light dawned. My earlier knock at his door had awakened him. Thinking it was the usual morning call, he had risen, shaved and dressed and was now ready to proceed to breakfast. Smiling sheepishly after learning the true state of affairs, he promptly returned to bed.

With another pair of chainmen, Ted and Keith, we were surveying a pipeline near Bow Island in southern Alberta. This was rattlesnake country, a new environment for us. It was very difficult to maintain an awareness of the danger for more than a few minutes at a time when one was not accustomed to doing so. I set a reference point on the survey line and was looking for something with which to mark it before moving on with the transit. Out of the corner of my eye, I saw a stick lying on the ground. Only half paying attention, I bent to retrieve it. Before my hand got there, the stick started to move. It was a rattlesnake, about four feet long. Disturbed, it moved slowly away in one direction; startled, I went rapidly in the opposite direction. It was a cool overcast day, so the snake was lethargic. I assume it had been lying out, sticklike, to absorb as much of the sun's heat as possible. For the rest of the morning the chainmen made snide remarks about my behavior in the presence of snakes.

At lunch time, I sat on the running board of our truck to eat my sandwiches. Ted and Keith found a huge flat boulder on which to settle. Ted was well into his first sandwich when something attracted his attention. Looking down to his side, he found he was sharing the rock with a very large, loosely coiled snake. Involuntarily leaping into the air, he shouted "Jesus Christ!" Ted was quite religious, so it didn't surprise me to hear him calling on his savior. What did astonish me was the height of his leap. I swear that Ted was able to repeat the same two words three times before he hit the ground again. His feet were making running motions while he was still in the air. Regaining contact with the ground, he set a new record for the hundred-yard dash. The snake uncoiled from its spot in the sun and slithered away under the rock. Upon returning to the truck, Ted adamantly maintained that there had only been two repetitions of his shout. The reptile was about six feet long and quite obviously not a rattler. It was later identified as a harmless bull snake, useful for keeping down the rodent population.

I have had chainmen leap into the air and dash off on other occasions as well, usually while cutting line through heavy underbrush. This always signaled the presence of a wasp nest. Wasps seem to have an unerring instinct for building nests right on the survey line. When disturbed, they can move a lot faster than snakes. The words uttered by the men on such encounters did not usually have much religious content.

Yes, surveying was a lot of fun. It was also a satisfying experience both physically and mentally. It involved hiking, climbing, snowshoeing and ax-work. The routine was always varied and never dull or boring. Sure, it was tough at times. In the winter, even at thirty below zero, with fingers and feet close to freezing and instrument mechanisms stiffened by the cold, we often had to keep at the job. More than once, the Jeep wouldn't start on a frigid winter morning. A tow didn't help—the lubricants were so congealed that neither the engine nor the wheels could turn over, the tires merely skidding along the roadway. The remedy was to play the flame of a blowtorch over the oil pan and the differential case to warm them up, a chore in itself. The Ford truck was better in that respect. It was equipped with a block heater—a recent innovation—that worked wonders provided that an electrical outlet was available, not always the case in the countryside.

In the summer, we occasionally found ourselves wading through chest-high water as we ran a survey line across creeks and sloughs. New chainmen, encountering such obstacles for the first time, would invariably wonder how to cope with them. Usually, the crew chief had to wade in to demonstrate the method before the new men were convinced that it was standard operating procedure. And always there were lots of insects to bug us, especially mosquitoes and black flies. In compensation for the working conditions, the wages were reasonable, and we got to see a lot of different scenery. But...

All that traveling meant much time away from home, sometimes many days. At first it wasn't too onerous, primarily because of time off for accrued overtime work once back in Calgary. Then Bob began asking us to take a detour on the homeward trip to do some newly commissioned survey. This meant more money in Bob's pocket because he was charging each job for full travel expenses from Calgary. Often we left home for an expected absence of two weeks and didn't return for three or four weeks. These diversions increased in frequency despite my complaints. The time spent with my family being whittled down to a fraction of what I wanted it to be, I proffered my resignation. Bob was loath to accept it and we came to a seemingly satisfactory accommodation which involved doing more local survey work. Unfortunately this informal contract was soon breached as Bob again began scheduling my crew for more and more out-of-town work. Eventually I found myself returned to the old situation of being away far more often than I was at home. Once again I submitted my resignation, with regret, but also with finality.

Nechako Dam

When I left Bob's employ, it was without immediate alternative employment in mind. I did have another iron in the fire, though, which I hoped would soon heat up. A few weeks earlier the federal government had placed a Canada-wide advertisement in all the major newspapers inviting applications for the position of game and forestry warden in the Northwest Territories. Here was the job for me! My response was mailed off without delay and, shortly thereafter, I found myself being interrogated by several civil servants. This led to an interview with the superintendent of game for the Northwest Territories, William Sloan. My foot was in the door.

There followed two months of nail-biting suspense while I waited to learn the result of the competition. When it came, it was rather anticlimactical. I had placed third in Canada on the list of eligible candidates, for which my survey experience was probably responsible, but—a disappointing reservation—there would be no hiring of any wardens until some indefinite time in the future.

Meanwhile, I found temporary work with the Calgary Natural Gas Company repairing leaky gas lines. Then an opportunity arose to go surveying on a huge hydroelectric project in British Columbia. This was part of an Aluminum Company of Canada development for the smelting of aluminum, a process requiring large amounts of electrical power. There were three major components: a giant smelter at Kitimat on a West Coast fiord; a powerhouse with seven turbines at Kemano, fifty miles inland, connected to the smelter by a substantial transmission line running across a rugged mountain range; and a massive earth dam across the Nechako River in the interior of the province.

I had read a magazine article concerning this enterprise which contained much hyperbole about bulldozing one-third of the adjacent mountaintop into the valley below to form the dam. The Kenney Dam (as it is now called) was to become the largest clay and rock dam in the world, with a height exceeding 300 feet. The reservoir behind the dam would take four years to fill and submerge an area of about 350 square miles. A ten-mile-long tunnel with a diameter of twenty-five feet, cut through bedrock, would drop the water a vertical distance of half a mile to the powerhouse turbines. It sounded like an exciting project.

Morrison-Knudsen, a major international construction firm, had overall charge of the engineering work, some of which they subcontracted to various smaller firms. When I learned that an engineer from Mannix Construction, one of the subcontractors on the dam, was in town for the purpose of hiring surveyors, I went for an interview and was taken on as an instrumentman. I was told that, after a probationary period of thirty days, family accommodation would be made available on-site.

I checked with the federal government concerning the present status of the game warden competition and learned that a position might be filled in the near future but, since I was third on the eligibility list, it was unlikely that I would be considered for it. So I left the gas company and headed first for Prince George and then to Vanderhoof, the jumping-off point for the Nechako Dam. Mary packed up our children and our few belongings, and went to stay with her parents at Nanaimo on Vancouver Island for, supposedly, a month's vacation before joining me at the dam site.

We didn't know it at the time, but we were leaving Calgary for good, never to return except for an occasional visit. I will always consider that city to be my hometown, though I've been away from it many more years than I ever spent living there. Sometimes I think that it would be nice to move back to Calgary again. Then I realize that the city and its surroundings which I delighted in during my adolescent years can never be regained. My Calgary—the one that I still picture in my mind—no longer exists; it is a phantom on the stage of history, engulfed by population pressures and the passage of time. As Thomas Wolfe advised, truly, "You can't go home again."

❖

Upon reporting for work at the Nechako dam site, I was interviewed by the chief engineer for Morrison-Knudsen, a gruff

Yankee whom I hadn't encountered before. He bluntly informed me that another person whose qualifications exceeded my own was there to assume the position of instrumentman and I would have to be satisfied to work as a chainman. No arguments accepted—take it or leave it! The Mannix engineer who had hired me originally, and who was to be my supervisor, was most embarrassed and apologetic.

What to do? In those days there was no official body to complain to about labor injustice. Had I followed an early suggestion from my father that I deposit a certain sum of money in a bank account to be labeled a "Go to Hell" fund, I might have made use of it then. As with my father, though, I had never accrued sufficient wealth for this purpose, so no such fund existed. After calming down, I decided to stick with the job for at least long enough to earn my train fare to the West Coast.

The survey work consisted of running location lines for the dam and ancillary structures, and of "cut and fill" measurements to determine the volumes of material to be removed from some parts of the site or added to other parts during the construction of the dam. I was pleasantly surprised to discover that a fellow worker was my ex-chainman from Alberta, Keith, the same person who had watched with amusement as Ted and I had reacted to the presence of snakes at Bow Island. He was a very competent chainman but, entertaining no higher aspirations, he had left McCutcheon's employ for the better wages to be found at the Nechako Dam project, where he had now been working for more than six months.

The first day on the job was a disaster—not for me but for the supposedly highly qualified instrumentman who had obviously greatly exaggerated his abilities. He didn't even know the proper operation of the transit. I offered him what assistance I could—albeit grudgingly, I admit, since it was due to him that I was on the payroll as a chainman instead of as an instrumentman. His performance on the second day was a repeat of the first. When we returned to the office, Keith apparently had a discussion with the Mannix engineer, who then had some conversation with the counterfeit surveyor and the crusty chief engineer. The net result of all the talk was that, on the third day, I was asked to assume the position of instrumentman. The previous holder of the post was fired and left for parts unknown.

It was fascinating to observe the procedures involved in building a huge earthen dam: the diversion of the river to permit the excavation of a core trench (the most basic component of the dam) across the original bed, the packing of impermeable clay into the trench as a seal against leakage, the subsequent layering of assorted rock materials over the core, and the blasting of "coyote holes" (tunnels) for various purposes.

Cold weather prevailed during the whole of my time at the dam site, with the temperature hovering around thirty below. I had two helpers to cut line through the bush when necessary. They always built a large bonfire at each new location where we anticipated working for more than an hour or so. It was nice to be able to warm up periodically at the fire but, when required to move out of range of its radiant rays, the cold seemed even more extreme.

Together with two or three new friends, I spent much of my spare time hiking the rugged Nechako River canyon. It was surprising to find that, despite the extreme cold, the river level still fluctuated on a daily basis. The water surface was at its lowest in the morning hours, but it rose later in the day due to increased snow melt after sunrise in the remote headwater region. Then the meltwater source would congeal again after sunset. On several of our little excursions along the river valley, the late-afternoon return journey was made more arduous by overflow saturating the deep snow on top of the ice. The moist snow then adhered to the webbing of our snowshoes, resulting in a partially frozen mass of cold heavy slush that made walking very difficult.

I missed my family, so, after a month, I started pressing for the on-site housing as originally promised. Now I was informed that such accommodation would only be made available to the people employed as engineers or in other lofty positions. An instrumentman didn't rank high enough on the social scale. This was another annoying shock, so, after due consideration, I resigned. On leaving, I was advised that I would be welcome back at any time on any Mannix Construction project, so I was pleased that no ill feelings had accrued as a result of my short stay. I took the local jitney from the dam site to Vanderhoof and then boarded a bus for Prince George and points south. Arriving in the lower Fraser Valley, it was quite apparent that spring was in the air. In Vancouver I was able to doff my parka and flight boots and walk around in shirt sleeves. It was as though winter had never been. I was soon reunited with Mary and the boys in Nanaimo and once again began seeking employment.

❖

I found an interesting position as instrumentman with Hewett & Smythies, a partnership of land surveyors in Victoria. The work involved laying out timber berths in the backwoods and making detailed topographic maps of some military bases on Vancouver Island, providing more new experiences for me. The timber berth work was especially tough, involving precipitous mountain slopes. The terrain often made it difficult to set up the transit tripod. Sometimes two of the three legs would fit normally on a small rocky shelf, but the third leg would have to be shortened and raised up high to rest against a cliff face. At other times, a perch might be found on the slippery round surface of a fallen cedar tree, six or eight feet off the ground. Once set up, it was even more difficult to maneuver around the instrument without sending it hurtling off to oblivion below.

On a number of occasions, oblivion was where I thought I might be headed, never mind the transit. It is a great thrill to round a bend on a narrow logging road and discover that an enormous truck, loaded with huge logs, is coming directly at one, full tilt on a collision course. There is no way that the truck can stop in time to avert a calamity even if the driver is inclined to do so, and I never met one who seemed so inclined. The logging trucks have their own travel schedules over roads on a timber berth. This keeps them from tangling with one another, but leaves no room for interlopers. When a truck is encountered, the only way to avoid disaster is to very quickly drive one's vehicle off the road. Hence it had better be at a spot clear of roadside debris and not immediately adjacent to the top or bottom edge of a cliff.

Fortunately for me, when confronted by one of these speeding behemoths, I always happened to be at a spot where I could swerve my four-wheel-drive Land Rover off the road without overly damaging it against rocks and stumps. This vehicle actually belonged to Hewett and he, having little experience of an active logging site, was voicing complaints about the increasing number of scratches and dents on it each time I returned to the office in Victoria. One day he paid me a visit on the site of a timber berth survey. I squired him around in the Rover, his car being unsuitable for logging road travel. On our first encounter with a loaded truck, I barely had time to throw the steering wheel hard over and goose the throttle to hurl our conveyance off the road. Hewett gasped in a manner which suggested that he might be experiencing a heart attack. However, he survived the moment and never again criticized the cosmetic condition of the Land Rover.

During this time, my family resided in Nanaimo while I stayed at the old YMCA in Victoria where I occupied a small room on the third floor. I was able to travel home for a visit on most weekends. However, on one weekend, a particular project required me to remain in Victoria, and gave me what I thought was my introduction to earthquakes. On Friday night, after a hard day's work in the field, I retired earlier than usual. Just as I was drifting off to sleep, I felt the room shaking, and the drinking glasses on the dresser jiggled around a bit. I debated putting my clothes on and dashing from the building. However, although the shaking continued for a while, it didn't increase in intensity, so I decided to ignore it and soon went solidly to sleep. The next morning I inquired at the desk as to whether there had been an earth tremor on the previous evening. "No," said the desk clerk, "that was just the regular Friday night dance."

When a real tremor hit a few weeks later, there was no doubting what it was. The dresser jumped around and the glasses almost fell to the floor. The bed shook dramatically. Before I could get up and come to grips with the problem, the shock was over, having lasted only a few seconds. In subsequent years in British Columbia, I have felt other similar shocks, at least one severe enough that I mistakenly thought a vehicle had rammed the house. Most were just mild shakers, rattling things for a very brief period of time. A quake on Vancouver Island, several decades ago, did do some substantial structural damage, but the really big one is yet to come.

❖

On one of my weekends back with my family, I was the recipient of mail from the federal government. It advised that two wardens were being hired for the Northwest Territories. Apparently the first two applicants on the eligibility list were no longer interested, so my name was now at the top of the heap. Did I still want the job? What a question!

I went for the requisite physical examination and was accepted. I was required to report at Fort Smith, N.W.T., in June. I was given the assurance that, later on in the year, I would be assigned to a warden district of my own, where family accommodation would be available. Where had I heard that story before? I hoped that this time the information was correct. I wound up my affairs in Victoria and away I went, once more facing an unwelcome separation from my loved ones for a little while. *Snowshoes and Sledges*, here I come at last.

Buffalo Country

I made my way to Edmonton by rail and then boarded a Canadian Pacific Airlines DC-3 for the flight to Fort Smith. CPA ran a weekly schedule from Edmonton to Aklavik, at the mouth of the Mackenzie River, landing at intermediate points if local weather and airstrip conditions permitted. Fort Smith was a small town built on the high west bank of the Slave River, at the lower end of a series of horrendous rapids, just north of the border between the Northwest Territories and Alberta.

At that time, the N.W.T. was completely controlled by the federal government, with Fort Smith the nominal capital and the site of the government offices. Fort Smith also included the headquarters for Wood Buffalo National Park, a large reserve straddling the N.W.T.-Alberta border. The park was formed in 1922 as a sanctuary for the last wild herd of buffalo (bison) remaining in Canada.

When the plane touched down on the Fort Smith airstrip, I was welcomed by a grizzled man with a three-day growth of whiskers on his windburned face. He was wearing a lumberjack shirt and black denim work pants, with moccasins on his feet and a baseball cap on his head. Stray strands of gray hair poked out in various directions from under the cap. He introduced himself as Billy McNeil. He immediately impressed me as being friendly and outgoing, with a wry sense of humor, but I had some difficulty with his accent. He was employed by the government as a patrolman, the term used to designate a warden's assistant. I was soon to learn that he was a respected old-timer in the district and was more experienced in the bush than any warden of my acquaintance, then or now. His accent turned out to be "Newfie," almost undiluted by the time span of forty years which had elapsed since his departure from the rockbound coasts of Newfoundland for Canada's northern wilds.

Billy, as I later discovered, left his Newfoundland home in 1911, a young lad of twenty years. He was hired as part of a three-man team transporting a herd of some fifty reindeer across Canada, by rail and barge, to Fort Smith. The reindeer had been part of a larger herd imported from Norway by Dr. Grenfell (of Labrador fame). Apparently, Grenfell had convinced the Canadian government that it should get into the business of farming these animals in the North, where the environment was supposedly similar to that of their native land. The project was doomed to failure. Only thirty-odd reindeer reached Fort Smith alive, where they were driven to distraction by the hordes of biting flies. They crashed their way out of the flimsy corral which had been constructed to contain them temporarily and scattered into the surrounding countryside. Some swam across the Slave River. Billy recaptured a few of the animals but, by 1916, the experiment was over. All of the original reindeer were dead and no offspring had been produced.

Billy liked the North so much that he stayed there, eventually marrying a local girl and raising a family at Fort Smith. Some time after the reindeer fiasco, he was engaged by the federal government as a buffalo warden to help protect those endangered animals, even serving as chief buffalo warden for a time. He estimated that, when he first came into the country, there were at most only a few hundred wood bison extant, split into two main herds. Billy was released from his position as a warden when the Wood Buffalo National Park was formed in 1922, so, under the tutelage of his father-in-law, he turned to trapping for a living and became very successful in this endeavor.

Billy was also engaged in various other work, being re-employed by the government in the summertime to maintain vital navigational buoys on the Slave and Mackenzie River systems. At one point he even had his own taxi service, using an old car to carry passengers over the portage road between Fort Smith and Fort Fitzgerald. When the government decided to move some plains bison into the park from more southerly regions, beginning in 1925, Billy was hired to help oversee the task, his previous experience in transporting the reindeer being a great asset.

Billy and I were soon to become good friends but, for now, he drove me from the airstrip to the administrative offices in town where I was introduced to some of the government people. These included Bill Sloan, superintendent of game (whom I met previously during my job interview), George Wilson, superintendent of forests (subordinate to Sloan), and Chief Warden F. A. McCall. All these people could boss me around if they felt so inclined but, according to protocol, my first level of contact was with the chief warden. After the introductions, I was left at the personnel office to get properly documented, a euphemism for filling out a bunch of forms in quadruplicate.

While I have used the term "game warden" to describe my position, the official designation was park warden. In fact, I was issued separate certificates stating that I was a game officer, a forestry officer, a dog officer, a commissioner for oaths, and perhaps one or two other things. The only position to which I couldn't lay formal claim was that of fisheries officer. Fisheries in the Northwest Territories came under the aegis of a separate Department of Fisheries, whereas my employer was the Department of Northern Affairs and National Resources.

Throughout the N.W.T. (and in the various national parks of Canada), park wardens enforced the hunting, trapping and forestry regulations, other laws pertaining to federal parks, and the International Migratory Bird Act. The whole of the country north of the sixtieth parallel of latitude was broken up into several large districts, with a warden allocated to each. I was to be responsible for one of these districts after a suitable period of indoctrination.

Almost immediately after signing the last copy of the final official document, I was directed to proceed to the site of a bush fire on the portage road between Fort Smith and Fort Fitzgerald, just south of the border in Alberta, and assume command of an N.W.T. fire suppression crew already battling the blaze. (Even though the fire was actually Alberta's responsibility, it was only common sense for the closest crews and equipment to do the job and worry about the jurisdiction—and the paperwork—later.) I arrived on the scene to find the situation completely under control. It was just as well, since I didn't know any more about fighting fire than I did about driving dogs. I grabbed a shovel and helped clear a firebreak around the smoldering residue.

The fire suppression crew actually came under the supervision of the Wood Buffalo National Park administration, with headquarters in Fort Smith. They were highly trained and permanently employed, as opposed to being a group commandeered from the first citizens to happen along at the outbreak of a fire. The primary justification for maintaining a standing crew during the fire season was the protection of the park's mixed arboreal forest and open meadowland environment, home to thousands of buffalo. However, the crew was also available for fighting fires outside of the park, within a hundred miles or so of Fort Smith.

Wood Buffalo National Park, where I spent some time that summer, was established to protect the indigenous buffalo herds roaming the meadows and forests west of the Slave River. These were originally purebred wood buffalo, a bison subspecies somewhat larger than the plains bison. The area of the park was about 17,000 square miles, largely in Alberta, but with the northern portion extending into the N.W.T. Years ago, the federal government saved the plains bison from extinction in Canada by purchasing a large buffalo herd from a private owner in Montana. Beginning in 1907, about 700 of those animals were shipped to Wainwright, Alberta, and held in a fenced enclosure. There they multiplied to such a degree that, in the years between 1925 and 1928, more than 6,000 of them were shipped into the park by rail and barge and set free to roam. The plains and wood bison interbred and, at the time I was there, it was thought that no purebred animals remained. However, in the late 1970s and early 1980s unhybridized wood buffalo were discovered outside of the park boundaries and apparently successful attempts have since been made to establish several purebred herds.

There were supposedly about 8,000 bison in the park in 1952, a figure arrived at by aerial counts and ground surveys. Billy, who referred to mammalogists, ecologists and others of that ilk as "bugologists," thought that no one really knew the correct total. He cited the case of a ground survey where a bugologist was maintaining a watch along a stretch of dirt road in order to count the number of buffalo tracks appearing on it. Periodically, a chain would be stretched across the dusty trail and dragged along it to eradicate any existing tracks. What wasn't known to the scientist was that a water hole existed on one side of the road, with a wallow—a place denuded of vegetation where the buffalo could give themselves a dust bath—on the other side. Several times a day the same group of animals would transit back and forth across the road between their two favorite spots, thus ensuring that the bugologist's count would be biased on the high side of reality.

The bison were sufficiently numerous that, once each year, some culling of the herds took place. This occurred at a place called Hay Camp on the eastern side of the park. Here there was a portable abattoir which could be moved around to various locations where buffalo were shot, with butchers following along to carve up the carcasses. Most of the meat thus obtained was given to the Department of Indian Affairs for distribution to Natives throughout the North.

A problem arose in that the butchers couldn't keep up with the hunters, so some carcasses weren't processed in a timely fashion, reducing the quality of the meat and resulting in some spoilage. Thus, it was decided to build a huge corral of stout logs, about a mile long on each side, into which a herd could be driven. Once inside this corral, animals selected for culling could be sorted into a smaller enclosure and efficiently processed. Aircraft were used to start the herd moving toward the corral. Pat Carey, a well-known bush flier, was one of the pilots taking part in this operation.

I wasn't involved in the proceedings of the first such roundup, but heard about the results from Pat and Billy and others who were present. It seems that, after several long days and much low-level flying, about 1,000 bison were safely ensconced within the confines of the big corral. Along came a private aircraft, piloted by someone who wasn't aware of the situation with the cull. "Jeez," I'm sure he thought to himself, "what's going on down there." He banked the aircraft steeply and went screaming down in a shallow dive to have a closer look. One thousand buffalo looked up to the sky and said to themselves, "Jeez, what's that up there? I'm getting outa here." The herd stampeded, ploughing through the log stockade as though it were made of matchsticks. So it was back to the old method for the time being.

Another year, when I was no longer at Fort Smith but in my own district, I learned that army half-track vehicles were used in the roundup, coordinated with the use of walkie-talkie communication sets. Some bureaucrat was shipped out from Ottawa, ostensibly to oversee the buffalo cull and look into other official matters but actually, according to my informant, to get him out of his superiors' hair for the summer. (I feel certain of the truth of this assertion having had some subsequent dealings with the person in question.) The bureaucrat made an amusing sight, standing up front in the leading half-track as it bounced along over the meadows and through the trees, hanging on tightly to the vehicle with one hand, using his walkie-talkie in the other hand to issue instructions to the troops, no doubt imagining all the while that he was the commanding general of some important military operation.

Returning to Fort Smith after the bush fire on the portage road had been extinguished, I made the acquaintance of a personable young man called Johnny. There were no government-supplied lodgings at Fort Smith for itinerant employees such as myself, soon to be moving on to my own district. There was the Mackenzie Hotel, owned by the Hudson's Bay Company Fur Trade Division and managed by Paul Kaeser. The hotel was probably established, many years earlier, to take advantage of business opportunities presented by the wearisome sixteen-mile-long portage around the Slave River rapids. However, I couldn't afford to reside there for some indeterminate period of time. Johnny had the solution. He set me up with a camp cot, a small table and a wash basin on the second floor of an old log structure which was originally the first administrative building in the town. He and

Billy had an office of sorts on the first floor. Nearby, a large new wooden-framed edifice now held most of the government offices, including those occupied by my supervisors.

Johnny's story was subsequently told to me by his friends. Some time previously, Johnny had been cashiered from the Royal Canadian Mounted Police for marrying a Native girl without obtaining the permission of his commanding officer. The girl had become pregnant and there was some question as to whether Johnny or another constable was responsible. In the face of this uncertainty about paternity, he had done what he felt was the honorable thing. Now Johnny, temporarily employed by the government, was staying at Fort Smith while awaiting the results of an application for reinstatement in the Mounties.

The Force (as members of the RCMP usually called their organization), and many white people, still had the "squaw man" mentality at that time, which is to say that they decried marriages between whites and Indians. I wasn't burdened by such notions. During my time with the HBC fur trade, living on the Sturgeon Lake Reserve and making friends there, I came to realize that— given similar circumstances, with allowances for cultural differences—Indians were little different from Caucasians in their actions, beliefs and aspirations. So Johnny's marital status didn't bother me. I respected his decision to marry the girl but objected to the price he had to pay for it.

Johnny was a nice person—helpful, kind and unpretentious. He had apparently been a fine police officer, dedicated to performing his duties in a rational manner. All lawmen should be imbued with Johnny's qualities. After I left Fort Smith, I heard on the moccasin telegraph (the northern equivalent of the grapevine) that he had been able to re-enlist in the RCMP. Some years later, I read in a newspaper that Johnny, responding to a complaint of domestic violence while on duty in a town in British Columbia, had been badly wounded by a shotgun blast. He hovered near death for several months, but eventually recovered.

It was Johnny, a few weeks after I had first made his acquaintance, who gave me the message that I was wanted at the local Canadian Army Signal Corps station. (Each settlement in the

N.W.T. had a small armed forces detachment which was responsible for wireless communications throughout the North.) I walked over to the Signal Corps establishment and was confronted by a person demanding a cigar. A telegram had just come through from Mary advising me of the birth of our third son, Richard Howard.

Flying Firemen

BOOM!! The cabin of the small Stinson floatplane exploded into flames. The startled pilot shoved the control column forward, putting the aircraft into a shallow dive. His passenger dropped the cigarette which he had been attempting to light and threw up his hands to cover his face. Except for the intervention of fate, I would have been that passenger. Instead, it was George Wilson, superintendent of forests.

Confusion reigned supreme for a few moments after the explosion until it became apparent that the resultant fire was confined to the cabin upholstery and there was no other obvious damage. Grabbing a portable fire extinguisher, George proceeded to apply its contents to the flames with some diligence and soon had them doused. Doug Rae, the pilot, eased back on the control column, bringing the aircraft onto an even keel again. Fortunately, there had been ample altitude available for a smooth recovery.

Now a new hazard appeared. The fire-extinguishing fluid was carbon tetrachloride, notorious for its noxious vapors. The fumes made the two men lightheaded and faint, and Doug was worried lest he lose consciousness before landing his craft on the Slave River, a thousand feet below. He cranked a small window vent open as far as it would go, then sideslipped the Stinson in such a way that the inrushing air helped to keep the fumes away from his face. At the same time, the sideslipping motion caused a rapid loss of altitude. Soon he had the airplane safely back on the water, taxiing up to the seaplane dock. He and his passenger climbed out, coughing and hacking, feeling quite done in from the combined effects of the carbon tetrachloride and the excitement. It had been a very close call.

Events of the past twelve hours had determined who was to ride in the passenger seat on that alarming flight. A fierce thunderstorm had swept through the area during the night. One of my duties as a warden was to go on a routine air patrol after such a storm and try to spot smoke from any forest fires which may have been ignited by lightning strikes. The Stinson had been chartered for this purpose. Doug Rae was a young fellow newly arrived from the southwest coast of British Columbia. His avowed aim was to become a bonafide bush flier.

I reached the aircraft just as Doug finished showering the cabin with fly spray. He didn't want to go aloft carrying any additional passengers in the form of the large horseflies which infested the area, known locally as bulldogs. These flies land gently on your bare flesh, take their time choosing a select cut of meat, then suddenly dig in and rip out a big chunk. This can be very distracting.

We climbed into the Stinson, which was tied up to a small jetty about a mile downstream from the forebodingly named Rapids of the Drowned on the Slave River. As we buckled up our seat belts in preparation for takeoff, a truck came roaring down the riverbank road and stopped near the dock. Out jumped George Wilson, waving at us to hold position. He had just received a report from a commercial airlines pilot who had flown over a fire that was burning some distance to the south of our location. It appeared to be heading for the big timber along the river.

Most of the forest in the Northwest Territories is just scrub brush and muskeg, and not of much concern with regards to fire suppression unless it is in a productive trapping area. But some good stands of commercial timber could be found along the rivers and every effort was made to save them from devastation by fire. The superintendent of forests was anxious to examine the situation personally, so he commandeered "my" aircraft. Regretfully, I climbed out and turned the seat over to him. Away they went. The aircraft got up about 2,000 feet above the river and George pulled out a cigarette. They gained a little more altitude while he searched his pockets for his lighter. Having found it, he flicked it once or twice and that was it—the aforementioned BOOM!! occurred.

101

On investigation, it was realized that the fly spray fumes had exploded and the residue of liquid spray on the cabin upholstery had taken fire. But Doug swore that it couldn't have been the fly spray because the blurb on the side of the can said that it wouldn't burn. However, what the label actually stated, in quite large letters, was "inflammable." Doug, thinking of terms such as "insecure," "insensitive" and "inseparable," where the prefix "in" means "not," had mistakenly assumed that inflammable meant not flammable, but it means just the opposite. When Billy McNeil heard about the incident, he said, "Of course it burns; I use that stuff every morning for starting a fire in my wood cookstove."

The superintendent of forests, whose hair and eyebrows were slightly singed in the incident, swore off smoking right on the spot. As far as I know, he never touched another cigarette. In retrospect, I was glad that he had commandeered the aircraft for that flight because I was a smoker at the time and probably would have tried lighting up immediately after takeoff, with who knows what consequences.

I went up with Doug on the following day to undertake the planned fire patrol, it having been deferred because of all the previous excitement. He didn't spray the interior with bug juice this time, but he did take the aircraft up to its ceiling—its maximum useful altitude. When I commented on this he replied that if anything untoward happened he would be able to glide a long way, so I figured he was still a bit rattled from his experience with the fire. We chased a lot of cloud wisps, since they often look like smoke at a distance, but didn't find any fires except for the one we already knew about from the report by the airline pilot.

On another occasion Doug had a job ferrying several people to a lumber camp some distance downriver. As I hove into view, I could see his passengers waiting on the jetty while he finished refueling. There were two men and a very robust woman. Two seats would have been required to accommodate her bulk on a regular airline flight. She carried a big suitcase. Evidently the woman was the new cook for the lumber camp.

102

When the okay was given, one man climbed in and sat on the rear bench seat. At Doug's request, to distribute the load according to his liking, the cook and her suitcase squeezed in there too. It was a tight fit indeed, the male passenger being almost engulfed. The other man sat up front in the copilot's seat. I observed that the aircraft's floats had sunk well below their normal waterline, portending a difficult struggle to lift the plane off the water. I also saw the doubtful look on Doug's face, but he had already learned that overloaded aircraft were part of the bush pilot's lot and he had to give it a try.

He taxied away from the dock, pointed the nose of his craft upriver into the wind and gunned the engine. He gunned it all the way up to the foot of the rapids without being able to get the floats "on the step" (riding higher in the water for reduced resistance), so he came back for another try. This time he rocked the control column back and forth with a vengeance, trying to break the suction so the floats could rise up, but all to no avail. After several more futile attempts the Stinson returned to the jetty. The cabin door opened and all of the passengers climbed out. Out, too, came the floats, out of the water to rest at their normal water line. Then the two men climbed back in and closed the door. Doug opened the throttle, and away went the airplane, up on the step in no time and off into the blue, leaving one dejected-looking woman standing on the dock. A second trip had to be made to get the cook to her destination. After all, a lumber camp is nothing without a cook.

I never saw Doug again. He flew a few more charter trips in the next couple of days and then packed his gear and headed south toward civilization, apparently disillusioned with life as a bush pilot in the adventurous North.

Airborne fire patrols were only one aspect of forest protection in the Northwest Territories in the early 1950s. As already mentioned, there was a highly trained fire suppression crew, made up mostly of local Natives. They were ready to tackle a fire at a moment's notice. Most fires in the North, away from roads and railways, resulted from two causes: lightning and careless hunters or trappers. Fires due to the latter were actually started in the late winter or early spring, when the ground was still completely covered with snow. Muskrat hunters would allow their campfires to burn down into the muskeg where they might smolder away for weeks and months. Then, in the summer, the fires popped to the surface again as the ground cover dried out, to start a conflagration in the brush and trees. Most of the trees were small, only a few inches in diameter at the butt. There were seldom any dramatic outbursts like the crown fires of the mountain country where, given the right conditions, flames can sweep at tremendous speeds through the tree tops.

Many fires were just allowed to burn themselves out, much of the country being covered only with scrub brush where suppression was a waste of time and money. The regions that were of concern were good fur-producing sectors and locations along the main rivers where the only timber of any consequence was to be found. Every effort was made to prevent such areas from being devastated by fire. Primarily, this involved flying a crew, with their grub and equipment, to the nearest suitable landing place and having them pack into the fire site.

Nowadays the availability of helicopters, with their ability to land at or near the fire site, not only simplifies the transportation of men and materials, but saves the firefighters many a weary mile of backpacking, leaving them with more energy available for extinguishing the conflagration. In my time the procedure usually consisted of finding the closest lake big enough for a floatplane landing (and a loaded takeoff, since the crew had to be recovered eventually) where the firefighters could be dumped off to go stumbling through the bush and muskeg for a few miles carrying heavy packs. If the distance to be walked was great, or the walking excessively difficult, then resupply during the course of the firefighting effort took place by means of airdrops.

A major item in our catalog of fire suppression equipment was the portable engine-driven water pump. There were two kinds. One weighed about sixty pounds and could be attached directly to a packboard for convenient transport by a human packhorse. The other was substantially heavier, and of a much more awkward shape, so that it was usually attached to the middle of a sturdy pole carried on the shoulders of two crew members. This arrangement formed a kind of pendulum whose bobweight—the pump—often swayed out of phase with the motions of the carriers, resulting in some strange maneuvers.

The hose which accompanied the pumps was slightly permeable to water. In use, the surface of the hose would sweat, staying moist enough to prevent it from being burnt through should the fire happen to sweep over it. This was a real possibility because there could be hundreds of yards of hose laid out over as-yet unburned ground between the nozzle, squirting water on the fire, and the source of supply where the pump and its suction line were located.

A small hand pump was also used, somewhat akin to a bicycle tire pump. It was linked by a short hose to a water reservoir carried on the back of a firefighter. Colloquially—at least on the fire line—it was called a piss pump, from the size of the stream thrown out. It was useful in knocking out very small localized hot spots. Axes and brush hooks were used to clear trees and ground cover from the path of the fire.

The most important tools of all, though, were—and probably still are—the lowly shovel and the Pulaski (a tool which combines an ax blade and a grub hoe, named after its inventor). Since much of the North is covered by muskeg, the successful suppression of nearly all fires requires a lot of digging to root out the hot spots. The procedure—using the shovel, the Pulaski and some form of water pump—was to dig and soak, then dig and soak some more. Even in modern times, with developments such as water bombing along the front of a fire to slow its advance, there is still no substitute for men slugging it out on the ground, especially for a fire in muskeg country.

One of my early experiences with resupplying firefighters by airdrop took place shortly after the bug spray incident. A brush fire had broken out at a rat hunter's campsite. The hunter had vacated his camp sometime in April, thinking his fire was out. Unfortunately, it was not. It smoldered away deep in the muskeg, resurfacing in July. The site was about fifteen miles east of the

Slave River, in good trapping country, and the nearest water suitable for landing a floatplane was a small lake about five miles from the fire itself. A fire suppression crew hiked in to tackle the blaze, packing some fire pumps and some basic necessities for setting up camp. My assignment was to fly (as a passenger) in the de Havilland Beaver aircraft and airdrop additional food supplies and fire hose to the camp, then land at the lake to unload other items, such as more pumps and the gasoline to run them, which couldn't be tossed out of the airplane as blithely as were potatoes, bread or beans. Members of the suppression crew would hike out to the lake to retrieve these items and pack them back to the fire site.

When I write about airdropping supplies, I am not referring to the military type of operation where parachutes fill the skies. In our case, there wasn't a single blossoming chute to be seen. We simply went in low and kicked stuff out of the aircraft's loading door. The items were cushioned in shredded paper packing material and then sewn into burlap sacks to prevent them from scattering all over the landscape. Lids of jam tins were soldered on so that they wouldn't pop off on impact and spew jam over everything. Butter came from the producer in hermetically sealed cans, so it was no problem. Eggs and milk, both in powder form, also came in cans. Beans, macaroni, rice and the like were packaged in cloth bags. Potatoes were tossed out in—what else— potato sacks. During a drop it was "heads up, everybody," because the parcels landed with a heavy thud and it wouldn't do to be under one at the time. The cushioning effect of the muskeg prevented them from bouncing much.

On this day I had the task of kicking the packages out of the aircraft at the pilot's command of "Now." Never having done it before, I didn't kick hard enough on my first attempt and, to my great chagrin, the bundle dropped out of the door and into the float support struts, where it became lodged. The amount of extra drag this caused was a real surprise. Coupled with the slow airspeed being maintained for the drop, it nearly resulted in a stall— a loss of lift—right then and there. With only a hundred feet of altitude, this would have been disastrous for us. Luckily, Pat

Carey, our pilot on this occasion, was one of great experience. He reacted automatically to recover control of the airplane. Then, tight-lipped in the proper tradition of Hollywood pilot heroes, he struggled to slowly gain altitude, limped back to the lake, and landed v-e-r-y carefully. Here the offending parcel was removed from the struts, a few choice words were said to me about kicking harder, and we returned to the location of the fire to finish the drop.

Pat was a veteran bush pilot of considerable renown. He was also a cautious pilot who usually avoided dicey situations but who took great delight in thrilling his passengers with unexpected side-slips during landings. I'm certain that his experiences would fill a book. Unfortunately, I was only associated with him for a brief period of time before being transferred further north, so I didn't get a chance to hear his life story. Many years later, though, I did learn about the final episode in his career as bush pilot, the one that convinced him to retire. Some embellishments may have been added to the story over the years but I will tell it just as I heard it.

It seems that Pat, getting on in years, was now flying charters in the Yukon. One day, returning to home base from a long trip in his Beaver aircraft, a blinding snowstorm caught him over the Yukon mountains. There was zero visibility in the blizzard and the daylight was fading fast. Without realizing it, Pat was flying down among the mountain peaks. Or maybe he did realize it, but couldn't do anything about it except to try climbing out above the rocks and the storm.

He didn't make it. The snow-covered ground in front of him rose up gradually toward a small gap separating two rocky crests. The Beaver flew into the cleft just at ground level. The wings met with the sheer walls on either side and parted company from the fuselage, reducing the plane's forward momentum as the crumpling aluminum ribs and skin absorbed some of the energy of the crash. The fuselage continued on a short distance, its progress slowed further by the heavy snow through which it was ploughing. It came to rest wedged securely in the crevice between the rocky cliffs.

The aircraft had decelerated smoothly, without causing much more commotion than a panic stop in an automobile. Pat was shaken but uninjured. The Beaver was crammed so tightly into the cleft in the mountain that he couldn't exit through the doors. He had to punch his way through the cabin roof, helped by the fact of the missing wings. As I heard the story, Pat was rescued the next day, somewhat weary and chilled. His first act upon being returned to home base—after getting warmed and rested— was to fill out his retirement papers.

Bush pilots like Pat, and earlier airmen like Wop May, Punch Dickens, Matt Berry, Herbert Hollick-Kenyon and Walter Gilbert, were my heroes. I envied them their accomplishments and would have liked to emulate them, combining the excitement of flying with a love of the outdoors.

I don't know what triggered my attraction to aviation. Perhaps it resulted from attendance at a school adjacent to the first Calgary municipal airport. This was just a large field, with no special runways, where small planes could take off into the wind no matter the direction from which it blew. Or perhaps the fascination of aviation was just in the air, in a manner of speaking. Almost everyone, no matter their age, was interested in things aeronautical as the closing years of the Golden Age of aviation mutated into the beginning years of the war.

Many children, myself included, were thrilled when the British-American Oil Company sponsored the Jimmie Allen Club in Canada. The latest issue of the Jimmie Allen newsletter, full of aviation doings, was distributed each month through the local B-A service stations. Jimmie Allen was a young American radio personality involved in various fictional aeronautical adventures. Club members could purchase a series of flying model airplane kits, starting with a small wooden hand-launched glider, then going on to a very basic rubber-powered propeller-driven model, and working on up through various degrees of constructional difficulty to the Jimmie Allen Air Racer, the epitome of stick-and-tissue models (but which cost the enormous sum of

$1.50 or thereabouts). I liked to build model airplanes but could seldom afford them.

One year, in the summer holidays, a Jimmie Allen Air Race was held at the old airport. Kids who had built the Air Racer competed with each other to see whose machine was the best in terms of distance covered or duration of flight. There was a spectacular mass launch of the models, most of which did an ungraceful pirouette or two before crashing to the ground, their builders being uninformed about the adjustments required for stable flight. The highlight of the meet was the appearance of the latest British fighter plane, the marvelous Hawker Hurricane, which made a low pass over the crowd at the tremendous speed of nearly 300 miles per hour!

My ambition to be a pilot was shot down by my inadequate vision, a handicap uncovered during the war when I joined the Air Cadets. This agency's (unstated) purpose was to provide partly trained replacements for the casualties of combat, including not only pilots but other flight crew as well. However, the organization was highly disorganized at that time. After spending a number of evenings hanging around the mobilization center (No.2 Wireless School of the British Commonwealth Air Training Plan) with no direction, I lost patience with the system and resigned.

Wolf Attack

Pine Lake, in the interior of Wood Buffalo National Park, was a sparkling body of water with a small sandy beach at the north end but otherwise surrounded by an abundant forest. It was connected to Fort Smith by a long winding trail encumbered with obstacles such as mudholes, sand traps and herds of buffalo. A substantial log cabin had just been constructed adjacent to the beach for the use of the warden service. Billy McNeil and I planned to spend some time there putting the site in order, checking out the wildlife, and generally keeping an eye on things. I was looking forward to the sojourn, not only to get out from under the thumb of authority at Fort Smith, but to listen to some of Billy's fascinating stories.

For the trip to Pine Lake, we requisitioned an old ex-army vehicle—a so-called four-by-four truck—from the government motor pool, rounded up some grub and, with Billy at the wheel, off we went. After some miles along the way, in aspen-dotted meadowland, we encountered several herds of buffalo, one such group containing about 200 members. I tried to obtain some photographs, but found it difficult to get close to the animals. They quickly got wind of me and stampeded away, a spectacular sight reminiscent of the Old West.

Continuing on our course, we rounded a curve in the trail and found a large bull buffalo confronting us. Billy slammed on the brakes. I took a photograph of the animal through the windshield and was ready to press on, assuming that the beast would move off the road to avoid us. But Billy informed me that he had tried that approach on a previous occasion and the buffalo had charged, hitting the front of the truck, raising it in the air and running its head and shoulders underneath the front suspension. Unbeknownst to Billy—nervously waiting for the beast to stand up and perhaps flip the vehicle on its side—it was dead of a broken neck. After a while, Billy surmised that this was the case and carefully got out for a look. Sure enough, the truck had won the joust. Billy was able to back off the critter and drive around it. So now we waited it out. After about fifteen minutes, the buffalo got tired of staring us down and wheeled off into the bush.

Farther on, now into a region of sandhills sparsely covered with jackpine, our vehicle had a breakdown. A bracket on the rear suspension system had come unshipped. We built a smudge fire upwind, in the middle of the trail, to combat the hordes of mosquitoes which were attacking us while we jacked the back of the truck up. Then we sat in the smoke and pondered our situation. As an old prairie boy, I figured if we only had some baling wire in our toolkit we could make a haywire repair. Unfortunately, we didn't have any wire of any description with us, but Billy had an inspiration. He knew that, many years before, a single-wire telephone line had been strung through the bush nearby, originating at some point in Alberta and terminating at Fort Smith. Its use had long since been abandoned. Billy took a pair of pliers and went off to search for some sign of the old line. About twenty minutes later he was back, dragging a length of telephone wire. We lashed up the bracket with it and were soon on our way again.

Arriving eventually at Pine Lake, we chased the mice out of the cabin and set up housekeeping. In the days to come we would build a stone fireplace, a picnic table, a small dock and other conveniences which local tourists could use. But, to begin with, there was a canoe stored at the cabin, so I put it in the water and made an exploratory trip around part of the lakeshore.

At intervals, as I paddled along, the weird trilling laughter of loons echoed wildly across the water. Once, I spotted the dark form of one of the feathered yodelers idling near the shoreline. Loons have a variety of unusual calls, some mournful and some maniacal. They become more vocal in the evening, or when a dark storm front is moving in, one bird calling and others responding, the notes resounding through the deepening gloom. As I cruised by a marshy area, the distinctive sound of a bittern boomed forth, but I couldn't locate its well-camouflaged form among the vegetation. After an exhilarating paddle I returned to the cabin to help Billy with some of the chores.

111

That evening as we were sitting down to supper in the cabin, we heard an airplane overhead and rushed outside in the hope of seeing it land on the lake and taxi up to our beach. There was nothing there. An hour later, we again heard the sound of an aircraft engine and dashed out to scan the sky. Still nothing. Was this the Flying Dutchman of the airways? After yet another such episode we became convinced that we were being deceived by a local noise and sought for its source. It turned out to be our chimney. When a breeze was blowing in just the right direction, at just the right speed, the air in the top of the sheet metal chimney pipe was set into resonance, making the most realistic imitation of an aircraft engine that I have ever heard.

❖

The next morning I prepared to hike down a new trail, recently bulldozed to assist fire suppression efforts. Two days earlier a severe electrical storm had lashed the area, flinging stupendous bolts of lightning from sky to ground. The storm might have started a bush fire, so I wanted to check for timber smoke. When the wind is right, it is possible to smell smoke from a smoldering lightning-blasted tree for several miles. I picked up a small ax and an old ex-army rifle of .303 caliber, put a few cartridges in my pocket and headed out. I was reluctant to haul the heavy rifle around, but I might spot a wolf. Wherever there were buffalo, there were often wolves too.

About three miles from the cabin I began smelling smoke. I followed the odor for another half mile to a point just off the trail where an old standing snag was smoldering away. The lightning had struck near the top of the dead tree and had traced out a charred twisting path as it followed the grain of the wood to the ground. About fifteen feet up, the tree was smoking quite heavily but, with everything still damp from the rain which accompanied the storm, the fire had yet to become well established. I spent some time chopping the tree down and then chopping it up to make certain that I found every last spark, covering the hot spots with moist soil to cool them down.

Having extinguished the smoldering snag, I decided to return to the cabin. I had only just started down the homeward trail when I noticed an animal some distance ahead of me. I couldn't quite make out what it was. I had recently acquired eye glasses to cope with poor vision but hadn't yet admitted to myself that I should be wearing them all the time. However, I did have them in my pocket. I assumed, from its size, that the animal was a young buffalo calf and decided to put my glasses on in order to keep a better lookout for the calf's mother which would probably be close by. I loaded a shell into the chamber of the rifle just in case she didn't take kindly to my intrusion on the scene. In the meantime, the animal apparently caught my scent, since I was upwind of it, and disappeared into the bush.

I walked up to the place where I had last seen it, and eyed the evidence on the ground. It was apparent from the tracks that the animal was actually a large wolf. It had been following along my back trail, more or less in my footprints, as wolves sometimes do out of curiosity. I assumed that this one was now long gone, since it had obviously spotted me, and continued on my way. A few minutes later, however, some sixth sense made me look back. There was the wolf, charging along toward me!

It is often said that wolves don't attack humans—or, as one old-timer maintained, "Any man that says he's been et by a wolf is a liar"—but I wasn't going to take a chance. In one motion, I dropped my ax, raised the rifle to my shoulder and released the safety catch. When the wolf was about seventy-five yards away, looming large in my rifle sights, I pulled the trigger and waited for something to happen. In the excitement of the moment, I didn't even hear the sound of the shot as the cartridge fired. The beast tumbled into the dirt and slid along on its snout for a short distance. I started to relax. Then...it got up and kept on coming!

I didn't have time to ponder the unusual behavior of this wolf, or wonder why it seemed bent on attacking me. Only later did I learn that it was in the early stages of a hopeless struggle with the rabies virus. But right now it was bounding closer and closer. I tugged at the bolt of my rifle to put another shell into the chamber. The bolt wouldn't budge! Something must be jammed! The wolf was almost upon me...

As the distance between us narrowed, I started getting very nervous. That wolf was still charging directly for me. I tried again to open the rifle bolt, to eject the spent shell and insert a live round, by moving the bolt handle up and back. I'd always used a bolt-action rifle and this motion was automatic for me. Again the bolt wouldn't budge! I tried harder. Still no movement!

Now, with the wolf much too close for comfort, I hit the bolt handle on the gun as hard as I could with my hand, assuming that it was just jammed. Still nothing budged. Desperately, I tried again. Time seemed to be ticking over very leisurely, like the television commercial where two lovers are running toward each other in slow motion, her long tresses undulating leisurely up and down as they stream out behind her, his...well, who's watching him. But you know what I mean. The wolf was like the girl's hair. Every bound seemed to take minutes to complete.

Suddenly my mind cleared as I felt the hurt in my hand from banging the bolt handle. I realized what the problem was. I had dealt with it only minutes before while loading the first cartridge, but it hadn't registered in my brain with sufficient intensity for automatic recall. The rifle was an unfamiliar old ex-Canadian Army Ross Mk.III rifle. The bolt handle on this abomination, unlike most respectable bolt actions, did not have to (and could not) move upwards first before traveling backwards. Its only motion was fore and aft. Some trick of the mechanism kept the bolt from flying backwards into your face when the shell fired. I learned later that this particular make of rifle was taken out of service (thrown out might be a better term) in 1916. The army rated its acquisition as an unmitigated disaster, the straight-pull bolt action being so easily jammed by dirt and grime. Why it was still in use with the warden service thirty-five years later is beyond me; another example of government parsimony, I would guess.

Now, realizing the cause of my difficulties, I succeeded in getting another shell into the chamber. I raised the gun, sighted swiftly at the oncoming beast and squeezed the trigger. Again the sound of the shot went unheard by me, blocked out by the panic of the moment, but the wolf tumbled into the dirt and lay still.

This time he was dead. I started breathing once more—and shaking almost uncontrollably from delayed excitement.

Judging by the aggressive behavior of the wolf, and its lack of fear, I thought that it might have rabies. We had standing instructions in the warden service to send the heads of any suspect animals to headquarters—an unavoidable pun for which I make no apology—for laboratory testing. I went back to the cabin and got a Swede saw, plus rubber gloves and a special metal container that had been provided for just such an eventuality. Then I returned to the carcass and carefully sawed off the head. This appendage was shipped by air, in its sealed container, from Fort Smith to the test lab. Months later, I was informed of the results and the wolf had indeed been rabid.

After that episode I concluded that, while wolves may not ordinarily attack humans, rabid wolves can't be depended upon to remember the rules of the game. I didn't know it at the time, but this incident signaled the onset of a major rabies epidemic that I had to contend with later on.

Hunger

After vacationing—for that's what it seemed like—at the Pine Lake cabin for several more days, Billy and I returned to Fort Smith. Here I was tutored by George Wilson, superintendent of forests, about the N.W.T. forestry regulations. This was in preparation for a check on a lumbering operation to verify compliance with certain requirements set out in the timber permit issued to the proprietor. George was a congenial person, well-versed in forestry law and lore, and a good teacher.

(As a footnote to history, George is the person primarily responsible for discovering the long-sought-for summer nesting ground of the whooping crane, a species on the verge of extinction. In 1954, he and his pilot sighted a pair of the birds as they returned from the scene of a bush fire in the northern part of Wood Buffalo National Park. Government mammalogist William Fuller performed the ensuing investigation into the nesting grounds, but to George must go the credit for recognizing the significance of the sighting.)

George and I subsequently flew in to the lumber camp on the Slave River. This operation, like most in the N.W.T., was a small one involving only a few people. Both the boss and crew resided on a barge tied up alongside the bank in the calm waters of a snye (backwater). As our floatplane nosed into the bank and the engine stopped, the boss gave a shout, inviting us on board.

It wasn't possible to transfer directly from the small plane to the barge since the latter sat high in the water. It was necessary to first step from the plane's floats onto land, clamber up the steep bank of the river, and then board the barge—much easier said than done. The deck of the barge was several feet lower than the bank elevation. The two were connected with a plank, two inches thick, ten inches wide and perhaps twenty feet long. It was bowed downward in the center by its own weight. There was no supporting structure of any kind, just that long limber piece of rough lumber. We both blanched when we saw it, but it was either walk that plank or lose face for the forestry service. I hung back, knowing that protocol required George to go first. If he fell in, it would give me an excuse to back down. He took a few tentative steps, the plank deflecting and bouncing under him. The downhill slope made the undertaking doubly difficult. Then George appeared to resolve himself to the venture, come what may. He strode quite boldly forward and made it onto the deck without mishap, the plank vibrating wildly behind him. There went my excuse. Fortunately, I was able to duplicate the performance, but not nearly so boldly, and only after mentally rejecting the option of sliding down the rough, slivery surface of the plank on the seat of my pants. After finishing our business with the camp boss, we found it easier to walk back up the plank knowing that, in case of an incipient fall, we had only to lean forward a bit to grasp the edges of the plank in our hands.

For anyone living and working along the Slave River, it was necessary to develop the agility and balance for walking narrow flexible planks to get from vessel to land and back again. The ice-gouged banks of the river were generally high and steep except in the delta area where the river emptied into Great Slave Lake through several channels.

Most of the supplies required to sustain the northern population moved along river and lake by tug and barge. On the river, tugs were rigged to push the barges rather than tow them. On a tow, if the boat happens to run onto an unseen sandbar, the barge can smash into the boat, driving it harder aground. By pushing, the barge encounters the bar first, leaving the tug free to pull the barge loose. There were lots of sandbars along the river, their position often changing from year to year. Most of the boats had sufficient crew that they could run without tying up at night, taking advantage of the long periods of summer daylight. Darkness descended only briefly, in the early morning hours.

Downriver from Fort Smith, there were some fast-water stretches on the Slave River but no rapids. Just upstream, though, was a whole series of dangerous drops, with names like Mountain Rapids, Pelican Rapids and the Rapids of the Drowned. The latter took its name from an accident in which five voyageurs lost their lives in the early days of the fur trade. Pelican Rapids was so designated because of a colony of nesting pelicans situated on a rocky island in midriver. The appellation of Mountain Rapids was due to a high hill encumbering the original portage trail around the tumultuous water, but it could have justifiably arisen from the mountainous standing waves, up to twenty feet high, occurring at the foot of the chute. The rapids were the reason for the existence of the towns of Fitzgerald and Fort Smith, which developed at either end of the portage trail.

During World War II, when the U.S. army was more or less given free run of the country to build the Canol Project—an oil pipeline proceeding west from Norman Wells toward the Alaska Highway—many of their supplies came down the Slave and Mackenzie River systems. The Yanks got impatient with delays engendered by the portage around the rough spots and tried turning several barges loose at the head of the rapids to make their own way through the turbulent waters. According to reports, nothing more than kindling wood was ever recovered at the foot of the rapids.

Returning from the Slave River lumber camp, I hinted around the Fort Smith headquarters that it was time for me to be assigned to a district of my own. Bill Sloan finally told me that he still had to resolve some problems concerning the transfer of other wardens to new locations. I went back to the routine of memorizing game regulations and making new acquaintances around town.

A few days later a fire was discovered burning in good trapping country east of the Slave River, so I flew in with a suppression crew to the closest suitable lake and prepared to pack in to the site of the blaze. Pat Carey was our pilot once again, with his Beaver aircraft. We had with us a local trapper, familiar with the region, who could not only guide us in on the best route to the conflagration, but would also help to fight it.

We shouldered our loads and struck out across muskeg and rock for the scene of the fire. Having only recently come from surveying timber berths in the woods of British Columbia, where most of the walking was on or around big cedar logs and soft forest mulch, I was still wearing my caulk boots. These had been a necessity in the B.C. environment, but I quickly found out that they were less than ideal for traversing the humped Precambrian rock outcrops of the Canadian Shield, and they weren't so good in the intervening areas of unavoidable muskeg either. The steel caulks on rocks behaved like skates on ice. I had been slipping and sliding around for a while, generating several broken blisters in the process, when I was offered the loan of a spare pair of moccasins by one of the crew members who took pity on me. I donned the moccasins and hung my fancy boots in a tree for retrieval on the return journey. I might just as well have left them there permanently, for I never wore them again. Moccasins are the best footgear for bush travel, summer and winter. No break-in required; in wet weather (or anytime), don rubbers over them to keep them dry and clean; in winter, switch to a larger size with warm duffle socks inside. Real comfort!

We got to the fire site late that night during the short period of darkness that was all that prevailed at that time of year. Two crew members set up a tent to shelter our supplies, and others started a small campfire to brew some coffee. Tired from the exertions of the day—packing a heavy load up and down the rocky outcrops and over the spongy muskeg took some getting used to—I just grabbed a blanket from the supply tent, rolled up in it on the nearest smooth patch of ground, and fell fast asleep.

The next morning I awoke to discover, with something of a shock, that the ground all around me was covered with ashes, soot and charcoal. We were camped in the middle of a burned-over piece of the countryside. It was not very clean living by any means—everything and everybody quickly acquired a dull black patina. A grassy meadow beside a gently flowing stream would have been more to my liking, but there wasn't much grass in that country and few proper streams. Upon reflection, however, our present location made sense. When you don't know where the fire may blaze up next, what safer place to be than right where the damage has already been done?

There were numerous small potholes in the area, full of brown-stained muskeg water which was quite adequate for our fire pumps and for cooking. We had a competent cook with us, always an asset on the fire line. After breakfast, we got busy trying to contain the blaze. It was well established in the muskeg, and had burnt all of the surface vegetation over tens of acres. We had a small portable two-way radio so we could communicate with headquarters if the need arose, provided that the atmospheric conditions were favorable. Later that first day, we had an air drop of additional supplies, with all the goods surviving the fall and none of them landing on a crew member.

Following a week of hard work, mostly of the dig and soak variety, we had the fire extinguished. The crew laid the hoses out to dry and cleaned the equipment as best they could. A proper cleanup would have to await the return to base. I sketched a rough map showing the extent of the burned-over area for the office records.

Meanwhile, our grub supply had run out and we were anxiously awaiting another air drop, overdue from the previous day when our area had been socked in with low clouds. To make matters worse, the summer had become one of widespread, rampaging bush fires throughout the North and a heavy haze of smoke hung over the whole countryside. The cloud and smoke combined to prevent Pat from locating us. We had heard him passing overhead several times but couldn't signal him—our radio gave us nothing but static. He had finally terminated his search and left the area, presumably to try again the following day.

So now, with the sky relatively clear, we anticipated Pat's return, but we waited in vain. As we later learned, he had been called away to haul equipment to the location of yet another fire. This one threatened some valuable timber along the Slave River. Thus, it got priority over hungry firefighters. After waiting until noon with no sound of an aircraft engine, we decided to pack our gear out to the rendezvous lake. Since we were doing this on empty stomachs, it seemed to be harder work than usual, and most of us felt quite fatigued on our arrival at the lake. It was going to take two trips to get everything out, so we resolved to wait for the appearance of some food before making the second trip. The cook set out several rabbit snares in the hope of capturing something for the stew pot, but had no luck.

We lay around in our blankets for the rest of that day, dozing off occasionally to conserve energy and to fend off boredom. The remainder of the time was spent discussing in detail the big meals we would have when we finally returned to civilization.

My thoughts turned to my childhood days during the Great Depression. Our diet then was quite frugal and uninspiring except for fresh vegetables from a garden plot. We ate a lot of rice and beans and hash. Our jams were homemade, of rhubarb or vegetable marrow. We could have either jam or butter on our bread, but not both at once. When we had syrup, it was diluted with hot water to make it stretch further. The bread was baked at home, a labor-intensive process but it saved a few pennies a day and the cloth flour sacks could be used for dish towels and other things.

Our staple fruit was stewed rhubarb, occasionally mixed with wild berries. Fresh fruits were a rarity at our house (and at many others), and all the more appreciated when some put in an appearance. We usually had oranges at Christmas and apples for a couple of weeks in November, the latter the result of canvassing the neighborhood on October 31 shouting "Halloween apples." The rest of the year any kid seen eating an apple faced the challenge known as "coresies." He had to surrender the core of his apple to the first person saying "coresies" to him. If he didn't leave a little "meat" on the core, he could expect some taunts about his stinginess.

I'm not complaining about the modest menu. We often had skimpy meals which lacked nutritional balance, but at least we were never really hungry. Occasionally I refused to eat the food set in front of me because of an intense dislike for the taste of it. This was especially the case in winter, when my mother persisted in trying to get me to eat various kinds of porridge "for the sake of my health." Unfortunately, my Scottish ancestors neglected to pass the porridge-loving gene down to me. Many were the times that I was late for school, or nearly so, through having to sit at the table until I finished the dreadful stuff. In fact, I never did consume a complete bowlful of porridge at a sitting. Sometimes I managed to throw up, a reasonably certain way of avoiding further demands to eat up.

Any grumbling I did about our food always elicited the same response from my mother: "The starving children in Europe would be glad to have this food; they're lucky to get a crust of dry bread." I did appreciate the fact that there were hungry people in the world. Just before the war started, I would see them almost every day—unemployed men roaming the country in search of work, knocking at neighborhood doors to ask if some food could be spared. My mother frequently responded to such requests with a sandwich or two, sometimes to be consumed on the porch steps with a cup of tea, sometimes carried away to be eaten later, but always accepted with gratitude. In a childish mean-spirited way I felt that those men should be grateful; at least they got butter on their sandwiches.

Now, dozing beside the lake, I recollected my mother's admonition about the children in Europe. I surely sympathized with those poor kids on that day as I waited impatiently for the arrival of our overdue provisions.

At some point during the day, while I was snoozing, the blanket which was covering me to help ward off flies and mosquitoes came askew so that my legs stuck out at the bottom. I was fully clothed but my pant cuff rode up, exposing my leg to a vicious attack by some insect of unknown ancestry. When I woke up there was a slightly swollen ring of flesh completely surrounding one leg, just at the top of my stocking. At first I thought a few bulldog flies had been feeding on me, but there was no indication of their individual bites—the missing chunks of flesh are usually obvious. The swelling continued to increase over the next few hours until it was as thick as my thumb and very painful. None of the crew, all locals, had ever seen the like. Even days later the swollen area was still puffed up and sore. It gradually turned black and blue, the pain and swelling subsided somewhat, and the itching began. Weeks later, taut bruised skin was still in evidence, fading only gradually away.

My guess is that I was bitten by some type of spider, a particularly barbarous and unsociable one to be sure, and certainly not one of the basement-variety spiders. (I was very familiar with basement spiders. Often, when I was young, I slept on an army cot in the basement of whichever house we were inhabiting at the time. Some basements were better than others—less dank and dingy—but all were bare unfriendly rough concrete. In those days, basements were just a place in which to put the furnace and hot water tank, not space for extra rooms. The inevitable result of bedding down in the basement was that my body was usually covered with spider bites, the spiders apparently objecting to giving up a portion of their abode to an outsider.)

There were other insects around besides the ubiquitous mosquitoes and bulldog flies. The tiny flies called "no-seeums," familiar to most people, were abundant in the North during the warm season. They can raise substantial welts, especially on the head at hat brim level, but nothing comparable to that resulting from the attack on my leg by the unknown bug.

At the rendezvous lake, there didn't seem to be many birds flying about in the sunlight to feast on the bounty of insect life. In the late twilight hours, though, flocks of nighthawks gobbled up any bugs bold enough to take flight as darkness was falling. The swift nighthawks, twisting and twirling in fantastic gyrations as they pursued the small bits of nourishing protein across the sky, could be seen only dimly in the pale light. With each bug swallowed, a quantity of air is also ingested by the birds. After a certain volume of air accumulates in their systems, the nighthawks go into a power dive. At the bottom of the dive, just as they initiate a pull-up maneuver, the air is expelled with a loud "whump," like a miniature sonic boom.

Early the next morning, under a smoky but cloudless sky, Pat and his Beaver finally put in an appearance. He landed on the lake and we unloaded some supplies for the unlucky crew members who were designated to make another trip to retrieve the rest of our gear from the site of the burn. That group immediately built a fire to start cooking breakfast. It was indeed break fast

123

time for them. They had been without food for almost forty-eight hours. So had the rest of us, but Pat was in too much of a hurry to wait while we shared the meal. We clambered aboard the aircraft and took off for home base.

I was looking forward to landing back at Fort Smith and dashing up the river bank to the hotel dining room to wrap myself around a large meal. Alas, it was not to be. At least, not the way I had imagined it. The Beaver touched down on the Slave River and taxied up to the jetty. As I climbed out, I was approached by Superintendent Sloan with the news that I was being posted a hundred-odd miles downriver to Fort Resolution. Apparently my earlier hints had been fruitful. I was to travel there by the government river boat, the MB *Buffalo*, which was leaving immediately. My personal effects had already been packed up for me and loaded aboard, anticipating my return from the firefighting job. So much for my big food binge at the hotel. I also missed out on bidding adieu to my friends at Fort Smith.

I boarded the boat, the lines were cast off, and away we went into the mainstream current of the big muddy river. The MB *Buffalo* was about forty feet long, manned by a crew of three: captain, engineer and deckhand. The deckhand doubled as cook. They were all busy getting underway, but I had only one thought in mind. I went to the galley and started rustling some grub. I downed a can of cold beans for an appetizer while warming up a main course of beef stew mixed with undiluted vegetable soup. This was accompanied by several slices of bread and butter. Next, a can of peaches and a handful of store-bought cookies provided dessert, the whole washed down with lots of coffee. At last my stomach felt full again. Those kids in Europe would certainly have been envious. With my hunger finally satisfied, I went forward to meet the captain.

Captain Bligh

The captain of the MB *Buffalo*, Larry Crozier, was new to the North and to the warden service. He had just arrived from the Pacific Coast where, according to him, he was prominent—even pre-eminent—in maritime affairs. It could be said of Crozier, as Mrs. Paul Gaugin is reputed to have said of her artist husband, that he was "wholly absorbed in contemplating his own magnificence." He began informing me of his greatness as soon as I presented myself to him. I was not impressed.

Subsequently, over the course of the next few weeks, Crozier so impressed the superintendent of game, who was his boss as well as mine, that he got himself fired. I always remember him under the sobriquet of Captain Bligh. There were two reasons for attaching this infamous appellation to him. One was his autocratic manner, something which didn't go over at all well in the warden service, where cooperation was the key. The other reason will become clear below.

For now, we were chugging downstream on a bright summer day. The engineer and the deckhand were locals, experienced in their work. The cook, however, lacked expertise, a fact attested to by every meal he served. (Recall that the deckhand and cook were one and the same person.) Moreover, he hated the chores that went with being cook. We hadn't made too many miles downstream when a solution to the problem came in sight, although we didn't realize it at first (and we tried to repudiate it later).

On the river ahead of us we saw a small canoe carrying two men. A load of gear was jammed in around them. The canoe had only an inch or two of freeboard, so even small waves were splashing over its gunwales. The craft was just eleven feet long; a sixteen-footer would have been more appropriate in the circumstances. The two paddlers hailed us as we approached, and the captain ordered slow ahead to allow them to come alongside. They did so cautiously to avoid being swamped by our bow wave. The *Buffalo*, like most larger river vessels, had a blunt bow to facilitate pushing a barge and it generated a substantial wave even at slow speeds.

As the men clambered aboard, they introduced themselves as two young Irishmen, straight from the "old sod," looking for adventure in the wild northland. One was tall and slender and the other was quite short, much like Mutt and Jeff of early comic fame. These Irish rovers had already been traveling for some weeks down the Athabasca River system and had been held up by wind on several occasions because of the insubstantial freeboard of their canoe. Their destination was actually the west coast of Alaska via the Mackenzie and Peel Rivers, with a portage over the mountains to the Yukon River system. They said they would welcome a lift as far as we could take them, which was Fort Resolution on the south shore of Great Slave Lake, a few miles around to the west from the Slave River delta.

An examination of the contents of the Irishmen's canoe provided some entertainment. For grub, they had only the dregs of a sack of flour, a small container of baking powder, a bit of rice, some sugar and some tea. These supplies were replenished from time to time at settlements along the way. They had planned to live off the land as much as possible and had equipped themselves with a shotgun and an antique rifle. Unfortunately, they hadn't known that it was illegal to kill game animals without a licence, that the hunting season was closed in the summer and that, basically, only residents of the Northwest Territories could obtain a licence. So their weapons were pretty much useless baggage. To cook the anticipated game, they had one large pot and a big cast iron skillet. These appliances probably saw more boiled rice and fried bannock than anything else. For bedding they carried several blankets, and a small tarpaulin provided them with minimal shelter at night.

The tall one wore a wide leather belt about his waist, with various sharp-edged instruments attached. Two sheaths on the right side carried knives, a runty one that was hardly even suitable for opening cans, plus the largest one that I've ever seen outside of a *Crocodile Dundee* movie, only slightly smaller than a machete. A sheath on the left side carried a fancy hatchet. All of these were just more useless baggage. Had the canoe tipped, that mass of metal would have ensured the wearer of a quick trip to the bottom of the river. What they didn't have was a proper ax, to

126

me the most valuable tool of all in the bush. I always carried a small HBC ax, sometimes called a boy's ax because of its size. With such an ax, one could chop firewood and tent poles, open cans, carve a paddle or do any other camp chore that required a sharp edge for cutting or a blunt back for pounding.

One of the first things the men did was declare their willingness to work for passage. The deckhand, ignoring the captain's prerogative, immediately asked, "Can either of you cook?" The short one volunteered he was a good cook and would be pleased to take on the position. Thus the matter was, seemingly, happily settled. I'm not aware of exactly what our new cook was used to dishing out in the culinary department, but it was soon apparent that it wasn't vegetables, meats or pastries. Perhaps it was porridge. I was against porridge on principal (stemming from childhood experiences), so I didn't try his variety.

On the second day at the job, the cook declared that one of the things he excelled at was the making of pies, any kind of pies. What did we desire? There being plenty of raisins aboard, a raisin pie was the logical choice. He couldn't locate any flour and didn't bother asking if we had any. Instead, he took some graham wafers, crunched them up, added water to the crumbs, and patted the gooey mixture into a pie pan. Several handfuls of dry raisins came next, with no sauce of any kind. He finished up with more of the wafer mixture over the top to hold the raisins in. Finally, he heated the concoction in the oven. At mealtime, he didn't appear to be at all upset or insulted when no one but he and his compatriot would eat the pie. He was either naive or had been too long in the bush, for he seemed to really believe that he was a good chef. Or perhaps they do things differently in Ireland. Unfortunately, the deckhand refused to re-assume the cooking chores, so we were stuck with what we had for the time being.

❖

The MB *Buffalo* finished traversing the Slave River and pointed its nose west as the journey to Fort Resolution neared its end. Everyone had survived the epicurean ministrations of the new cook, but the crew members were muttering among themselves about Captain Bligh's arrogant and peremptory manner of command. Further, it was apparent that the captain was determined to be the master, not just of the ship but of all its operations, with everyone else his servant. In truth, his position actually required that he be at the beck and call of the wardens, to perform whatever services they required.

As the boat swung around Moose-Deer Island, the village of Fort Resolution came into view in the distance, sprawling along the low foreshore of the lake. Flags were flying from the Hudson's Bay Company store, the RCMP detachment buildings and the Canadian Army Signal Corps establishment. Near the latter, two antenna towers reached high into the sky. Other small buildings were scattered about, residences of the local inhabitants. To the south of these were the larger buildings of the Roman Catholic mission, gleaming white in the sunlight.

Fort Resolution was established in 1786 as a Northwest Company trading post, an organization that eventually merged with the Hudson's Bay Company after many years of fierce competition between the two rival firms. For well over one hundred years the village had been a crossroads for travelers in the North, including such historical figures as Peter Pond, Sir John Franklin, George Back, Warburton Pike, Ernest Thompson Seton and John Hornby. Now it was just a backwater, bypassed by most people in favor of the new northern metropolis, Yellowknife, on the north shore of Great Slave Lake.

Coming alongside the wharf, we were met by Bill Day, the incumbent warden. Fort Resolution was the headquarters for his district. Now I was to assume command here and he was to be transferred to another region, although there was apparently still some uncertainty about just where that would be. He took me to the warden establishment where I settled in, temporarily, to a small office building containing a cot to sleep on. Bill was especially pleased at the arrival of the MB *Buffalo* because it was scheduled to ferry him and his family across the lake to Yellowknife, where they could all receive some much-needed dental care and indulge in some shopping and visiting. Subsequently they would be ferried back again to pack up their belongings and proceed to their new posting, assuming that Superintendent Sloan would finally arrive at a decision on it.

Before leaving for Yellowknife, Bill hurriedly introduced me around town. As he boarded the boat at departure time, I apprized him of the captain's uncooperative attitude.

The Irishmen rested for a day at Fort Resolution and then continued on their way. I heard later they were windbound on the south shore of Great Slave Lake for many days. This was not surprising when one considers the meager freeboard of their craft and the great fetch available to any northerly wind. For hundreds of miles the wind was free to blow without hindrance from dense forests or high hills, obstacles which might otherwise absorb or divert its energy and slow it down. Even a light breeze from the north, blowing steadily, could roughen the water surface sufficiently to impede travel in a small canoe. Calm days on the lake were few and far between.

Eventually the two men made it to the Mackenzie River and headed downstream. However, it was then much too late in the season to contemplate the portage over the mountains, let alone the long journey from there to the coast. When they reached Norman Wells, they decided to stop for the winter. The Imperial Oil Company had a crude-oil refinery at that location, where the men sought employment. In this they were successful, being hired on as—you guessed it—cooks! I never heard the rest of their story, but I hope that they did eventually win through to the Yukon River and Alaska. Despite my disparaging comments about the pair, I greatly admired their spirit of adventure.

Several days after the departure of the Irish rovers, the MB *Buffalo* returned to Fort Resolution. I only became aware of the event when Bill Day, grim-faced and cursing, dashed into the office where I was checking over some trapping records. He declared that Captain Bligh had just filed a complaint with the local RCMP detachment, charging him with mutiny on the high seas! Well, to be truthful, I'm not certain now about the high seas part, but the charge of mutiny was real enough. As if that was not sufficient, there was an additional charge against Bill of theft of ship's stores. Shades of HMS *Bounty*!

As Bill calmed down slightly, he explained the events of the past few days. After arriving at Yellowknife and discharging his passengers, the captain had ignored Bill's injunction to tie up at the government wharf and await further instructions. First, Bligh became intoxicated and took the MB *Buffalo* to a different wharf, well removed from town, where he managed to cause some damage to both dock and boat by ramming one into the other. Next, he left the boat there and sought out some more alcohol. When the time came for the return trip, Bill spent hours tracking down the vessel's whereabouts. Finally locating it, he then had to go looking for the captain, who was found in a speakeasy, sloshed to the gills. He was hauled back on board with great difficulty.

Captain Bligh was in no shape to operate the vessel on the homeward journey, so Bill took on that task. A severe storm, with high winds and mountainous seas, was encountered as the boat neared the lake's south shore. The captain had begun to sober up, reaching the stage where he was once again ambulatory, but still mean, argumentative and overbearing. He adamantly insisted that they seek shelter in the mouth of the Slave River to await the cessation of the wind and the waves. From Bill's long experience in the region he knew that the many sandbars surrounding the river mouth, hidden by the confused seas and blowing spume, were just waiting to grab any unwary vessel trespassing there. The safest course was to continue on their present heading, breasting the unruly waves toward Fort Resolution. Bligh, although not conversant with the hazards around the river mouth, continued to argue the point. Then he tried to take over the helm by force and had to be physically restrained until the vessel was past the delta area. Shortly thereafter the storm passed on, disappearing to the east. The more violent surface motions quickly dissipated and the MB *Buffalo* continued on under the command of "Captain" Day.

On arriving at Fort Resolution, Bligh hurried off to the RCMP office, where he laid the aforementioned charges against Day. Then he visited the Signal Corps and sent two telegrams off to Ottawa, one to the minister of shipping and another to the Seaman's Union, attempting to have the boat put under an injunction to remain tied up to the dock, preventing its further use. This, of course, wasn't the approach recommended by Dale Carnegie and didn't win the captain too many friends. It did influence people though.

Bill, on his way home from the wharf, also went over to the RCMP office. That's when he discovered that Bligh was charging him with mutiny—for taking control of the boat and refusing to relinquish it—and with the theft of government property, to wit, one gray army blanket missing from ship's stores. This latter complaint was ludicrous. Army blankets were ubiquitous throughout the North. They were war surplus from World War II. The government shipped large quantities of them to every department in the North. The warden service issued them to firefighters, wardens and anyone else who could use them. Some of the blankets on the MB *Buffalo* had likely been put there by Day, taken from the warden's warehouse. The local RCMP had a stockpile of these blankets in their own stores. There was no way that the charge of theft of an army blanket could be made to stick against a government employee.

The Mounties, quite reasonably, had to keep a straight face about the whole affair and try to treat it seriously, but they really knew it was a farce except perhaps for the possibility of some physical damage to one or more of the participants. Bill asked them directly what the result would be if he went and, in the vernacular, punched the guy out. The response was that the captain could then lay an assault charge and this could not be taken so lightly.

Bill came back to the warden's office and sat thinking for a while. After calming down somewhat, he went to the Signal Corps establishment and sent off a message to Superintendent Sloan at Fort Smith to inform him of the problem and request advice. Sloan immediately chartered an aircraft and flew into Fort Resolution. He interviewed Bill, the ship's crew, the RCMP and Captain Bligh. Results quickly followed. The superintendent fired the captain precipitously, with the words: "You've got twenty minutes to pack your gear and get off the boat." Bligh did as suggested, all the while uttering dire threats about what the Seaman's Union would do.

It was all an anticlimax, though. Nothing more ever came of the affair. A warden was appointed to succeed Bligh in the captaincy, and the boat and crew continued to do the work required of them without further ado. Thus ended the Mutiny on Great Slave Lake.

131

Fort Resolution

At the time of Superintendent Sloan's visit to Fort Resolution in connection with the infamous "mutiny," he advised me that the issue of warden transfers was still unresolved and so was Bill Day's move. Naturally this was disappointing news, with the heartache of separation from my loved ones gnawing at me again. After waiting for an additional week or so, every day becoming more weary of the procrastination at the Fort Smith headquarters, I decided to stir things up. I sent Sloan a letter which said, in effect, "I quit."

The letter had the desired result. Bill Day received a telegram from Sloan requesting that he convince me to hang on for a while longer. Later that same day, Bill received another message advising him of his immediate transfer to a location down the Mackenzie River, displacing a warden who was to be sent to the Liard River station to replace the warden who had superseded Bligh as captain of the MB *Buffalo*. With Bill and his family finally gone to their new district, I occupied the warden's house and sent Mary a telegram to hurry in with the children on the first available aircraft. Soon we would all be together again. I could hardly wait.

It wasn't an easy trip for Mary from Vancouver Island to Fort Resolution, by rail and air with two youngsters and a babe in arms. To make matters worse, they were "bumped" at Fort Smith because the airstrip at Fort Resolution was temporarily unfit for landing. The airline had neglected to advise Mary of this small problem before departing from Edmonton, where she could have visited relatives. After spending several dreary days in a small room at the Mackenzie Hotel, she boarded a Douglas DC-3 going directly to Yellowknife but scheduled to touch down on the reopened strip at Fort Resolution on its return trip.

On the ground at Yellowknife, Mary asked the crew to be absolutely certain that her luggage was not unloaded there since it contained all of the necessities for caring for a six-week-old baby. Of course, such a request was like waving a red flag at a bull. On arrival at Fort Resolution, the luggage had disappeared, obviously off-loaded at Yellowknife. It was retrieved a week later when the next airliner touched down on our airstrip. In the meantime, some of our new neighbors very helpfully pitched in to round up sufficient baby clothes, diapers and bottles to see us through.

We had a nice two-storey house, the best we had yet lived in. There was a big cistern in the basement which held water—and a large amount of sediment and bacteria—trucked up from the lake. From the cistern, water was pumped up to a steel drum in the attic. This acted as a gravity-feed reservoir to provide running water to the kitchen and bathroom taps. For drinking purposes, the less-than-pristine water had to be boiled. Electrical power was supplied to us, and to the various other government buildings in Fort Resolution, from a generator operated by Department of Transport personnel on the airstrip, a quarter of a mile north of our residence.

In the summer, to answer nature's call, we used an outhouse in the back yard. Outhouse holes in Fort Resolution could only be dug with great difficulty because of permafrost which was within a few feet of the surface. It was necessary to dig a bit, let the exposed surface thaw, then dig a bit more. This procedure was continued until the hole was of a suitable depth. In winter we used a small indoor toilet containing a bucket whose contents had to be emptied daily into the frozen hole outside. At least the seat was warm!

Firewood for cooking and heating was obtained via a contract with local Natives. Such fuel had to be barged in from miles away, nearby stands of suitable wood having long since disappeared. The wood-burning cookstove in the kitchen had a copper heating coil in the fire box which provided hot water to the plumbing system while the stove was being used. For winter use, our house had a form of central heating. There was a furnace in the basement which provided hot air to the main living area through one large vent in the living room floor. A hole in the ceiling of the living room allowed some of the air to rise into the second floor bedrooms. This system worked quite well except for one problem. The furnace was not designed for burning wood. It was actually a converted coal burner, with a diminutive firebox which could only be loaded with a few small, and rapidly consumed, logs. In very cold weather, it had to be stoked several times per hour.

The RCMP detachment buildings stood to the west of our yard, with a house for the married officer-in-charge, a warehouse building for various stores and equipment, and an old edifice holding the office, a cell and facilities for a single constable. The married quarters were occupied by Corporal Tom Auchterlonie, his wife Alberta and their small daughter. Don Devries was the constable.

The Territorial day school lay just to the east of us. A government policy in the North required that a teacher in any settlement be of the same religious persuasion as the majority of the residents. At Fort Resolution, Pentecostal preachers had made some inroads and there were a few Church of England adherents, but the principal religion was Roman Catholicism. The language of instruction was English. The first teacher met with during our stay in the village was from Quebec and was so deficient in the use of English that we could only understand each other with great difficulty. I suspect that the educational experience must, at that time, have been rather traumatic for the children. Subsequent teachers had English as their mother tongue, so the children fared better in their pursuit of knowledge.

Several private residences were just across the road to the south of our house, acting as a buffer between us and the main part of the town. A short distance away, a free trader named George Pinsky had his store and residence. (A free trader is one unaffiliated with any company, working only for himself.) Further along were the Canadian Army Signal Corps buildings, the Hudson's Bay Company store and the small shack used for a post office, near the government wharf.

❖

A visit to Pinsky's store was an experience to be remembered. It was a typical frontier establishment, with goods of every conceivable type piled on the floor, stacked on overloaded shelves or hanging from the walls and ceiling. We called it the store of the three wonders—you wondered if he had a certain item, he wondered where it was, and you wondered how he ever found it amid the clutter.

Pinsky was a longtime resident of the North, arriving in about 1920. Apparently most of his family emigrated from Europe then—his stepfather, his brother Bill (who established a store at Fort Fitzgerald), and his sister and her husband (both of whom subsequently returned to Russia to live). His mother came some time after the rest. George was well-established in Fort Resolution by 1922, when he completed construction of a new house and store there. He also operated several outposts at various times, in particular one at Fort Rae on the north side of Great Slave Lake, employing local people as managers.

A few individuals seemed to hold old grudges against George, suspecting that he had bested them on various deals in the past. I suppose, human nature being what it is, such disagreements are probably an unavoidable part of most businesses. I never found him to be anything but fair-dealing and kindhearted. I have to admit that I was probably in a privileged position—everyone wanted to stay on the good side of the game warden. George did exhibit certain idiosyncrasies. He was known locally as "Second-gear" Pinsky because he never drove his truck in anything but second gear, even from a dead stop. This made for some jerky starts, and for some high engine revs when he was zipping along the airstrip at top speed. Second gear was about right for most of the mile or two of local roads, though. I believe George always drove in second gear because he had never learned how to use the clutch to shift gears while underway.

With all of the old-style goods in his store, George was still very interested in new product developments. On one occasion when I visited his establishment, he had just returned from a buying trip Outside (a term referring to civilization south of the N.W.T.) where he had discovered plastic dishware, then new on

135

the market. A salesman had demonstrated the durability of plastic dishes by bouncing them off the floor. George, after enthusiastically describing this latest scientific advance in his usual voluble manner, wanted to give me the same demonstration. He went out to his warehouse, where he was in the process of unpacking the dishes, and came back into the store carrying a dinner plate. "Watch this," he chortled, as he hurled the plate to the floor. Instead of bouncing it shattered into a dozen little pieces. Then...silence. George's visage took on the most crestfallen appearance I have ever seen. He was stunned. "George," I said, trying to sound sympathetic while struggling to suppress my laughter, "I think the problem is that the plate was very cold, which made it brittle." After all, the temperature in his unheated warehouse was the same as the temperature outside, a chilly thirty-below zero. "Well," George replied sadly as he collected the broken pieces, "the salesman didn't tell me anything about that."

❖

Our family's staple food supplies were ordered once a year from suppliers in Edmonton and shipped in by riverboat and barge during the summer. Most of these supplies were also available at the local stores, but at quite exorbitant prices. In the winter, at substantial expense, it was possible to haul nonperishable goods in to Fort Resolution by bombardier, a self-propelled tracked vehicle with an enclosed cab (incorrectly, but acceptably, pronounced "bombadeer" almost everywhere in North America except in Quebec where it is manufactured by the Bombardier Company). Bombardiers traveled across the lake ice from Hay River, a winter road making that town accessible to shipments from the south.

We did without many perishable food items because they could only be obtained by air at a cost of five to ten times what they commanded back in civilization. Fresh milk and fresh fruits were two examples. To provide fresh milk for our family of five would have required the expenditure of at least one-fifth of my annual salary. Instead, we got along with powdered milk, which came packed in fifty-pound drums. When reconstituted by adding water to the powder, it looked like real milk but tasted like chalk.

The manufacturer suggested aerating the mixture by whipping it with an egg beater, but it still tasted like chalk to me.

For adding to coffee and tea, we used canned milk. It came in liquid form and was relatively imperishable so long as the can remained unopened. It could also be watered down slightly to make a palatable, but expensive, milk for drinking with meals. For the latter purpose, our family persevered with the powdered stuff. One young Signal Corps child, familiar only with the canned variety, was once on a trip Outside when he saw a cow in the countryside near Edmonton. He asked his mother about the bag hanging under the back end of the animal. When told that the udder was where the milk came from, the youngster queried, "How do they get the cans out of there?" A reasonable question for a literal mind.

When ordering groceries, we considered the likes and dislikes of each family member. If tastes changed, and some food was suddenly looked on with disfavor, too bad—there was up to a year's supply of it to be consumed. Such a problem might have arisen on one occasion when I discovered small black bugs in the canned raspberries, one of our favorite fruits. The bugs were floating dead among the berries but were so tiny that they didn't really upset anyone. In fact, no one but me had even noticed them until I pointed them out. However, I decided to write about it to the fruit packing company in British Columbia. I enclosed several samples of the bugs with a humorous letter suggesting that they were no doubt sterile and probably nourishing, but not very appetizing. There were more comical statements in this vein, and I concluded by speculating about a switch to peaches if the company was unable to keep the bugs out of the raspberries.

I was surprised to receive a prompt reply from the company, telling me how meticulous they tried to be in cleaning the fruit, but they just couldn't find a suitable method for capturing all of those wee beasties before they got cooked and canned. They asked for advice as to the best method of shipping something to me. I responded, expecting that they might send a few replacement cans of raspberries. However, as soon as the ice was strong enough, a bombardier from Hay River chugged up to our house and delivered a case of twenty-four large cans of delicious peaches! Unfortunately, that company no longer exists or we would still be among their loyal customers.

In spite of the very short growing season, vegetables could be cultivated at the latitude of Great Slave Lake, if one had access to a suitable plot of ground. The long summer hours of daylight made this possible. The year following our arrival at Fort Resolution, I planted a garden in some good soil at the front of our house. It consisted mostly of potatoes, sown in early June. Thick green foliage, about six inches high, was showing after a few weeks. Then one morning at the end of the first week in July, I walked out to the garden and found the potato tops had disappeared. My first impulse was to blame it on vandalism, thinking that someone had pulled the tops off during the night. Closer inspection, though, revealed that this was not the case. Instead, a heavy nighttime frost was the culprit. It had caused the tops to shrivel up and blacken, matching the color of the soil. This appeared to be the end of my agricultural efforts for the year but, a week or so later, I was astonished to find the potatoes pushing up new shoots. They rapidly regained their original growth, and provided us with an excellent crop of spuds when I harvested them in the fall.

Great Slave Lake

Now that my family was together again, I faced the task of familiarizing myself with the warden district and the people in it. The district itself comprised about 40,000 square miles, some of it in the Barren Grounds. The southern boundary ran along the sixtieth parallel of latitude (the dividing line between the provinces and the Northwest Territories), beginning at the same longitude as the eastern border of Saskatchewan and extending westward to the Buffalo River, just east of Hay River. Then the boundary headed north across Great Slave Lake to Gros Cap, an Indian fishing village on the north shore of the lake. From that point, it followed the lakeshore for some distance before continuing on in a straight line northeastward out into the Barrens. At an appropriate point, it headed east to encompass the Thelon Sanctuary (then much smaller than its present-day size), finally regaining the starting longitude of Saskatchewan's eastern border and continuing south to close the circuit by once again touching the sixtieth parallel.

I was expected to cover this territory by canoe, boat and dog team, with the occasional aircraft flight thrown in. Most of my efforts revolved around the western sector, this being the region where the majority of the people resided. The Barren Grounds were not of much concern then, because the low price for white fox fur meant that little trapping was being done there. The Thelon Sanctuary was the home of a large herd of musk-ox, but no one seemed to be disturbing them. Even so, it was fortunate for me that there was a two-man RCMP detachment located at Fort Reliance, near the extreme eastern end of Great Slave Lake, about 200 miles from Fort Resolution. They were ideally located, on the main travel route to the Barrens, to observe any comings and goings. As part of their duties—with the assistance of a Native patrolman—they engaged in long winter patrols, even into the Thelon region, thus relieving me of the immense task of monitoring that far-off portion of my district. In fact, I could only have done so by dogsled with great difficulty and at enormous expense because of the need to establish food caches at reasonable intervals along the route. The round-trip distance from home base could exceed 800 miles, involving many weeks of travel. In particular, great quantities of hard-to-obtain fish would have been required for the dogs since it was illegal to feed them on caribou.

I found some maps in my little office building which were intended to provide information about my district and beyond. They showed large areas of incomplete charting, especially away from the rivers, the main arteries of transportation in the wilderness. They reminded me of my youthful trips to the library when, in addition to browsing books, I found fuel for my imagination in perusing maps of the North. Most of these had designated certain areas as "unmapped," "unknown" and "unexplored," especially away from the well-traveled routes. I used to plan rugged expeditions while pouring over those blank spaces, wondering what the terrain was like, what native plants and animals existed there, how dangerous were the river rapids and did a lost tribe dwell there? Anything was possible. And Robert Service used to implore me, with his words from "The Call of the Wild":

Let us probe the silent places, let us seek what luck betides us;
Let us journey to a lonely land I know.
There's a whisper on the night wind, there's a star agleam to guide us,
And the wild is calling, calling...let us go.

Some portions of my maps were still based on George Back's exploration of the Great Fish River (now called the Back River) in the early part of the nineteenth century. Worse than the insufficiency of detail, they also included some incorrect features, derived from hearsay or inaccurate travel diaries. As far as I know, no real tragedies resulted from these map errors, but it is certain that some travelers in the bush and the Barrens were confused on occasion. After World War II, the Royal Canadian Air Force had begun a program of aerial photography to help fill in the blank spaces and to rectify old errors, but nothing had filtered down to the warden level then. Today, complete and accurate maps of Northern Canada are readily available. They still leave some scope for an active imagination, but forget about lost tribes; the ground has been too well covered for any major new discoveries.

❖

The main thrust of my work, besides watching over my precinct, was to issue trapping and hunting permits, to check on trap lines and institute a procedure for registering the lines, and to maintain a visible presence throughout the populated areas to discourage abuses of the game and forestry regulations. I had the assistance of a patrolman named Harry Balsillie, who acted as guide when necessary, looked after the dogs most of the time and did other chores around the place.

My boat was a small twenty-four-foot cabin cruiser, with narrow benches that could sleep two. My canoe was an eighteen-foot freighter type with a substantial beam and depth for good carrying capacity. It had a square stern for use with a "kicker" (as an outboard motor is called throughout the North). The canoe was used for short investigatory trips, for fishing for dog food or as a life boat towed along behind the cabin cruiser. I always carried several ten-gallon drums of extra gasoline on the rear deck of the cabin cruiser, since there were no filling stations around. (My fuel supply came in by barge in the spring.)

I also carried a fire pump on the boat. It was driven by a small gas engine. This pump did more than just help douse any small fire encountered by chance as I cruised around my district. Some of my boat travel involved traversing the various channels of the Slave River delta, where the sandbars (actually mudbars) could change form and position from week to week. A bar lying just under the surface was invisible in the opaque brown water, and wind and current conditions could conspire to hide any other clue to its presence. Occasionally, I would run the boat up on such a hidden bar and could not back off with the engine in reverse gear because of the sucking power of the silt. Not to worry—I would just throw the suction line for the fire pump over the side of the boat, crank the pump to life, and use the high-pressure water stream emitted from the hose nozzle to wash away the mud beneath the boat. It worked like a charm.

I nearly brought the boat to grief once when Harry and I were returning from a voyage to the settlement of Rocher River, on the south shore of Great Slave Lake about sixty miles east of Fort Resolution. The weather was all that could be desired, amply warm with a clear blue sky. Then the slightest indication of swell, the long-wave forerunners of a distant storm, appeared on the surface of the lake. When a storm lashes an area, piling up mountainous seas of all descriptions, water waves travel away from the center of the disturbance. The waves of greatest length from crest to crest travel faster than the shorter-length ones, and so are the first to be observed at some distance from the storm. I hoped that the swell now being experienced was really just the dying embers of some storm far to the west.

It was a false hope. Within minutes, shorter waves were tossing the boat about, making my stomach queasy. As we approached the Slave River mouth, the interaction between the storm waves and the river current resulted in horrendously steep pitches, threatening to roll and swamp our puny vessel. Even a good swimmer could not survive for long if tossed into those icy waters. A few years previously, a warden had fallen from the float of a small aircraft as he was preparing to moor it to the lakeshore. He was immersed for less than ten minutes, but succumbed to hypothermia because of the low water temperature.

We had little choice but to head for shelter in the river mouth. We knew that the Department of Transport had set out buoys marking the channel. After an anxious search we finally spotted one just to the south of our course and headed toward it. Soon the next buoy in sequence appeared and we knew we were nearing the entrance to the river. On each side of us were shallows, to be avoided at all costs. As the boat rose on the crest of a wave, the buoys seemed to recede into the bottom of a deep valley. When the boat was in the trough of a wave, the buoys could not be seen at all. In fact nothing could be seen except great walls of water roofed over with a small patch of blue sky. In between the crests and troughs, the boat was slewing wildly about, difficult to control.

Soon I lost sight of the marker buoys completely, unable to spot them even when the boat was high on the peak of a wave. With these visual references gone, I tried to set my course by compass. But the boat's violent motions were causing the compass to rotate erratically, rendering it useless. As another trough rolled by, the boat slammed hard onto the shallow mud bottom. I changed the course by a few degrees, but still the boat found bottom with every passing wave. Harry, with his lifelong knowledge of the region, thought he could find the channel again by the appearance of the trees along the foreshore, so I passed the helm over to him.

A few more thuds against the bottom and Harry had us safely back in the channel, whence we proceeded without further ado into the river mouth. Here we nosed into a snye for several hours until the waves abated on the lake and we could continue our cruise. It was fortunate that the bottom where I had bumped the vessel was composed of light sediment and not rocks. Even so, the boat developed a slight leak alongside the keel, making it necessary to pump the accumulating bilge water more frequently than usual. A bit more pounding into the mud might have opened up the seams of the hull and allowed the water to rush in.

So much for the hazards of lake travel. I was soon to learn that traveling by cabin cruiser on the Slave River also had its trials, one of which was having to tie up to the shore at night to get some rest. Zillions of sadistic mosquitoes would swing into action as soon as the door to the cabin was opened. Such were the swarms attacking one's face that it was almost impossible to see one's hands at work while trying to tie the mooring line about a tree or a clump of willows. I could well believe stories about these pests driving men crazy in the bush. On the lake the mosquitoes could be avoided by staying well offshore and only making landfall on points exposed to a breeze. But there was no way to steer clear of the hordes along the river.

The mosquitoes were bad enough in the settlements. When we went from our house in Fort Resolution to the airstrip to meet incoming aircraft in the summertime, we often wore our winter parkas with the hood up as protection against the throngs of mosquitoes. It was rumored that, once upon a time, the airport attendant had rushed out and put thirty gallons of gas in a flying machine before he realized it was just a big mosquito!

❖

The boat trip described above was actually my second one with the cabin cruiser on Great Slave Lake. My first such trip was also to the settlement of Rocher River. According to any map one may consult, Rocher River village is on the Taltson River, a couple of miles upstream from its mouth on Great Slave Lake. However, I never heard anyone use the map name. The translation of the French word *rocher* is "rock" and the river was supposed to contain more than a few of these obstacles to safe travel. Billy McNeil, in his Newfie patois, called them "sunkers," an apt terminology, especially if one should run a canoe into them at full tilt.

It was my intention to ascend the river for a distance of about twenty miles to another small settlement called Rat River. (In the north country, the use of the name Rat—a contraction of muskrat—for rivers, creeks and lakes is widespread for the obvious reason that someone has been impressed by the local abundance of the creatures. The same applies to the use of beaver, moose, gull, loon, jackfish and sturgeon in the creation of place names.) For some reason now forgotten, Harry wasn't available for this trip and, since it was all new territory to me, I hired one of the Natives from Fort Resolution to act as a guide. I wasn't anxious to bounce off too many rocks on the way to Rat River, so I made certain to inquire of my new guide as to his knowledge of that part of the country and was assured that he had been up the river "many times."

Our trip around the lakeshore was uneventful, the weather being fine and the wind negligible. We were towing my canoe behind the cabin cruiser. As we approached the wharf at Rocher River, I could see several buildings along the shore. The most obvious one was the Hudson's Bay Company post, the store and house painted in the traditional colors of white with red trim. Just to the north of it was a ramshackle building belonging to a free trader, Ed Demelt, a longtime inhabitant of the Northwest

144

Territories. To the south, and some distance back from the river, was the new two-storey wood-frame building housing the Territorial day school, with the teacher's residence on the upper floor. The school was closed for the summer and there was no teacher living there just then. Beyond the school were some Native residences, most of them constructed of logs. We tied the boat and canoe up to the wharf, and the guide left for a visit with some acquaintances of his in the village. I proceeded to the HBC store to introduce myself.

The HBC post manager's name is long gone from my memory. He was a sociable fellow who welcomed an exchange of news and views. After inviting me for supper and serving an excellent meal, he provided some gossip about local events and personalities. This led us rather spontaneously into a discussion about "characters" (eccentrics), who seem to be abundant in the North.

Characters are generally people whose behavior deviates from the accepted norm in some way. Such individuals seem to have a penchant for life on the frontiers. Perhaps they are unable to cope with the hectic pace of urban life and seek their own way of doing things. Some are friendly, open and harmless. Others may carry a large chip on their shoulder and subjects or actions which annoy them must be carefully avoided. Some have a preoccupation with a particular subject that almost borders on lunacy. The occasional character is simply looking for adventure, if that can be considered an oddity. Whatever the case, the North had many characters in residence. Quite a few of them had made their way there after serving in the armed forces of various nations in World War I, finding themselves footloose and fancy free upon demobilization at war's end.

One eccentric I had heard of (because he had a relative living in Fort Resolution) was an English remittance man. His type was familiar on the prairies during the days when homesteading had been a way of attracting settlers to a sparsely settled land. Often a ne'er-do-well scion of an upper class British family would be shipped overseas to make something of himself, supported by a periodic remittance of funds from home. Now, with homestead

145

land no longer available, remittance men had to explore other avenues for advancement.

The character alluded to here lived on the Arctic coast. He was a very lazy individual, according to all reports. He lived on eggs because they were easy to cook. Empty egg crates were stacked all around his shack. He was known by the nickname "Dynamite" due to an episode resulting from one of his infrequent periods of gainful employment. A local mission had hired him to split some firewood for use in heating their buildings. Dynamite obtained a quantity of blasting caps from somewhere, and, true to his indolent nature, he found it easier to use the caps for splitting the wood rather than the usual ax and muscle power. The problem was that some of the caps remained unexploded until the wood was loaded into the mission furnace. Then the furnace door was blown loose from its hinges!

Billy McNeil, introduced previously, was a character too, but one of the nicest kind. His eccentricities were harmless and amusing, his behavior whimsical rather than weird. Perhaps his deportment was the norm for a Newfoundlander. Billy was a hard worker when the occasion required it. He helped his fellow man when the opportunity presented itself and his knowledge of the bush won him renown and respect throughout the North.

Now, at Rocher River with the hands of the clock approaching midnight, my discussion with the Bay manager continued for another hour or more. He stated his firm conviction that the free trader Ed Demelt was definitely a character and he furnished some supporting evidence. His stories about the man, some of which I had heard before and hadn't quite believed, were often derogatory. They described a certain style of outlandish behavior which fully justified the classification of Ed as a character. The manager was quite knowledgeable with regard to Demelt's affairs, no doubt because of a need to be well informed about the competition since they both vied for the same trade. He said that the two of them got along well, at least to outward appearances. I delayed forming a definite opinion about Demelt until the morrow, when I planned to meet him in person.

Free Trader

Ed Demelt was indeed one of the North's more unusual characters, a designation not easily earned or lightly awarded since there was an abundance of characters of high degree residing in the Territories. He must have come into the country at the end of World War One. Frederick B. Watt, in his book *Great Bear* (Yellowknife: Outcrop Publishers, 1980), mentions meeting Demelt in 1932 on Great Bear Lake where they were both staking mineral claims, and states that it was fourteen years since the latter had been south of Fort Smith. Demelt had established a successful fishing business at Hay River on the south shore of Great Slave Lake. Watt comments that Demelt had a "forceful character" and a voice with a "proprietorial tone to it, though it was not unfriendly."

Fred J. Peet was another person who made passing acquaintance with Demelt in those earlier days. In his book, *Miners and Moonshiners* (Victoria: Sono Nis Press, 1983), Peet mentions that, in 1933, Demelt was hired by the government to install navigation beacons along the south shore of Great Slave Lake. Peet described the man as "powerful, rough, uncouth and hard as nails," and he claims that some member of the RCMP said that "Demelt could live and survive where a wolf would starve to death."

I never did determine how Ed ended up as a free trader in Rocher River. He was considered to be an old-timer in the community, so perhaps he had gravitated there after the excitement of the uranium rush to Great Bear Lake had faded away. He was the proprietor of a small store or—for those who prefer a more romantic label—a trading post. He was also something of an entrepreneur, pursuing any moneymaking opportunities that chanced his way, usually in the form of government contracts for such things as local road maintenance.

The Bay manager told me about a contract issued to Ed for supplying the school with water. The school building, like our house in Fort Resolution, had a cistern in the basement. Demelt had a team of horses and a large tank mounted on a wagon, so he was able to haul water from the river to the cistern. The contract was written in terms of the number of trips, rather than the number of gallons, that it took to fill the cistern. It so happened that the tank used for hauling the water had a hole drilled in it at a level where it was just half full. How the hole got there is anyone's guess. The tank was pumped brimful at the river but, by the time it arrived at the school, it was half empty. *Voila!* Twice as many trips to the river—and double the pay. When school was in session, the cistern probably needed filling at least twice a month. The time required for the extra trips was inconsequential; a local Native was hired to drive the team, and there was no minimum wage regulation.

The day following my conversation with the HBC manager, I visited Ed Demelt at his log cabin store. The front door was wide open, the day being warm, but little light penetrated the interior. I walked tentatively into the darkness and was greeted cheerfully by a loud voice from an unseen source. As my eyes became accustomed to the gloom, I made out a great hulk of a man lying on a store counter, his head resting on a roll of brown wrapping paper. Ed had been having a little snooze. His wife was engaged in a similar activity on another counter. I introduced myself, and was invited to sit down on one of the several chairs scattered around the premises.

I was careful to avoid sitting close to the low two-hole cast-iron heater in the middle of the room, not because it might be hot—there was no fire in it on such a warm day—but because Ed was reputed to sometimes use it for a toilet. I never verified the story personally, and there was no particular odor emanating from it on this day. However, on the basis of subsequent experience during the following winter, I can vouch for the fact that Ed would open the front door just a crack and then urinate through the opening. On a typical cold day the urine would freeze almost immediately. Gradually an imposing pillar of yellow ice was built up just outside the door. One had to be careful not to stumble over it on entering or leaving the store.

We commenced an interesting, but rather one-sided, discussion in which I was given Demelt's version of local events and personalities, not always in agreement with the information I had received from the Bay manager on the previous day. I soon began to form an opinion of the man that was very close to that voiced by Fred Watt and Fred Peet. When the conversation started to lag a bit, I introduced the topic that was actually the main reason for my visit.

I had been notified by the chief warden at Fort Smith that Demelt was suspected of trading in shot beaver pelts, an offence under the game regulations. During the spring hunt, it is more difficult to trap beaver than it is to shoot them swimming in open water, but it was assumed that many of the shot animals were lost because of the inability of trappers to recover the carcasses of those which dived or sank to the bottom of their ponds. Therefore, the practice of shooting beaver, and of trafficking in shot pelts, had been outlawed.

So now I had a little rhetorical discussion with Demelt about people with shot pelts in their possession, and he declared vehemently that I would never find him in that position. He was quite right; I never did. To get ahead of my story, the following spring there was another report that Ed was buying illegal beaver skins from the Natives so I went over to Rocher River after the lake opened up and searched his premises. I found only two bales of beaver pelts. There may have been others which I overlooked; all kinds of possibilities for hiding them existed. The bales were about to be stowed onboard a Hudson's Bay Company vessel whose departure from the local wharf was imminent. I made myself very unpopular by insisting that the bales be opened for inspection. This was done after some protest, and I had a careful look at the skins. All were legal; not a bullet hole in the bunch. Demelt then had the chore of hurriedly rebaling the furs. Ever afterwards, I was told, he referred to me as that "Gestapo" of a game warden, usually prefaced with a few other choice words. To my face, though, Ed was always polite.

149

Our discussion about shot beaver at an end, I wanted to get started on my trip up to Rat River as quickly as possible. My anxiety in this regard was used as an excuse to decline Ed's invitation to stay for a meal. The Pentecostal preacher at Fort Resolution, Howard Peever, had told me of a time he and his wife stayed with Demelt overnight. The preacher said that supper consisted of a big pot of steaming-hot caribou stew set in the middle of the table for everyone to help themselves. Even before the diners were through loading their plates a cat jumped onto the table and began eating directly from the pot! Demelt made no move to shoo the animal away, so it was apparently an acceptable practice in his household. Oh well, caribou stew invariably had a lot of caribou hair in it in any case, so what difference would a few cat hairs make? The preacher also mentioned other instances of uncleanliness, shaking his head all the while, and vowing to find somewhere else to stay the next time he had to travel to Rocher River. From such events are a character's reputation formed.

Taking leave of the Demelts, I rounded up my guide preparatory to heading up the Talston River. It wasn't feasible to take the cabin cruiser through all the rocks, with channels of unknown depth and a strong current flowing, so we resorted to the eighteen-foot canoe. Going upstream was easy. The canoe was driven by a five-horsepower kicker and our relatively slow progress against the current allowed us to spot rocks in time to avoid them. Going downstream would be a different story.

Along one stretch of the river, we encountered a swimming caribou, well to the west of its usual habitat at this time of year. It held to its chosen course as it paddled across the river, but its head turned to keep us under observation. We continued on upstream, losing sight of the caribou before it had completed its swim.

Nearing our destination, the kicker suddenly conked out. One minute we were making fair progress and the next we were being swept rapidly back toward Great Slave Lake by the river current. I checked the fuel in the tank—plenty of that—and then ascertained that the spark plug lead was properly attached. I yanked incessantly on the starter cord, but couldn't restart the cursed thing. Not having a tool kit along, it was not possible to take the motor apart to see what ailed it. We picked up our paddles, lying in the bottom of the canoe, and strenuously stroked our way upstream for the last few miles to Rat River. Two more lessons learned. Never go up the creek without a paddle and, if dependent on any kind of mechanical contrivance, always carry a screwdriver and pliers.

The first of several people I encountered at Rat River was Jimmy Donovan, a longtime resident of the Northwest Territories, about seventy years old at the time. I had been advised by various people to accept Jimmy's hospitality when visiting Rat River. There wasn't any doubt in anyone's mind that it would be offered, and they were right. Even as we pulled our canoe alongside the small dock at the river's edge, Jimmy was there insisting that I bring my sleeping bag up to his cabin and stay with him for the duration of my visit to Rat River.

Once inside the cabin, which was neat and clean compared to some that I'd been in, Jimmy began putting supper on the stove. The ensuing meal was delicious, consisting of a variety of freshly cooked vegetables. Jimmy had his own garden which produced magnificent specimens of all manner of vegetables, even luscious tomatoes. All were helped to attain a large size by irrigation water pumped from the adjacent river and by the long hours of daylight. Jimmy was not only a good cook but an excellent baker as well. Some of the best bread I ever tasted was cooked by him in an old wood stove, using empty five-pound lard pails for bread pans. These being round, perhaps six inches in diameter, the loaves came out in cylindrical form which could be cut into nice circular slices.

Jimmy had one handicap, perhaps a result of his advancing age. He was nearly deaf in both ears. Sitting around a table, one had to shout loudly at him to get a response. After doing this for a while, it was hard to avoid shouting loudly into the ear of any other person who might be sitting beside you.

In his younger days Jimmy had been a trapper and, like most people in the North, had also engaged in whatever other work he could drum up. In the 1930s he had run mail and fur packets south from Fort Smith to Fort McMurray on the Athabasca River. During the course of a conversation, I mentioned the city of Edmonton. "Boy," Jimmy exclaimed, "that Edmonton sure is a big place." I was under the impression that he hadn't been south for quite a few years, but perhaps I was mistaken. "When were you there, Jimmy?" I bellowed in his ear. "Nineteen hundred and twenty," was the response! If he thought Edmonton was big then, he should have seen it thirty-odd years later.

Jimmy had a good dog team of his own and raised a few sled dogs for sale to other people. Just now he had some pups wandering loose around his place. They had the run of the house if they wanted it. He treated them kindly, fed them well and showered them with affection which they returned in good measure. Strangely enough, though, they were very wary of anyone else and would hide away from visitors. Bill Day, my predecessor, had contracted earlier to obtain two older pups from Jimmy to replace two dogs which had died in the spring before I arrived at Fort Resolution, so I accepted delivery of them now. As it unfortunately transpired, the new members never did learn to fit in with the rest of my team and became quite vicious. I guess they missed the carefree life at Jimmy's place. (I use the words "my team" but, of course, all of the dogs actually belonged to the government, for use by the incumbent warden.)

I got a bitch from Jimmy, too, part wolf and part husky. It was subsequently bred with one of my dogs in order to have some young sled dogs to replace team members who were getting along in years and would soon be too old to work. Actually, Jimmy presented the bitch as a gift to my oldest son because he felt that the government might want to lay claim to it if I, a government employee, accepted the animal. He was upset with the government because of a bureaucratic problem concerning payment of the above-mentioned contract.

The next morning I borrowed some tools from Jimmy and operated on my kicker, finding a broken coil wire and burnt prongs on the sparkplug. After fixing these problems and reassembling the various pieces, the kicker started with just a couple of pulls on the starting cord. Meanwhile, several Natives wandered up to see what was going on. They were staying at Rat River for a little holiday out in the bush. They would return to Rocher River before freeze-up to get their trapping outfits ready for the winter.

I also spoke with two other residents of Rat River—two more characters. They had come into the country just after World War I. One of them was a Cockney Englishman, small in stature but carrying a big grudge against the world for no good reason that I could ascertain. He kept insisting that he was an excellent first-aid man—no doubt part of his wartime training—and advised me that he would be happy to treat me should the need arise. He also invited me to stay at his cabin, but added that I should bring my own grub. I thanked him but declined the invitation.

Ed Demelt had told me a story about the little man. Years before, two prospectors coming down the river had upset their canoe in a whirlpool somewhere upstream from Rat River. It wasn't a question of carelessness, of not being on the lookout for danger. Some whirlpools aren't in continuous motion but are generated from time to time by vagaries of the current. What appears to be smooth fast water will suddenly turn into a maelstrom and, a few minutes later, will just as suddenly revert back to relative calm. The prospectors had been caught in such an event. All their supplies had been dumped irretrievably to the river bottom in the deep water at the center of the vortex. The whirlpool collapsed as the men surfaced, gasping for air. The canoe drifted away on the swift current before they could recover it. They managed to save themselves by swimming to a small island in the middle of the river.

Hours later, the Cockney happened by in his canoe. The castaways, shouting and waving, caught his attention. Backpaddling against the current to stay level with the island, he shouted, "Have you got any grub?" When he heard the negative response, he just continued on downstream. As luck would have it, Demelt came by a short while later and plucked them from the island. Score one for Demelt; at least he looked out for his fellow man. Jimmy told me that the little Englishman was a "real miserable cuss," and when kindly old Jimmy had a bad word to say about anyone it had to be believed.

As my guide and I readied our canoe for the return trip down-river, Jimmy stowed aboard several sacks of vegetables, gifts for myself and other people back at Fort Resolution. We loaded the three dogs in, shoved away from the dock, fired up the kicker, and off we went in the middle of the stream, anticipating a swift passage back to the cabin cruiser which we had left tied up at Rocher River.

It soon became apparent that the guide couldn't remember for certain just where the channel was along any segment of the river. Obviously the last of his "many times" had been some years in the past, or else he had a short-term memory. So I sat in the stern operating the kicker and steering, while the guide knelt in the bow and used a paddle to fend off collisions between the canoe and wayward rocks along our course. The end of the paddle became somewhat worn in the process. We managed to avoid direct contact with all but two or three of the obstacles and struck those with only a glancing blow—no damage to the canoe except for scraped paint and roughened canvas. We got safely back to our cruiser and returned uneventfully to Fort Resolution.

Dog Team

Life was hectic as I hurried to become acquainted with all the goings-on in my district before the fall freeze-up, that period in late autumn when traveling any distance from home base wasn't feasible because ice was forming on the surface of the lake. I also had to allot several weeks for the fall fishery, at which time Harry and I would attempt to harvest sufficient fish to feed our dogs from freeze-up right through to the end of the spring breakup, when the lake would be free of ice again.

I soon found out that being a game warden didn't mean always being out in the open air. I had to issue trapping licences, hunting licences, wood permits and such. I had to file reports on trap lines, fur returns, fire hazards and related items. But worst of all, I had to respond to moronic bureaucratic missives from Ottawa, usually relayed through the chief warden at Fort Smith.

The powers-that-be in Ottawa had no understanding of life in the North and, consequently, often made ludicrous requests or rulings. One such decree involved items on the warden station inventory. Such items could only be disposed of, for whatever reason, with permission from Ottawa. This consumed much time and produced a long trail of quadruplicate red tape, as in the following example.

Some time before my arrival at Fort Resolution, two dogs from the warden's team had to be put out of their misery after a temporary hired hand abused them through overwork. Apparently he ran them nearly to death, to a point beyond a reasonable prospect of recovery. It is possible to do this with sled dogs because those team members which are fit and healthy will keep charging along without letup, especially if forced to do so by a cruel or unthinking driver, and any unfit animal in harness is compelled to keep moving with the rest, perhaps until it collapses. Any dog driver worthy of the name can readily see when an animal is ailing or laboring unduly, and will turn it out of the team long before it becomes incapacitated.

Now it so happened that dogs were inventory items and couldn't be destroyed without first obtaining permission from Ottawa. It mattered not that the animals were suffering and in great distress. Ottawa hadn't been consulted, so Ottawa refused to acknowledge the fact that the inventory was two dogs short. As far as they were concerned, the complement of dogs was right up to the mark and no funds would be made available for the purchase of replacements for the dead animals.

However, there was usually a way. Replacements were needed for the ensuing winter season so Bill Day made the previously mentioned arrangement with Jimmy Donovan to obtain two dogs on credit, the method of payment to be determined at a later date. By the time of my arrival, Ottawa still hadn't relented, but a ploy for getting the money to Jimmy had become apparent. A bush fire had occurred near our village in the spring of the year and several local people had been commandeered to extinguish it. One extra firefighter wouldn't be remarkable. In collusion with Superintendent Sloan, Jimmy was added to the list of people earning wages on the fire line. Since Day was leaving, the paperwork was left to me to finalize. A check for Jimmy arrived eventually, no one in Ottawa having questioned the payment because no one there was aware of his advanced age and his physical unsuitability for battling fires.

Another case that Bill told me about involved a warden in the town of Yellowknife, where some miles of bush roads existed that were suitable for traversing with a motor vehicle, providing splendid opportunities for poachers. The warden wanted a Jeep to patrol the roads. He put the request in his annual budget submission but was told by Ottawa that it couldn't be considered until he turned in his old Jeep. Since he didn't have an old one, or any one, he was caught in the trap of a circular argument: he couldn't have a new vehicle until he turned in his old one, and he couldn't turn in his old one because it didn't exist.

Ottawa had overlooked the fact that there had never been a vehicle on the warden's inventory. What to do? Solution: borrow a worn-out write-off from the local Department of Transport personnel, who had both a new vehicle and their old one, which was still in their possession pending a "board of survey." (A board of survey comprised several officials who were supposed to come around every two years to verify that certain equipment was junk and could therefore be taken off inventory and hauled away to the dump.) So the warden got his new Jeep. I don't know what happened when the board finally showed up, presumably expecting to find two broken-down vehicles.

The bureaucracy in Ottawa would occasionally send telegrams directly to me, usually making what I considered to be frivolous requests. The messages would always terminate with the requirement to "reply by return wire," meaning immediately. One such missive asked for the size of all the government buildings in my district—not just my home settlement, but including places such as Snowdrift, almost 150 miles to the east and accessible only by floatplane or a long boat journey. I did reply by return wire, suggesting that they should look in their own files in Ottawa for the blueprints of the various buildings. Surely drawings must have existed for the buildings to be constructed in the first place. Eventually, the chief warden advised me that Ottawa had misplaced the blueprints.

Another time, the question involved two bathtubs, shipped to the warden station five years before. Ottawa couldn't find them on my inventory. Why not? I wired back that one of them had been built into the warden's house and that it was hooked up and in constant use. I disclaimed any knowledge of the second one. (Actually, Bill Day had traded it for something that was needed at the warden station, but for which Ottawa wouldn't provide any funds.) Later I was told by the chief warden that Ottawa had complained about the tone of my telegrams. He suggested that I be less sarcastic in my replies, even when sarcasm was warranted.

As if telegrams weren't sufficient, sometimes a bureaucrat would appear in the flesh, often with no advance notice. The only warning might be when a pilot ferrying in such a visitor buzzed the settlement, this action being a request for someone to come to the wharf or the airstrip with a vehicle to provide taxi service. On one occasion when the buzz job was neglected, I was sick abed with a raging case of influenza. With our three kids in various stages of the illness too, Mary hadn't been able to keep up with the housework. A knock came at the door. There stood the district commissioner, the titular head of the Northwest Territories! The less said about that visit, the better.

I've previously mentioned, in connection with the buffalo cull in Wood Buffalo National Park, the bureaucrat who was shipped out from Ottawa so that his colleagues could have some summer relief. My first introduction to him came one morning after breakfast when I was hard at work in my office on some official correspondence. A knock came at the office door, followed by the entrance of the bureaucrat's aide-de-camp. He came with an urgent message—my immediate attendance was required down at the wharf. The bureaucrat had arrived late on the previous evening aboard the Department of Indian Affairs vessel *Peter Pond*, which had been lent to him for a trip around Great Slave Lake.

I walked down to the wharf and went on board, to find the bureaucrat eating breakfast. He made some small talk while he finished his meal. Then he said that "my men" were having trouble with the kicker used on a dinghy carried aboard the *Peter Pond*. It kept breaking shear pins, a little metal pin used in the drive mechanism to help protect the propeller from damage if it should hit an obstacle in the water. They had used up their available supply of pins and needed some more. Could I help? (This was so urgent?) I suggested that brass welding rod, cut to suitable lengths, might serve the purpose for substitute pins. I said I would check with the Department of Transport at the airport, where they had a welding outfit. As I climbed on deck to leave the ship, his exalted highness began to lather his face, preparatory to shaving.

I got to the landward end of the wharf just as the Department of Transport boss arrived there on another mission. I explained that I was looking for some brass welding rod and wondered if he could spare some. The man, not the most friendly person in the world, asked, "What do you want it for?" I started to reply, "That SOB from..." when some sixth sense made me look around.

There he was, the clean-shaven SOB of a bureaucrat, right at my shoulder. I quickly started over, "That SOB of a kicker keeps breaking shear pins." However, I knew that the bureaucrat knew that the epithet was really intended for him. He'd had a quick shave and I'd had a close shave.

❖

Bureaucrats, boats and baloney (the BS kind) occupied much of my life that first summer, but I made certain to reserve some time for attendance on my dog team. They had to become familiar with their new boss or they might not give of their best when out on the trail. And I needed to learn something of their individual traits to help them do their best. For a start, I began serving them their daily allotment of food, as well as going out to quiet them in the evening when the nightly "howl" started in the village.

Many people in Fort Resolution maintained dog teams to assist them on their winter trap lines. More than 200 dogs were resident in the village in the summer months, doing nothing but lazing around and making the occasional noise. Sled dogs don't bark, they howl; and every time one dog starts, all of the others join in. A communal howl always got underway in the early evening, when many of the teams were being fed. Imagine the sound of all those dogs howling at the same time! Fortunately, it seldom lasted for more than ten minutes or so.

Two hundred-odd voices raised in doleful cry were easy to accept when one considered the way it used to be. Previously the dogs had been allowed to run loose in the village, making a great nuisance of themselves, stealing, scavenging, fighting and, of course, howling. Ernest Thompson Seton had some scathing comments to make about the situation when he visited Fort Resolution in 1907. He derisively called it "Dogtown." This famous naturalist was in the country to study caribou, buffalo, musk-ox and other denizens of the North. He reported on the trip in a book called *The Arctic Prairies* (New York: Charles Scribner's Sons, 1912). Therein, quoting from his daily journal, he had this to say about the village: "It is the worst dog-cursed spot I ever saw; not a square yard but is polluted by them; no arti-

159

cle can be left on the ground but will be carried off, torn up, or defiled. There is not an hour or ten minutes of day or night that is not made hideous with a dog-fight or chorus of yelps." And that was from an animal lover!

The dogs also presented a threat to people, especially to children. By the late 1930s, an ordinance had been enacted that required the dogs to be under control at all times; they had to be chained or fenced when not working in harness. Still, on one occasion a small child wandered too close to dogs chained in the RCMP dog compound and died as a result of being bitten and mauled. Children had to be taught about the danger of approaching seemingly friendly dogs, and even adults could be at risk from a strange team.

Dogs were just called "dogs" in the North, and not normally differentiated by names relating to their breeding, like Husky or Malamute. It might be different nowadays, with all the publicity given to dogs bred for racing, fed on fancy diets and put through comprehensive training routines. Ours were strictly everyday working dogs. The local Indian dogs—mostly of the type known as Heinz 57 varieties—were usually quite small and relatively short-haired compared to my dogs and those of the RCMP. The lineage of my team was primarily Husky. The name is said to be a corruption of "Esky," an early slang designation for Eskimos, so that Esky dogs eventually became Huskies. Likewise, Malamute is derived from an Eskimo tribe known as the Malemiut. Actually, the dogs called Huskies include Malamutes (with their typical black face mask around the eyes), Siberian Huskies (originally imported from Asia), and intermixtures of these two breeds.

I will describe my dogs as I came to know them during that first summer, while they idled away part of the year in the dog compound, and later, on the winter trail after I learned how to handle them properly. My team comprised five dogs; at least that was the number normally hitched to the sled. Sometimes there was a spare dog or two in the compound being considered as possible replacements for older team members. Each dog had its own unique personality, being no different from people in that respect.

Dogs, like many people, are averse to sudden changes in the status quo. So, when I first introduced myself to my new team, they expressed their displeasure by growling ferociously, and by jumping and snapping in my direction whenever the opportunity presented itself. I began their conversion to the new regime by personally giving them their daily feed in their compound in a clearing behind the warden station. Soon I had gained the trust of several of them, at least to the extent that they looked forward to seeing me at mealtimes and I could walk up to them without facing exposed canine teeth and vicious snarls.

Skipper was the smallest dog of the bunch, golden brown in color and weighing about seventy-five pounds. There wasn't much Husky in him. He served as wheel dog in the team, occupying the position immediately in front of the sled. Usually a large dog is chosen to handle this job, part of which consists of controlling the sideways motion of the sled and helping it to track properly around any bends in the trail, tiring work at times. Skipper was small for the job, but handled it without undue exertion, especially if the driver helped out when necessary by manipulating the handlebars of the sled in an appropriate fashion. Skipper had been raised as a pet by Jimmy Donovan and was very friendly.

The next dog in line was Dusty, one of the heavier dogs in the team at ninety pounds or so. He had black fur, tipped with gray. He was already ancient for a working dog, twelve years old according to the office records, and most dogs of his age would have been pensioned off. Yet he still gave yeoman service for the next couple of years. Dusty was definitely one who did not appreciate change. For more than a month I had to stay out of his reach when feeding him, for fear of being bitten. After that I was able to go up to him with his food, but I still had to back cautiously away. When I turned around after getting safely beyond the length of his chain, Dusty would lunge and snap at my posterior. The situation gradually improved until, after about three months, I could ruffle his fur with my hand or turn my back without fear of repercussions. Soon he gave his allegiance to me (shared with Harry, of course). Dusty remained selective in choosing his

161

friends though. The Mounties, who fed my team when I was out patrolling by canoe or boat in the summer (in exchange for my returning the favor when they were away), always complained that they had to be very careful around him.

Another member of the crew was Ricky, similar to Dusty in size and age, but with milder manners and no unusual characteristics. He was quite content to be a follower and do whatever the majority were doing, so one could almost call him a "sheep" dog. To give him his due, he was a good worker and a faithful team member.

The dog that I, at first, thought was the prize of the collection was Silver. He was a magnificent specimen, with spectacular creamy-white fur. Silver had only one fault, but it was a big one for a sled dog. He was very insecure. So long as he was with the team in his accustomed position, everything was fine. But change his position in harness, especially try to train him for the lead position as I did once or twice, and he just fell to pieces. Too bad, because he would have made a most imposing sight at the head of the team.

The true prize of the team was the lead dog, Spider. He weighed about eighty pounds and had mostly black fur with multicolored accents. I would have immediately realized that he was something special had I known anything about sled dogs initially. It is by virtue of an outstanding character, including both dominance and intelligence, that a dog becomes a team leader. Spider had that character. As foreman of his crew, he was a stern but fair taskmaster. He pulled his own weight, and wouldn't tolerate any dog doing less. He had merely to turn his head back and give a slight snarl to get a shirker pressing his shoulders into the harness again.

Spider had a fantastic memory. He could remember the location of every spot where the team had turned out of the trail for a tea stop or an overnight camp for at least the last couple of years. Every time we approached such a place he would slyly try to turn out again in the hope of convincing me that a rest was due. Then I would have to shout "hew" or "cha" (right or left) loudly two or three times, and occasionally even run up alongside of him with raised fist, to get him to change his mind. So I guess if Spider had a fault it was that he was a bit of a conman who kept trying to play the boss for a sucker. Perhaps it would be more equitable to call him an optimist. He certainly compensated for his tricks by the tireless way he kept the team going for hours and days on end when necessary.

The dogs were condemned to a life of inactivity during the summer and fall months, a period which they spent chained up to posts in the dog compound. They each had their own wooden house of suitable size to protect them from the elements. The houses were shaped like a basic box, not only for ease of construction but to provide a flat roof. The roofs, covered with tar paper to shed moisture, enabled a dog to lie on top of his house out of the dust or mud if he so desired. Most of the time when the weather was warm, the preference was for lying on the cool earth. In fact, the dogs spent a substantial amount of time rearranging that earth to suit their liking. Our compound usually looked like a World War I battleground, full of craters and mounds. The craters were almost large enough to bury the dog houses in, which gives some idea of the energy put into the excavations. Since the permafrost was only two or three feet below the surface, it was possible for the dogs to stay nearly as cool as they wished, the only difficulty being that the exposed frozen ground became mucky as it thawed. However, it quickly dried out and warmed up in the summer sun. Then the dogs would just dig a little deeper.

Part of the dogs' leisure time was spent devising methods of unchaining themselves so that they could have a promenade around the countryside, their compound not being enclosed by a dog-proof fence. The chains, about eight feet long, were strong enough so that they couldn't be broken by the direct application of brute strength. However, Spider conceived the plan of jumping straight up with his chain stretched taut, so that the loop of the chain around the post was hitched upward ever so slightly with each jump. By maintaining tension on the chain, he prevented the loop from settling back to the bottom of the pole between jumps. Repeating this procedure many times, he succeeded in moving the loop right over the top of the pole. Thus he was free to roam about at will, albeit dragging his chain with him.

These escape attempts were foiled by driving several spikes part way into the top of the post, with the body of each spike pointing down at an angle to the post. Then the chain could not slip freely over the top. However, Spider was unconvinced at first and kept trying the same routine until, eventually, a link of his chain caught on a spike. Thus, even when he slacked off the tension, the loop did not drop back to the base of the pole. Spider took advantage of the situation by moving in close to the pole and then lunging out to the full length of his chain. The geometry of this arrangement provided a substantial leverage at the base of the pole. After repeated lunges, Spider succeeded in uprooting the pole completely. Now he was free again, although this time he had to drag both the chain and the pole around with him.

The final solution to the problem was to put in a sturdier post as deep as possible, chipping the bottom of the hole into the permafrost, while retaining the spikes in the top. Spider kept trying his old tactics for a while thereafter but, being the smart animal that he was, soon recognized the futility of it all.

My visits with the dogs in the compound made me impatient for the arrival of some snow and cold weather so that I could start getting the team (and myself) in shape for winter traveling. This would be accomplished by starting out with short trips, then gradually increasing their length and frequency. It would also be the time for breaking new dogs into the team if necessary, for checking out camping gear and heavy clothing and for planning some of the longer patrols to study game conditions, register trap lines and visit friends living out in the bush. By the time the lake and its tributary streams and rivers had a thick enough coating of ice for safe travel, both the dogs and I would be raring to go. Before any of this could happen, though, there was the fullness of autumn to come and, with it, the fall fishery.

Fall Fishery

Autumn arrived in all its glory, announcing its entrance on the seasonal stage with a fanfare of icy blasts out of the northwest. One brief flurry caught the MB *Buffalo* out on Great Slave Lake a few miles west of Fort Resolution, where the lashing waves washed a freighter canoe from its deck. The new captain (Bligh's replacement) sent a telegram from Hay River requesting that I keep a lookout for the craft, which would likely blow ashore somewhere along the south edge of the lake. Harry spread the news among the local people and soon thereafter a Native informed us that he had seen a large red canoe being battered by waves on a rocky beach near Pine Point, some twenty-five miles away. Storm conditions still prevailed at the time of the sighting so he'd had no inclination to approach too closely in his own boat. Almost certainly, it was the missing government canoe.

Harry and I headed across the bay to check out the sighting, using the cabin cruiser with our own canoe in tow. We anchored in the mouth of the Little Buffalo River, there being no good landing site for a boat along the lakeshore, and then traveled westward in our canoe in search of the derelict craft. After navigating several miles toward Pine Point we spotted a big red mark on the landscape and pulled into shore. There was the missing canoe—with a fist-sized hole in the bottom from being bounced on the rocks by waves, plus a few minor punctures and scrapes.

We explored the nearby bush for some birch bark and spruce gum with which to repair the damage, and soon found ample quantities. Harry built a small fire while I got a frying pan and some lard from our grub box. We tossed the spruce gum into the frying pan after first heating a bit of lard to keep the sticky gum from adhering to the pan. As soon as the spruce gum melted to a syruplike consistency, we spread it around the hole in the canoe and slapped on a birch bark patch, applying extra spruce gum all around the edges of the patch. Then, to be certain of a good glue job, we held a burning torch of bark against the patch to remelt the spruce gum and smooth it out.

Soon we had the wreck in shipshape condition but, before towing it back to the cabin cruiser, we decided to continue on to Pine Point and have a look around. The area had been the scene of some claim staking activity at the time of the Klondike gold rush and again in the 1920s. We found a few of the sampling trenches blasted into the rock by those earlier prospectors. Unknown to Harry and me at the time, interest in the mineral prospects of the region was even then reaching new heights. A town site, a wharf and a railroad to link the place to civilization were on the drawing boards in the main offices of the Consolidated Mining and Smelting Company.

Pine Point subsequently became well known as the site of a very large base metals (lead-zinc) open-pit mine and a substantial settlement, the population reaching 2,000 at its peak. Production got under way in 1965 and continued for twenty years until the ore body was exhausted. Today, Pine Point is reported to be almost a ghost town, with only a few people residing there.

Harry and I had no visions of future prosperity for the region; we saw nothing but bush. The following year though, an engineering camp was set up at Pine Point, and surveyors began to lay out building sites, roads and a dock.

Returning to Fort Resolution, it was time to organize our fall fishery. One of the first things I discovered about dog teams, even before learning how to drive them, was that they consumed a lot of food. Now I was to learn just how much effort was required to secure that food. We had to catch approximately 3,000 fish to supply our dogs with their energy requirements for the winter. While working during those cold months, they were always fed several pounds of frozen fish each day, usually whitefish, their favorite food. They would sup on some other species if absolutely necessary, albeit only after sniffing disdainfully at the meal for a while instead of gulping it down immediately as was their usual wont. The whitefish spawning run occurred in the fall. It was relatively easy to catch the fish then as they schooled up near the shore, as opposed to the summer when they were scattered all over the lake.

In the off-season, when the dogs weren't working, their once-a-day meals consisted mostly of dog mash, with an occasional treat of fresh fish thrown in. Since summer was an interval for repair and maintenance work, for patrols by water, and perhaps for firefighting, there wasn't much time left for fishing. Dog mash was easy to cook up. It was a dry material, packaged in hundred-pound sacks, whose nutritious constituents I have long since forgotten. We boiled it in water to the consistency of thick porridge and, after letting it cool a bit, served it to the dogs. The cooling period was important since the dogs usually wolfed food down immediately upon it being presented to them, and the ingestion of boiling hot mash into their mouths and stomachs did not make for contented mild-mannered animals.

From time to time a little fish oil was added to the pot of mash. This came in fifty-gallon drums and was quite expensive. The dogs liked the oil and mash mixture better than the straight mash, and we were convinced that the oil kept their fur looking healthier. However, given a choice between mash and fish, it was no contest. The dogs much preferred the fish.

Even if the dogs didn't always appreciate their mash, other animals weren't so fussy. It was difficult keeping field mice from helping themselves at every opportunity. I even knew of a black bear that seemed to like the stuff. When I was in Wood Buffalo National Park, I saw a two-storey log building where dog mash was stored in a room on the upper floor. There was evidence, in the form of numerous claw marks in the bark, that a bear had scaled a nearby tree in an attempt to reach a window of the room but couldn't quite make it, the tree being a little too far away from the wall of the building. How the bear knew the mash was in there, I don't know. The window was closed, the between-log cracks were all well plastered, and I didn't think the mash had that much of a scent. But I don't have the sensitive nose of a wild animal.

On a subsequent attempt, the bear actually clawed its way up the side of the building, smashed the window, and climbed inside.

It then proceeded to tear open the sacks and gorge itself on mash. Presumably the bear also gobbled down a substantial quantity of the broken window glass, since the sacks were in a position where the glass would have fallen on them, and the amount of glass found later during the cleanup was far from sufficient to account for the original window area. The bear never showed up again, so perhaps it got a very bad case of indigestion from its meal.

The fall fishery was conducted during the whitefish spawning season, usually beginning in late August. At this time, with the whitefish running close to the shore, it wasn't too difficult to find a productive location for setting nets. Harry and I used to set out four nets, each about eight feet deep and three hundred feet long. We would check them (or "fish" them) every day for about a month. During this time we hoped to catch the 3,000 fish needed to feed the team right through to the arrival of the spring thaw.

The weather usually sported a touch of Indian summer when we first put the nets in the water but would shortly thereafter run rapidly downhill toward winter. We would find ourselves having to break our way out through a bit more shore ice every morning in order to get our canoe underway. Once or twice, after a calm night, a skim of ice would appear over a large area of the lake, reaching from the shore to some point well beyond our nets. Except for the certainty of more stormy winds to break up this early offshore ice, we would have been in a panic to save our fishing gear. The shore-fast ice, though, just kept getting thicker. Altogether, the weather around Great Slave Lake was fairly accurately described by an old prairie joke about ten months of winter followed by two months of tough sledding. Our fishing started just at the end of the tough sledding period. The ice cover in the bay in which we fished, once firmly ensconced, didn't disappear completely until the beginning of June, and the first feeble attempts to freeze over again started in September.

Our nets caught mostly whitefish, quite a few conies (inconnu), too many jackfish (pike) and ling (burbot), some pickerel and suckers and, very occasionally, a nice lake trout. There were always a few volunteers waiting around on the dock who were more than willing to haul the delectable trout away for us. Ling were unwelcome catches because they would roll around in the net and wrap up many yards of it, preventing other fish from being caught in that section. When taking them out of the net, they would drape themselves around your arm like a big eel. My dogs disdained to eat them at all, which is saying a lot. Pike were even more unwelcome catches because, with their mouthful of sharp teeth, they could ruin large segments of the net. They could also ruin your benumbed fingers as you fumbled to get the fish out of the net, so you had to be extra careful when dealing with them. Conies were the largest fish caught, some so heavy that it was a difficult task to throw them from the canoe onto the dock, but they didn't seem to be nearly as nourishing, pound for pound, as whitefish. Consequently, the dogs were only fed conies when they weren't engaged in hard work.

The business of fishing the nets was, without a doubt, one of the more trying jobs that I've encountered in my working career. Each morning, the temperature only slightly below freezing on the good days, Harry and I headed out in our eighteen-foot freighter canoe. A trip of a mile or two in the chilly air brought us to the nets. Donning rubber bib overalls, we would pick up the float and its anchor at one end of a net, lift them over the canoe, and put them down again on the other side so that the net lay amidships over our laps. Then began the chore of extracting fish from the meshes of the net.

As we finished one section, we would pull some more of the unfished portion of the net over the gunwale on one side and drop the emptied part over the other side. In this way, we passed along the net from one end to the other, fish flopping in the bottom of the canoe and cold water splashing freely about. Our arms were quickly soaked to the shoulders and our hands were freezing and raw. We had light cotton gloves to wear, which were fine for disentangling most whitefish from the net, but were much too cumbersome when it came to stripping the fine mesh threads from the gills and teeth of jackfish. The threads made nasty gashes in the puffy flesh of cold, moisture-saturated hands. To add to the dis-

169

comfort, finger ends would crack wide open when the soaked skin dried out, exposing raw flesh to the frigid air.

Reaching the end of a net, we pulled the anchor there, stretched the net taut and dropped the anchor again. Then the whole process would start over on the next net. It usually took us about four long, cold, miserable hours from the time we first left our moorage in the morning until we returned again with our load of fish, depending on how much ice we had to break passage through and how many jackfish had to be untangled from the snarled-up net.

After hauling our catch back to the warden station, Harry and I put the fish on willow sticks for convenience in hanging them on the drying rack, or fish stage. With a knife, we made a slit in each fish just forward of the tail. Next we shoved a stick through the slit so that the fish hung head downwards. No attempt was made to clean the guts from the fish; the dogs probably considered them to be the best part. Ten whitefish were put on one stick, and this was then hung up on the log-frame fish stage to dry in the sun and the wind. A "stick" of dried fish used to be one of the standard units of barter in the North.

Once we started hanging fish it was fervently hoped that the weather would remain cold. If it suddenly warmed up for a spell, the fish would start to rot and eventually drop off the stick as the decaying flesh near the tail gave way. This not only created a slight aroma in the neighborhood but, if too many such losses occurred, it meant that nets would have to be reset and fished some more, weather permitting, in order to be certain of an adequate food supply to carry the dogs through to spring.

A scarcity of fish might also result from a period of unusually cold, but calm, weather during the fishery. Then a layer of ice would form over much of the bay, preventing access to the nets. One had to hope for a sufficiently strong wind to break up the ice, while praying that the nets wouldn't get carried away. Otherwise, the task of fishing through the ice might have to be faced—once it thickened up—in order to procure enough fish for the winter. Thankfully, I was never confronted with this prospect, although I understand that some people Outside actually do it for sport.

Perhaps winter fishing is more fun when you can do it with a line and sinker from inside a little shack than it is when it must be done with nets on the open ice.

❖

During my first fall fishery I encountered another impediment to the retention of an adequate supply of fish. Gulls! These birds would land by the dozens on the peaked roof of our warehouse, which was immediately adjacent to the fish stage. From there they would drop down at their leisure to take a few pecks at a fish. The trouble was that those few pecks were right near the tail where the stick went through, and the fish would often break free of the stick and fall to the ground. Soon fish were rotting away all over the ground under the stage. I tried tying rags and tin can lids to the stage to flutter and rattle in the breeze, but they were completely ineffective. I tried going out every hour and making all kinds of noise, but the birds just ignored me.

One day the sight of all our work going to waste drove me mildly insane. I leaned a ladder against the front of the warehouse and climbed up for a look. The gulls fluttered up when my head appeared over the edge of the roof, but they settled right back down again in the same place along the ridge. With a maniacal gleam in my eye, I went and got my twelve-gauge shotgun, put a shell in the chamber, and climbed back up the ladder. Carefully, I sighted down the ridge line. Slowly, I squeezed the trigger. Bamm!! There was a great flurry of feathers, shrieking birds taking wing, and carcasses rolling down the roof to land on the ground below.

Badly shaken by the whole affair, as I suddenly awoke to the realization that I—the local game warden, protector of animals and enforcer of regulations—had broken one of those laws, I hurriedly picked up the dead birds and buried them out in the bush. I had accounted for eleven birds with one shot, but at what risk! The penalty for a game warden illegally shooting gulls was much more severe than for an ordinary citizen committing the same offense, which is as it should be. Had I been apprehended and convicted, I would have been fined a minimum amount equivalent to about one-quarter of my gross annual salary. In addition, I could have been sentenced to two years in jail, and would certainly have seen my career as a game warden vanish, literally, in a puff of smoke. All of which goes to prove that the gulls *must* have driven me berserk.

Fortunately, if anyone witnessed the deed, they kept their own counsel, no doubt in sympathy with my predicament. Looking back on the event with intermingled shame and horror, I don't understand how I could have resorted to such an extreme act, even though I'm aware that most of the Native fishermen would have considered it to be normal behavior, having indulged in similar protective measures themselves on occasion. However it might be regarded, it was my only indiscretion during my tenure as a warden. I can report, though, that the gulls never bothered my fish again that year.

Once 300 sticks of fish were safely hanging from the stage, the nets were pulled from the water and dried, any needed repairs were made, and then they were stored away to await the next fall fishery. The canoe was cleaned of fish scales and slime, which encouraged wood rot if left in place, and put in the warehouse for the winter. The cabin cruiser was hauled out on the lakeshore, at a spot some distance from the village where a windlass had been constructed by the RCMP, so that there would be no chance of the vessel being crushed later on when a solid layer of ice formed on the lake surface. Then I looked forward impatiently to the first substantial snowfall of the season. A few inches of dry snow was all that was required to start getting the dog team in shape for winter travel.

Cold Comfort

It will be recalled (from the first chapter) that my initial attempt at driving a dog team ended with me stretched out on the snow, while the dogs traveled cheerfully onward by themselves.

After picking myself up from the frozen ground and finding that I could still move all of my limbs without causing undue pain, I followed in the wake of the team. I caught up with the miscreants at a spot about two miles away where they had stopped to relieve themselves. After lifting their legs, and then milling around to sniff at each other's contribution, the dogs had become so tangled up in their harness they couldn't proceed any further.

Fortunately, they hadn't started to fight among themselves, as would most entangled teams. I was to learn that my lead dog, Spider, maintained a taut ship—if I may use that analogy—having previously made the rest of the crew understand that he, as captain, would tolerate no fighting unless he was the one doing it. Since no other crew member was anxious to argue with him, I never had any trouble with my dogs chewing on each other. The occasional snarling match and threatening gestures, maybe, but nothing serious. Mind you, when we encountered another ship sailing on a reciprocal course, that could be a different story. The captain wouldn't stop his crew from assaulting the complement of a rival vessel. Then I would have to wade into a snarling mass of fur, ax-handle swinging, and exert my authority. Most often, though, other teams we met on the trail would swing off into the snow on the command of their driver and let us pass peacefully by.

I loaded the sled with some heavy rocks from the lakeshore to reduce the speed at which it could be pulled, ensuring that there would be no recurrence of the recent accident while on the return journey. After I untangled the traces and said a few harsh words to the team, we proceeded home without further incident. I had the uncanny feeling that the dogs were laughing among themselves at the entertaining way in which the day had gone. Back at the dog compound, I unharnessed the animals and chained them up again. Then I made straight for the house of the local seamstress where, feeling greatly embarrassed and humiliated, I ordered another parka to replace the torn rag I was wearing.

As a novice with dogs, I soon found that there was much more to the game than I had originally thought. From observing Hollywood movies in my youth, I knew that when the Mounties went out to get their man in the dead of winter, their dog teams would stand submissively in harness while the sled was loaded, moving off nicely at the command "mush." Unfortunately, my team hadn't seen those movies. The dogs were so anxious to get out on the trail for a run that they wouldn't listen to any command while the gear was being piled onto the toboggan. They would lunge into their harness, restrained by the anchor rope, making such an unholy uproar that I doubt if they could even hear any commands above the yapping and howling.

Once the anchor rope was loosed, the noise ceased and away went the team like an arrow from a bow. On several occasions, Mary tried to take a photograph of the team at the moment of departure. Despite my warnings about the speed of takeoff and her repeated assurances that she had the picture composed in the viewfinder and was ready to snap the shutter, the dogs always beat her to the draw.

Unlike the movie dogs, mine never responded to the command "mush." After any stops along the trail (following on from the initial unrestrained dash), just stepping on the back of the toboggan was usually sufficient to indicate to them the desire on the part of the driver to be moving along again. Otherwise, the command "alright" would suffice, if said in the appropriate tone of voice.

Fortunately for me, I had Harry for a tutor in driving dogs. He was very capable, both in showing me how to handle the team properly on the trail and in guiding me on trips into unfamiliar territory. His only fault was that sometimes he would imbibe too well the night before a planned outing and so be unfit for travel the next day. In such a case I might go without him but, more often, I would just delay the trip for a day to bring him to the realization that the work couldn't be so easily avoided.

❖

The appliance used in the bush country is usually a toboggan, rather than a proper sled, although it is often referred to as a sled or tobaggon, interchangeably. The toboggan is typically made from two oak planks, each about ten inches wide and fastened together in parallel by a number of cross braces. A high curl is formed into the front end of the planks, rising up like the prow of an ancient ship. The toboggan works more efficiently in the deep, soft snow of relatively level bush country than does a sled with conventional runners, since the planks allow it to ride up higher in the snow, creating less drag. It also stands up better to the occasional encounter with a tree. For sidehill travel, though, toboggans are tougher to handle because they tend to slide downhill, whereas the runners of a sled dig into the snow for a better purchase.

During the spring thaw, the snow in the bush is very sticky for much of the day, but forms an icy crust at night after the temperature drops. Then most toboggan travel is done in the early hours of the morning before the crust begins to thaw again. Rudimentary steel runners, just narrow strips of metal, are then fastened on the bottom of the toboggan to provide directional stability over the snow. Some spring trails are very hard to travel, even with runners attached, because of the way the thawing process takes place. It's the same thing that happens with the path to the outhouse. The hard-packed snow in the middle of the track melts more slowly than the softer snow along the edges, resulting in a slippery path that slopes down on each side from a high center crown. In fact, the snow in the middle still marks the path for some time after all the rest of the ground is bare. On such a trail, the toboggan keeps trying to slide off to the side and must be continuously manhandled to keep it on track. This is laborious work even with a light load.

A backboard, with handlebars at a convenient height, is hinged to the toboggan about a foot or so from the rear end of the bottom planks. The hinges give some flexibility to the backboard while in use, and permit it to be folded down for storage in the summer. In the upright position, it is supported by ropes tied fore and aft near the edges of the planks. When riding on the sled, the driver stands on the rear of the planks and hangs onto the handlebars. Again contrary to Hollywood movies, if the sled is loaded with gear, the driver only rides for perhaps half the distance of any trip. The rest of the time is spent running behind the sled to reduce the workload for the dogs.

A topless canvas container called a carryall is rigged between the backboard and the curled-up front end of the toboggan. Most of the gear is packed into this container, a tarpaulin is laid across it, and the whole load is securely lashed with rope. An ax and rifle are usually slipped under the top ropes, where they can be gotten at in a hurry if need be. The makings for the midday meal are also carried outside of the tarpaulin to avoid having to unlash the ropes until camp is made at the end of the day's travel. The fish for the dogs are packed separately in a canvas sack hanging from the backboard to avoid contaminating the rest of the load with a fishy odor.

At the rear edge of the toboggan planks, there is usually a homemade braking device. In my case, it consisted of a barndoor hinge with a portion of one leaf bent in a right angle so as to dig into the trail when pressed down by the driver's foot. When not in use, a screen door spring held the bent part up out of the way. This kind of brake can sometimes be useful to slow the dogs down in critical situations if the driver is on the back of the sled and the snow on the trail isn't too soft. I mostly used it when going down steep slopes or approaching open water.

On one backwater branch of the Slave River that we traveled frequently during the winter, there was an area of several hundred square feet that never froze over at all. Perhaps there was a relatively warm spring entering at the bottom of the channel whose efflux intermingled with the river water, because the water current at that location didn't seem to be strong enough by itself to keep the surface free of ice. Whatever the cause, my lead dog's favorite stunt was to dash toward the open water, wheeling away at the last possible second. This had a crack-the-whip effect on the toboggan. On more than one occasion I found myself teetering on the brink of disaster, foot pressed hard on the brake, desperately throwing my relatively light weight around to keep the rig out of the water. The more I berated Spider for this behavior, the more delight he seemed to take in repeating it at the next opportunity. Besides being smart and cunning, he was a great practical joker.

Whenever the foot brake proved to be ineffective, the ultimate solution was to throw the sled on its side and sit on it. This created enough drag to bring the dogs to a rapid halt. The sled was also put on its side during lunch stops, or brief hunting stops, to keep the team from carrying on by themselves. However, if my team sensed caribou in the vicinity, even this expedient would not prevent them from dragging the load for several hundred feet in the frenzy of the chase. They had been indoctrinated into caribou hunting before I acquired them and had probably been allowed to feed on such delicacies as caribou intestines. Now, whenever these animals were sighted, or even if a rifle was loaded in the dogs' presence with no caribou around, they went wild with excitement. In fact, so conditioned were they, the mere "snick" of the rifle bolt moving into place would set the team into more rapid motion in anticipation of caribou on the trail ahead. I often took advantage of this Pavlovian response when I was in a particular hurry to get somewhere. No matter how often I clicked my rifle bolt, the dogs would always speed up for at least several minutes. I considered this stratagem to be just retribution for the tricks they played on me.

The most important accessory on the toboggan is the anchor rope—a conviction which was reinforced by my first undignified experience with dog driving. The rope has a diameter of about five-eighths of an inch and is about thirty feet long, more or less depending on the driver's level of confidence in his own abilities. It is fastened permanently to the front of the toboggan. The primary purpose of the rope is to keep the dogs from running away with the sled before the driver is ready to go. To accomplish this, the sled is first positioned near a large post or tree to which the free end of the rope is tied, using a slip knot. Next, the sled is fully loaded and the covering tarpaulin is lashed on. Then the dog harness is laid out in place. I used dog collars, like small horse collars, which slipped over a dog's head and fetched up against its shoulders. A cinch strap went around the belly. Leather traces connected the dogs and sled together, going from the lead dog's collar and cinch to the collar of the dog next in line, and so on, the last traces being fastened to the front of the toboggan.

I always hooked my dogs in tandem, that is, single file. This was partly because I normally ran only five dogs, but mostly because some of my travel was over narrow bush trails. Also, the tandem arrangement is the only way to go when deep snow requires the driver to break trail for the team. The gang hitch, or double tandem, where dogs are aligned in pairs, is useful for running seven or more dogs in fairly open country. The fan hitch, where each dog is fastened by a separate tug line to the sled, is used in the Barren Grounds or the High Arctic where the snow is mostly hard-packed and the countryside is free of trees.

As the dogs are hooked up one by one, they begin leaping in their harness, trying to start the sled. They are enthusiastic about their work and want to get moving immediately. By the time several dogs are in harness, there is enough combined muscle to actually start the nose of the toboggan bouncing up and down with each forward lunge of the animals. Finally, with five dogs hooked up and everything else ready, the driver plants himself firmly on the rear of the planks, foot pressed heavily on the brake. He slips the knot on the restraining anchor rope and hangs on for dear life. The dogs delight in going at top speed at the start of any trip, and even the brake can't hold them back. If the going is really good, they can briefly achieve a speed of nearly twenty miles per hour.

This is when the anchor rope serves as insurance against losing the team while miles from civilization. After slipping the knot, the rope is left trailing behind the sled until the initial burst of speed has dissipated. This could take five minutes or so. It often seems longer, especially in rough going. Then, if the driver gets bounced off during this period, there is a chance of getting the dogs stopped if he can manage to catch the rope as it goes whistling by. Of course, he might also get his parka destroyed, or even worse.

❖

You haven't truly experienced Nature's law of the survival of the fittest until you've made an overnight camp about a quarter-mile in from the lakeshore—where it may sometimes be necessary to go to get into a timbered spot for a decent campsite, with much of that quarter-mile piled high with accumulations of drift logs—and then tried to drive the team back over the jumbled mess of wood the following morning when the dogs are full of pep and raring to go. That's how it can be for travelers along the south shore of Great Slave Lake, especially to the east of the Slave River delta.

Each spring when the ice in the river breaks up, it scours the riverbanks as it progresses downstream, knocking whole trees into the current. Some of the trees even come from the faraway Peace River system, beginning in the mountains of British Columbia and joining the waters of the Slave River near its exit from Lake Athabasca. Many tons of silt are also carried along in the raging waters, to be deposited in relatively quiescent locations where the slowing current no longer has enough energy to maintain the particles in suspension. Year by year, these geologic processes cause sandbanks and driftwood to pile up on the foreshore of Great Slave Lake, separating the bush from the water by a goodly distance in some places.

Fortunately, when faced with the necessity of driving my team over the tangled mass of trunks and roots—the intervening spaces filled with varying depths and densities of snow—I always managed to hang on and keep the sled upright. There were moments of great anxiety, some high-angle tipping and violent swaying, some jolting and banging with splinters of wood flying, and some very close calls indeed, but no unrecoverable upsets. So I never did find out whether I would have been able to catch the anchor rope in such a circumstance and get the dogs stopped before they bashed my brains out against the driftwood.

After the first hectic minutes of the day's journey the dogs throttle back slightly to a fast lope of ten or twelve miles per hour and the anchor rope can be reeled in. Then the novice driver begins to learn something about the dogs' biological functions.

The evening before, they dined on their usual meal of frozen fish. Now, with their first activity of the day, they want to rid themselves of the useless residue. However, they don't all come to that decision at the same time. One of the world's funniest sights is that of one member of a dog team trying to evacuate its bowels while the remaining members insist on maintaining a hell-bent-for-leather pace along the trail.

Picture a dog running along as fast as possible on his two front legs, his rear legs raised up out of contact with the ground and his hind feet hovering around his ears. His bent rear knee joints project above his backbone. Imagine the look of intense concentration on his face as he tries to attend to his business without getting his behind rubbed raw on the hard-packed snow of the trail. Every so often he is forced to thrust one of his rear legs down to provide some additional upward momentum. Finally the task is accomplished and he is able to settle back to a fast gallop on all four legs again. Only the lead dog is safe from this daily trial. When he wants to stop, everybody stops.

This is not only a trying time for the dog attempting to attend to Nature's needs, but also for the driver. The driver must be ever on his mettle in order to tip the toboggan slightly on edge at the critical moment, thus avoiding the goop laid down on the trail by the dog. If he doesn't take avoiding action in time, the goop smears out over the bottom of the planks, freezing almost instantly into a rough drag-increasing surface. Then the driver must stop the toboggan, tip it over on its side, and painstakingly scrape the frozen mess off the bottom with the blade of his ax. Will the rest of the dogs take advantage of this stop to evacuate their bowels in relative peace and quiet? Not at all. They will just chomp at the bit until the sled is moving again, and *then* it is the next dog's turn.

While on the subject of natural functions, I might as well describe the problem of emptying the bladder (for the dogs, that is). Dogs don't seem to be capable of urinating on the run, so the one with the most urgent need suddenly moves sideways to the bushes at the edge of the trail, pulling his teammates with him, and applies his brakes. The rest of the team knows what is intended and, the leader willing, they all come to a halt. The dog in need

180

lifts his leg and lets fly, and then the rest of the team try to parade by, take a sniff, and mark the spot themselves. Unless the driver can persuade the dogs to maintain their positions, the result is usually a tangle of harness. Perhaps you think the whip could be used to keep the dogs in line, but that's only for Hollywood movies. I never saw a whip the whole time I was in the North, although I believe the Inuit do use a whip crack alongside a recalcitrant dog to encourage him to work a little harder.

The bowel problem only occurs once a day, in the morning, but the bladder problem takes place at intervals throughout the day, often simply as an attempt by the team at marking spots already claimed by another team traversing the trail before them. One might think that bladders would soon become empty, but the dogs replace body fluids by eating snow during rest stops, or even scooping it up on the run.

There is a related problem, too. Sometimes, when traveling the south shore of Great Slave Lake, where the north wind has a fetch of 100 miles to the north shore and then several hundred more unobstructed miles to the polar sea, the wind chill is so bad that the dogs' external plumbing almost freezes up. The dogs stop to urinate, each one lifting its leg in the expectation of marking the trail, but nothing happens. Then it is necessary to halt for a spell while the dogs lie down, curl into a ball, and start licking some warmth into the appropriate part of their anatomy. The driver must, perforce, stand around, stamping his feet and jumping up and down, because his own plumbing isn't all that warm either. After a short wait, one dog stands up, lifts its leg in anticipation, and manages to produce a stream. One can almost hear the animal say "ahhhhh" in relief. Quite soon all of the dogs are content again and everyone can go merrily on their frozen way.

After the initial superspeed burst of a few minutes duration, and the fast lope period which might last twenty minutes or so on a good trail—or road as it is called in the backwoods—the dogs settle down to a steady trot of five or six miles per hour. At this point, especially if the weather is very cold, the driver may feel like trotting a bit himself. He hops off the back of the sled and starts running. As soon as the dogs feel the load lighten, they step up the pace, so the driver had better have some speed in reserve to enable him to catch up and climb aboard again when the desire strikes. It can be difficult to run in heavy winter garments, even on a good road.

With my team, if I began to fall behind, the worst thing I could do was to start shouting "whoa." The practical joker in the lead position, sensing my lack of control of the situation, would immediately increase the pace. The more I shouted, the faster went the team. When I finally managed to climb aboard the sled again, I was usually well warmed up. I swear the leader would look around at me, his lips curled in a smile, his demeanor speaking for him: "Almost got you that time, boss!"

Lost in a Blizzard

When out on the winter trail, it was my practice to avoid riding on the dog sled as much as possible. It aids the team immensely if they don't have to pull the driver's weight along with everything else. In general, each dog can pull nearly twice its own weight when the going is good. For tough sledding or faster travel, lighter loads are advisable. So I would run whenever it seemed appropriate. I often ran fifteen or twenty miles per day behind the dogs.

Early on in my days as a game warden, I gained a modicum of fame as an exceptional trail runner. Harry spread the word that I was one of the best runners he had ever traveled with and soon the Natives were referring to me by an Indian nickname which I could neither spell nor pronounce, but which meant "the runner." I didn't mind being known as a strong runner—a reputed strength of any kind often provides a psychological advantage to a game warden in the performance of his duties—but I had to work hard to live up to my reputation.

In the North, the unit of distance used for winter travel was often given in terms of time. For example, a certain destination would be said to be three days away, meaning that it took the average dog team three days to make the journey, traveling at a normal pace. The magnitude of my unit, translated back into distance, was usually about thirty-five miles per day on familiar well-used trails, so I might describe Rocher River as being two days from Fort Resolution. The length of the traveling day wasn't necessarily constant, though. In fact, it could be quite variable, depending on the physical well-being of the team (and driver), the weight of the load, the condition of the trail, the topography (flat or hilly, treed or open), the time of year (cold January and warm March both make tougher sledding), and the weather (facing into a blizzard slows the team down). Other factors could be the locality (known versus unknown territory) and the availability of shelter (convincing oneself that only two or three more miles would bring one to the comfort of a cabin could extend an already arduous day).

The time spent traveling might also depend on the amount of daylight or nocturnal illumination available. At night, sufficient light can be provided by the moon or by a bright display of the aurora borealis, or Northern Lights. The availability of substantial auroral light is usually restricted to a band which encircles the globe like a ribbon, centered on the magnetic pole. The seasonal duration of daylight depends on latitude. In the High Arctic, where there is little or no daylight for part of the winter, it is necessary to travel mostly by moonlight unless the area is a familiar one. Near Great Slave Lake, there were about five hours of full daylight in midwinter which, with an early start, easily allowed thirty miles of travel on a good road and still left a little twilight in which to make camp.

Sometimes—if all the conditions seemed right and I knew pretty well where I was, and especially if I was traveling alone so that the dogs had a lighter load—I would keep on for a much longer time, covering a distance of up to sixty miles in a day's travel. At the end of such a stretch, both dogs and driver would be dragging along at a rate of about three miles per hour or even less. Occasionally, a dog wouldn't be quite up to pulling for such a long distance, so I would have to take him out of harness and let him follow along at his own pace. This, of course, threw a greater weight on the remaining dogs, so we slowed down even more. Once, Skipper suddenly went lame and, after being turned out of harness, showed no inclination to trot along in the rear. Even after leaving him some distance behind, I could see that he remained motionless on the trail. This left me no recourse but to go back and load him on the sled to be hauled along by his fellow team members, further increasing their burden. Since this took place well out on the lake ice, with miles to go before a suitable camp site could be found, it ended up being one very long day of traveling, nearly eighteen hours in all. The lame dog recovered after a day's rest, and so did the driver.

If I was in unfamiliar country, with no good roads, I would always try to make camp by dusk, even if it meant breaking off the travel early at some suitable campsite. To do otherwise would be an invitation to getting lost or, at least, to becoming bewildered, and then having to waste time getting reoriented on the following day.

It was also easy to develop a certain degree of perplexity by continuing to travel in a blinding blizzard, especially at night or if the trail was poorly defined. On one occasion, after leaving Fort Resolution very early in the morning, I had gone about fifty miles in an easterly direction, much of the distance along the lakeshore. Normally, I would have stopped about thirty miles out, at a regular gathering place on Stoney Island, but this day I was traveling light and hoped to make the whole distance to Rocher River before halting for the night. I had a little shack there, so I wouldn't have to camp out or impose on the HBC manager's hospitality. I was traveling alone because Harry had been on one of his binges the evening before and I didn't feel like waiting around for an extra day until he was back in shape for mushing. The night was dark except for stars, both the moon and the aurora having failed me, but the road was a familiar one.

The village of Rocher River was some distance inland from the lakeshore. The winter route to it didn't follow along the river but approached through a large, deep bay to the west of the river mouth. Each year, after freeze-up, local people would mark a path across the bay with small spruce trees stuck in an upright position in the snow. These led to the start of the bush trail in the bottom of the bay. At first, these markers would stand about five or six feet proud of the snow but, after a month or two, drifting flakes blowing in off the vast expanse of the lake, piling up more or less uniformly throughout the bay, would cover all but the topmost part. Sometimes the trees would even be completely hidden.

Now, in the darkness, I couldn't find the markers. Any pre-existing sled track which might have helped to show the way had been filled in by blowing snow, and the wind was rapidly getting stronger. I knew the bay was several miles across from point to point on the lakeshore and was of a like depth. From the west-ernmost point, I imagined that I could see deeper shadows mark-

185

ing the tree line away off in the bottom of the bay but, after staring hard for a while, I had to concede that it was not so. My mind was just trying to play tricks on me. I took a guess at the proper direction and swung the team into the bay. Soon the vigorous wind turned into a blizzard, lifting the snow high above the surface of the lake, blotting out both the stars and the indistinct shadows. At first I tried to maintain a course at a constant angle to the direction of the wind but soon gave it up as a lost cause because of the spiraling gusts. I lost my bearings completely. The dogs, too, were hesitating, uncertain of the trail.

We—the team and I—had to find some kind of shelter before stopping for the night, preferably among trees because I wasn't packing a portable gas stove along and wanted wood for a campfire. Nor did I have my tent on this trip because I'd been expecting to make the settlement at Rocher River in one long day, and every bit of weight that I could leave off the toboggan meant a reduction in travel time. I was worried, initially, that we might unwittingly swing around and head offshore, with nothing but miles of ice and an uncertain future ahead of us. Then I realized that pressure ridges in the ice, beyond the near-shore shallows where the lake was frozen right to the bottom, would serve as a warning sign. So we just kept plodding along, getting wearier by the minute.

Finally, out of the night and the swirling snow, a dark shape loomed, a little darker than the rest of our surroundings. We had stumbled onto a grove of trees which, later, turned out to be growing on a small island near the river mouth, not far off our correct route but outside the bay into which I thought we were proceeding.

I unhooked the dogs and fed them. They were happy, this night, to settle for their whitefish supper right off the sled, unheated and unthawed. I did make a number of incisions in each fish with my ax, so that the dogs found it easier to bite off frozen chunks. Then I erected a brush lean-to for shelter from the wind, made a fire, and heated a meal for myself. I unrolled my sleeping bag between the lean-to and the fire and climbed in.

Just as I started to doze off, the dogs gave a few whimpers. In the last light of the dying campfire I could see that they were all standing, ears pricked up and noses pointing in the direction from which we had come prior to bumping into the island. There was something out there all right, but I wasn't sure what it might be. Most wild animals were unlikely to be traveling in that blizzard, except perhaps for a few caribou drifting along with the wind. The dogs would have reacted differently to caribou scent, though, even as tired as they were. Whatever or whoever it was, they wouldn't find our track into the island—that had long since been erased by the drifting snow. After a while the dogs snuggled down again, noses tucked under tails, and we all went to sleep.

In the middle of the night the frost penetrated my sleeping bag and brought me half awake. The wind was dying down and my fire had long since burned out. As I struggled to doze off again, shivering with cold, I envied Sam McGee, who had gotten happily warm during his cremation on the marge of Lake Lebarge (according to Robert Service). I wasn't willing to go that far but I did start wondering why I hadn't chosen a different career. I could have continued working at Whitburn's Nursery, where it was always balmy inside the greenhouses. Better yet, and more remunerative, I might have been a chemist and studied reactions involving heat, ones like coal gasification or steam recovery of petroleum from tar sands. That would have kept me warm. I was good in chemistry at high school. I actually paid attention in class and learned how to balance the equations that govern chemical reactions—a certain number of grams of ingredient X, interacting with a certain number of grams of ingredient Y under the right conditions, would yield so many grams of a product Z. Sometimes energy had to be added to make the reaction go, and sometimes energy would be liberated in the form of heat. For an efficient reaction, all the proportions had to be just right.

"Aha," I had thought then, "this wonderful knowledge has certain possibilities. Perhaps I can apply it to the making of gunpowder?" I was interested in rockets and pyrotechnics at the time. A little extra research provided the names of the required ingredients, all readily available at my local drugstore in small cardboard canisters containing a cupful of chemical, at costs ranging from ten cents to twenty-five cents for each package. I used the balanced reaction equation to calculate the correct proportions and carefully mixed up a batch of black powder. Would it work?

That night, under cover of darkness, I put some of the powder in a large empty can and took it out to the middle of the field in front of my house. This field was a block long on each side, with houses facing it across the road on two sides. I stuck a fuse in the powder but I didn't put a lid on the can. I wasn't ready for an explosion just yet; I merely wanted to check on the accuracy of my calculations. I lit the fuse and backed off to a safe distance. Whoosh! A huge flame roared out from the can and lit up the surrounding area like daylight. I could clearly see all of the architectural details on the house fronts. Fortunately, the flame was of brief duration and the quick return to darkness allowed me to leave the scene before any local citizens could come around with embarrassing questions.

A few days later, I took some of the mixture to school in a small bottle, capped by a lid with a tiny slit in it through which a fuse could be inserted. During a period when I was supposed to be studying in the school library, I went out to the back of the school. In a moment of thoughtlessness, I decided to set my little bomb off. It was very little; I thought it would make no more sound than a big firecracker. I put the bottle under the solid wooden steps at the back of the school so that any flying glass would be contained. Then I lit the fuse and went around to the front of the stairs, out of the line of fire. The noise of the explosion was much louder than I expected. Much, much louder.

Before I could leave the scene, the door over the steps was thrown violently open and a teacher rushed out to see what calamity had occurred. How lucky for me that it was my chemistry teacher. He had been conducting a class in a nearby laboratory. As a cloud of smoke drifted away from the area, I was subjected to a severe dressing down. But he was a nice guy. In the end, he said that the incident would not be reported to the principal—primarily because it had been carried out in the interest of expanding my knowledge of chemistry—provided that I forthwith abandoned any similar experiments. I agreed to this condition, realizing that my ignorance about explosive mixtures was great and I could have seriously injured myself.

I got a lot of heat from that experiment—mostly from the teacher. Just thinking about the tongue lashing he gave me must have warmed me up for I finally dropped off to sleep again.

❖

The next morning dawned bright and clear and cold. There was no wind at all. The sun was peeking over the horizon, shining through the trees. Tired from the strenuous effort of the previous day and compensating for the fitful rest in the nighttime cold, I had overslept. Everything, including myself in my sleeping bag, was drifted over with six inches or more of snow. Each time that I exhaled—lying on my back looking upward to the cerulean blue of the sky overhead—my breath froze into tiny ice crystals which drifted slowly downward, shimmering with reflected sunlight, right back onto my face. I decided to skip breakfast for the time being, since I knew that the settlement couldn't be too far away. I hurriedly got up and looked to the dogs. Their presence was only betrayed by their breathing holes in the blanket of snow. With half-frozen hands, I harnessed them to the sled and broke camp. Once the team was clear of the island and back on the lake ice, I was able to determine our location from the lay of the land. In less than an hour we arrived at our destination and I was soon stoking up the fire in my little shack.

Shortly after arriving at Rocher River, I heard the sound of a bombardier pulling up outside. I thought it might be a fisherman coming into the village with a catch of fish for sale. Bombardiers were popular vehicles with people engaged in winter commercial fishing, which took place miles out on the lake ice. They traveled much faster than dog teams and could carry a bigger load. However, this particular bombardier disgorged the RCMP corporal who asked if I had seen any sign of a fellow traveler on the trail. Apparently a missionary had started out from Fort Resolution shortly after me, hoping to follow my tracks to Rocher River, but he hadn't shown up yet. Since he was a novice at winter traveling (who wasn't!), his fellow missionaries had become a bit concerned about him and had notified the police. The corporal, in a commandeered vehicle, had just made a fast trip with it over much the same route I had followed on the previous day. The missionary was nowhere in sight along this trail.

Immediately I realized what it was that had caught my dogs' attention the previous evening. It was the missionary and his team passing close to the island in the darkness. Evidently his dogs had been prevented by the fury of the storm raging around them from sensing the presence of my team. On and on he pressed, as the story unfolded later, eventually stopping miles beyond the point at which he should have turned inland, but at least he had regained the lakeshore. Pulling up to a timbered spot, he had rested for a few hours.

At first light the missionary was on his way again, still heading in the wrong direction, not realizing he had overshot his destination. Then he had happened on an Indian encampment, where he was informed of his error. It was a fortunate meeting for him, since he had been carrying sufficient dog food for only one night, and there is no telling what additional difficulties he might have encountered. The bush in winter is no place to make mistakes of any kind; in the words of the old cliché, Nature can be truly unforgiving. The exhausted traveler finally arrived at Rocher River on the following day, approximately twenty-four hours overdue, and the search for him—just about to get underway in earnest—was canceled.

Winter Travel

After a fresh snowstorm in the bush, or after any strong northerly wind along the lakeshore, all the roads are filled in with snow, often to the point of complete obliteration. They have to be reestablished by some hardy soul and his dog team. This is called breaking trail. Sometimes the job is so tough that it can almost break one's spirit. The lakeshore itself is seldom much of a problem because the fierce winds compact the top layers of snow into a hard crust that is usually sufficiently strong to bear the weight of a loaded toboggan.

Sheltered areas in the midst of the bush or along the river are quite another matter, whatever the wind conditions. The snow is often so soft and deep that even unharnessed dogs can only move in it by leaping up and forwards. A team in harness can't leap very well with a sled hanging on behind even should they manage to launch themselves in unison, a feat with very low probability. The only feasible solution is for the driver to put on his snowshoes and make a trail for the dogs to follow. This isn't quite like ordinary snowshoeing; smaller "trail" shoes are used instead of regular ones. Trail shoes sink more under your weight and help pack the snow. This makes the process a lot tougher for the driver than if he could use larger snowshoes to provide more buoyancy, but it is easier for the dogs to negotiate the resulting track.

Any time there is much road to be broken out, a distance traveled of ten or fifteen miles traveled represents a very good day's work and, if the going is really tough, one is fortunate to make five miles. Breaking a trail is such hard work that, after a fresh snowfall, everyone in the village who has some reason for traveling tries to hold off as long as possible in the hope that the other guy will get the job done first.

My lead dog Spider always considered the necessity for breaking trail as an opportunity to indulge in some more practical joking. Conditions permitting, he would walk up close behind me and tread on the tail of my snowshoes. The effect of this was to pitch me forward onto my face in the soft snow ahead, much to his apparent amusement.

The snowshoe harness in widespread use throughout the North consists of a length of lampwick, of the coal-oil lamp variety, about three feet long. This is wrapped over the crossbar and around the foot in such a manner that the foot can be readily slipped in and out of the harness. As long as the lampwick remains dry, it is flexible in the coldest weather.

I didn't look forward to the first session of snowshoeing in each new dog-sledding season because it involved the use of muscles which hadn't been exercised since the previous winter. Picking snowshoes up high enough to clear the snow and move the feet forward without getting them all tangled up puts a strain on certain leg and foot muscles. In particular, the Achilles tendon, at the back of the heel, is subjected to undue stress, leading to the notorious and painful affliction, *mal de raquette*. However, like most muscle problems, relief is just a day or two away provided that the part is given some rest.

A spell of very cold weather can also keep one off the trail. I made it a practice never to set out on a trip if the weather forecast called for temperatures colder than thirty-five below. However, the forecasts in the North are no more accurate than those in any other part of the country, and I would sometimes leave in relatively balmy air of perhaps minus fifteen, only to have it quickly turn much colder. A lot depends on the wind, too, mostly because of the effect on the dogs. They don't wear parka hoods for face protection, with an extra set of winter woollies to help keep the plumbing warm. Even for the driver, with a deep parka hood, it can be a real hardship to have to keep moving into a bone-chilling north wind, so imagine what it must be like for the dogs.

The best range is plus five to minus twenty degrees. Temperatures much colder or warmer make for tougher sledding, even on a well-traveled road. As the temperature decreases, the drag of the sled increases because the snow hardens into sharp-edged ice crystals which cut into the toboggan boards. The sound of the motion changes too, with a high-pitched squeal of protest being emitted as the angular crystals massage the toboggan's bottom. The drag also increases at warmer temperatures due to the sticky melting snow which results when the pressure from the weight of the loaded sled reduces the melting-point temperature below thirty-two degrees.

The coldest temperature I was ever caught out in was about fifty-five degrees below zero, on a trip in January. Fortunately there was no wind to make it feel even colder. Harry and I had been on the trail for a week, with fairly good mushing weather. Then things turned nasty when some really cold Arctic air rolled in. However, we were just one day away from home on the return trip and thus suffering from what seamen call "channel fever," so we kept traveling on. Because of the difficulty in breathing the cold air while undergoing any exertion, we set an easy pace for the sake of ourselves and the dogs. We kept checking each other's faces for white patches of skin, indicating the onset of frostbite. When fingered, the icy flesh had no feeling left. It had to be warmed up under the wool mitts which we wore inside of moosehide gauntlets. Bare hands couldn't be used for this purpose without fear of fingers freezing too.

Had there been any significant breeze we might have been tempted—or even forced—to make camp and try to wait the cold weather out, as we had done once or twice previously on forty-below days when a gale was howling down from the north, blowing its gelid breath across the lake ice and into the bush. There are definitely easier ways to make a living. Nothing is more frustrating than to be weather-bound on the homeward journey. Luckily for us, we didn't try to wait for warmer weather on that occasion. On each subsequent day, for the week following, the temperature dipped under minus sixty—more than ninety degrees below the freezing point! There would have been no possibility of staying in camp for the duration of that cold spell; food supplies for ourselves and the dogs, as well as our patience, would have long been exhausted before it was over. (The mean temperature for the whole month of January that year was minus thirty-three degrees. Sam McGee would have hated it.)

Making camp at the end of a day of slogging along the winter trail involves finding a suitable location—one sheltered a bit from the wind, with a supply of trees for firewood. Then the dogs are unharnessed and chained in positions out of reach of each other and of anything chewable that they shouldn't be chewing on, like the harness, the grub box and the toboggan. Some spruce boughs are cut for their bedding. Even though hungry, the dogs lie quietly without making a fuss, their eyes following my every move. They know the sequence of events, including the stage at which they will be fed.

Next, a substantial fire is built for warmth and light, first scraping the snow away to ground level using a snowshoe for a shovel or, if the snow is too deep, constructing a platform of green logs to support the fire and keep it from melting its way into a big hole. For starting the fire, a layer of old dried bark from a birch tree ignites easily no matter the weather. Lacking this, dead tree limbs are whittled into kindling. If the kindling is reluctant to respond to the heat of a lighted match, a candle from the grub box is a good persuader. Soon a hearty blaze is crackling away, casting a yellow glow on the dogs and the surrounding bush.

Frozen fish for the team's evening meal is set by the fire to thaw for a while, making the repast a little easier on their teeth and stomachs. Time then for a quick warmup for myself, standing close to the fire with bare hands outspread, watching out for burnt spots on my clothing from the sparks being tossed by the blazing wood. When the air near the fire warms up, an occasional "whump" sound is heard as an overloaded branch on a nearby tree dumps its burden of melting snow to the ground.

Usually I carry a small floorless sidewall tent. After choosing a tent site—between two trees where a rope can be used to suspend the ridge of the tent—the snow is tramped down and any snags cleared from the ground. If no suitably placed trees are available, four poles are cut and lashed together to form a pair of V-shaped supports. Another pole, to which the tent ridge will be attached, joins the supports at the top. Since the use of tent pegs is not tenable in the deep snow, two heavy poles are laid in the

194

snow, one on each side of the site, to serve as attachment points for the sidewall ropes. Then the tent is pitched. Green logs are cut on which to support a light sheet-metal stove inside the tent, the stove pipe protruding through an asbestos collar sewn into the roof of the tent. (The stove is a wood-burning one whose metal ends and sides fold together for easy transport.) Spruce boughs are cut and arranged for a mattress and, finally, the sled is unpacked.

By the time all this work is done, the frozen fish are slightly flexible so I toss each dog his share. This is their moment. Powerful jaws crunch the partially thawed fish into a few large bites which are wolfed down without additional chewing— bones, ice and all. A few gulps and their evening meal is over. Next they pad about for a bit within the confines of their chains, organizing their beds for a night of rest. Then each dog turns around once or twice, lies down and curls up, bushy tail around its nose. The last sound from them is a contented sigh. Some fall asleep almost immediately. Others, one eye closed, follow my motions with their other eye for a while as I move about in the flickering light of the fire.

After cutting extra firewood and kindling, in readiness for the following morning, I make my own supper. This typically takes the form of caribou meat cut up into bite-sized chunks and fried in a frying pan. I don't care much for the flavor but I'm usually hungry enough that taste isn't the prime concern. When the meat is about done, I add some precooked beans or stew to the pan to thaw out. These items were cooked at home to save time and trouble on the trail, frozen solid by putting them in the back porch for a while, and then broken up into small pieces. In camp, I need only haul some bean or stew chunks out of the grub box and warm them up in the frying pan.

While the main course is getting ready, some bannock or biscuits (also precooked and frozen) are toasting on a stick by the fire, and snow for tea water is melting in a billy can. This last operation requires a certain amount of finesse since it is possible to scorch snow, ending up with water that has a horrible burnt taste. It depends on the consistency of the snow, the heat of the fire and the attention paid to keeping the snow packed down as it melts. I know that "burnt" water might sound like a tall tale, but it can happen easily enough. Tea (the most common beverage on the trail) is not my favorite at the best of times, and I can't stomach it at all when made with scorched snow water. Some of the Natives just add a large spoonful of butter to each such cup, stir until the butter dissolves, and then gulp the mixture down. Yechhh!

After supper I crawl into my sleeping bag and read for a while by candlelight. (If Harry is with me we play a few rounds of cribbage and, of course, we share in all of the aforementioned chores.) During the night the fire probably needs to be stoked up once or twice to get a little warmth in the tent again. My sleeping bag is one of the best available, a Wood's Arctic bag, but I can't keep comfortably warm in it if the mercury in the thermometer dips too low.

In the morning, it is just a matter of reaching over to the stove from the security of the sleeping bag, throwing in a handful of the previously-prepared kindling, touching a match to it and adding a few sticks of heavier wood. Soon the stove sides are radiating with a bright cherry-red glow, signaling the beginning of another day on the trail. It also signals the start of one more of life's little annoyances. In cold weather, all the moisture given off by the body through respiration or transpiration condenses on the inside surfaces of the tent and freezes there as the air cools down. With the stove blazing away in the morning, the icy condensate returns once again to the liquid state, causing an indoor shower when the tent fabric is touched. It is possible to beat some of the ice off the tent before it melts, but it is nearly impossible to collect the chips and granules to dispose of them. Besides, it means getting out of the sack before the fire is roaring away, something which most people are loathe to do, and I am no exception.

After getting dressed and downing breakfast—more caribou meat and beans, together with some questionable toast made on top of the stove—the tent is taken down, the sled loaded, the dogs harnessed and away we all go for another delightful romp in the snow.

❖

In the springtime, traveling conditions change. Frigid temperatures are no longer a problem, but the warmer weather and the alternate periods of freezing at night and thawing during the day cause some difficulties. For one thing, the dogs, with their heavy winter fur, don't appreciate the (relative) heat wave and fatigue easily, so it may be preferable to travel mostly in the cool of the night and early morning. Also, the mushy melting snow squishes up between their toes and starts forming icy pebbles. At rest stops, the dogs can be observed licking their feet, trying to clear away these annoying accumulations that, if allowed to build up, could cause foot or leg injuries. In addition, the recurrent melting and refreezing cycles cause the snow to form into sharp needlelike crystals which lacerate the pads on the dogs' feet. The solution to the last two problems takes the form of little "booties" or dog moccasins, made of moosehide or canvas, which can be fastened onto the dogs' feet at the first sign of trouble.

Sometime in April, travel on the frozen surface of the lake becomes dangerous. The heat of the sun, and the meltwater runoff from tributary streams, weakens the near-shore ice. Time then to pack the toboggan and accessories away again and begin looking forward to a few months of traveling by water. On Great Slave Lake, spring winds break up the rotting ice cover into drifting pans of various sizes, allowing some water-borne traffic to resume by mid-May. However, the dock at Fort Resolution was usually not accessible until the first week in June, the ice in the bay being some of the last to disappear.

Rabies Epidemic

My first experience with the scourge of rabies was when the wolf charged me in Wood Buffalo National Park. It was a precursor of things to come, for it was followed in a few months' time by a major outbreak of rabies over much of the Northwest Territories and northern Alberta. During the ensuing winter, I encountered several additional instances of that dreaded pestilence.

Rabies has a long history, going back into unrecorded time in Europe. It is not certain how it arrived in the New World, but possibly it was brought in by the canine companions of the Spanish Conquistadores. Subsequently, the disease was transferred to wild populations from whence new epidemics still spring from time to time. In North America, the primary host animals are foxes, skunks, raccoons and bats. All warm-blooded animals are susceptible to rabies, including domestic livestock, humans and even birds.

Rabies is caused by a virus which attacks the central nervous system. The virus is carried in the saliva of infected animals and is usually passed on through a bite. However, even a drop of saliva falling on an open scratch in the skin is sufficient for transmission of the disease. The virus travels from the wound site up the nerve fibers to the brain. Once there, it causes encephalitis (inflammation of the brain), then it follows along the nerves to the salivary glands.

In animals, the incubation period for the disease—the time before external symptoms develop—is usually only a few days after exposure. It used to be thought that the same time frame applied to humans, but it is now known that this is not the case and that the incubation period can extend to at least a year. If exposed, and no medical treatment is obtained, a human has nearly a 50 percent chance of developing rabies. If exposed and suitably treated, the likelihood drops to less than 10 percent. Once the disease does develop, death is inevitable—instances of people surviving a full-fledged rabies attack are unknown.

For both animals and humans the symptoms are quite similar. In the early stage of rabies there is usually a loss of appetite and the onset of restlessness and irritability. Painful throat muscle spasms occur on attempting to swallow, leading to a rejection of liquids. Just the sight of water can bring on a spasm, hence the old name of hydrophobia for the disease. Saliva accumulates in and around the mouth, giving a foam-flecked "mad dog" appearance. Wild animals seem to lose all fear of humans and may wander into populated areas. In the next stage, the victim of the disease can become very aggressive and even vicious, attacking objects and other animals or people without provocation. Forcible restraint is necessary. Convulsions, paralysis and failing vision ensue. Finally, death arrives, usually within five days after the onset of the first symptoms. The whole process is unpleasant in the extreme and very traumatic, both for the victim and for the persons who care for the victim.

❖

The outbreak of rabies began in my district in 1952, after the first good fall of snow, when a resident of Fort Resolution stepped out beside his woodpile to relieve himself. A fox approached him, snapping its jaws together in a strange fashion. The man picked up an ax lying by the woodpile, despatched the fox with a blow to the head, and reported the incident to me. After letting the carcass freeze for easier removal of the head, I sent that appendage off for laboratory examination. The lab was apparently now geared up for rapid processing of such specimens, for it took only weeks, rather than months as for the wolf from Wood Buffalo National Park, before the results came back. The fox was rabid.

The next instance happened on my own doorstep. A fox came out of the bush into the schoolyard, wandered over to the adjacent warden station property and up on the back porch of the house, as evidenced by the tracks in the light snowfall which had occurred overnight. Then the fox staggered over to the nearby RCMP dog compound where it wandered within reach of one of the chained sled dogs. The dog killed the animal with a single bite to the neck. This fox was subsequently found to be rabid too. As nearly as could be determined from external examination, none of the dogs received any bites or scratches in this encounter. Fortunately, all of the RCMP dogs, as well as my own, had been previously vaccinated against rabies.

Most of the dogs belonging to the Natives of the country had not had rabies shots at this juncture and, since it now appeared that there was an epidemic building up in the wild animal population, the Mounties arranged for a supply of vaccine to be flown in. Together we organized clinics throughout the area to try to vaccinate every dog. In the village of Fort Resolution alone, there were more than 200 dogs, with perhaps as many more in outlying districts. Even as we were giving the shots to one group of dogs, a Native came up and reported that his lead sled dog, normally somewhat of a pet in its behavior toward him, kept trying to bite him. When I went to where the dog was chained, I found it exhibiting a constant chomping motion with its jaws so that it chewed—in a very mechanical way—on anything that got near its mouth. By the following day the dog had succumbed to the ravages of rabies.

More cases of rabid foxes showed up locally and some villagers were quite frightened, reporting shadows as animals on occasion. One person saw two foxes in the moonlight, chasing each other around in circles on the nearby lake ice. When Tom Auchterlonie and I went to investigate, the foxes turned out to be two tree stumps, immobile—frozen solidly into the ice. However, people were right to be wary. All over the North there were reports of rabid animals—foxes, wolves and dogs.

Headquarters in Ottawa sent periodic telegrams to all the wardens throughout the Northwest Territories, warning of the gravity of the situation. Initially, they advised that the incubation period of the rabies virus in humans was thought to be about one week to ten days. Then, a few weeks later, they wired to advise that the period could be as long as a month. In the following weeks, the figure kept being revised upwards, first to six months and then to one year. Finally, it was indicated to us that the course of the disease was very uncertain and that an indefinite incubation term should be assumed.

It was not only the canine populations that were being affected during the epidemic. One hundred miles southwest of our village, there were reports of crows attacking cows, and of cows dying of rabies. A little further south still, a truck driver on the winter road to Hay River was changing a flat tire when a rabbit charged him. The driver climbed into his cab and closed the door. The rabbit jumped up on the engine hood of the truck and tried kicking in the windshield with his feet. I'm not making this up, as a review of the Edmonton newspapers of the time will show. I'm certain that the truck driver wasn't making it up, either. He may have misinterpreted the behavior of the rabbit, but the actions are not inconsistent with the aggressive stage of rabies. Imagine, charging rabbits and divebombing crows!

The most horrendous case with which I was involved occurred the following summer. Jimmie Donovan—the old retired trapper from Rat River—had spent the day visiting friends at Rocher River. After the evening meal was finished, he climbed into his canoe, fired up the kicker, and made his way twenty miles back upriver to his cabin. It was late when he arrived home, but still light, and his dogs had to be fed. Jimmy got several fish from his cache and carried them over to where his animals were chained. Just as he began tossing the fish to the dogs, a wolf appeared out of the bush and made a frontal attack on him. Fortunately Jimmy was leaning slightly forward at the time, so he wasn't carried to the ground by the attack. Otherwise he might have been killed then and there. As it was, the wolf chewed on his arm and side for a while, inflicting some savage wounds. Then the beast turned away and disappeared into the bush. Jimmy dragged himself back to his cabin and passed out on his bunk.

He was discovered by some neighbors early the following day. Their dogs had also been attacked by the wolf. They transported Jimmy by canoe to Rocher River, where a larger vessel continued on with him to the mission hospital at Fort Resolution. The whole trip took a very long, grueling day. On arrival at the hospital, Jimmy's wounds were cleaned up and he was given penicillin injections to ward off septic infections. According to the information I was given, he received no specific antirabies treatment, possibly because there was none available at the hospital or perhaps because the medical officials there decided against it for reasons unknown to me.

Subsequent investigation revealed that the same wolf, on the same day, had attacked at least thirteen other dogs in the surrounding area, as well as a horse. All of those animals died of rabies within one week. The only signs of the attack exhibited by the horse were a few small scratches on its muzzle. I was very worried about Jimmy's condition, not only because he was a good friend but especially because I knew that he might still come down with rabies even long months after his wounds had healed. But he didn't, so he was one of the lucky ones.

A government mammalogist proposed that I should submit an article about the foregoing episode to a scientific journal as an authenticated wolf attack on a human. His supervisor vetoed the suggestion on the grounds that, lacking the carcass (which was never discovered), we couldn't prove that the culprit was actually a wolf and not just a large sled dog on the loose. However, if anyone could tell a dog from a wolf, it was old Jimmy—and he had a particularly good look at this one. Besides, no one ever reported a missing dog in the area. The same skeptical person thought that I was mistaken in believing that "my" wolf—back in Wood Buffalo National Park—was charging me with malicious intent, but he wasn't there facing it.

The rabies epidemic in the Northwest Territories gradually faded away, most likely due to host animals being largely killed off by the virus they had been harboring. It seems that, when animal populations are put into stressful circumstances—such as those that arise from overpopulation for example—they become more susceptible to organisms that had previously existed in their bodies without causing harm. There have been subsequent recurrences of rabies as the fox population rebuilt to large numbers again, but nothing quite as bad as the 1952–53 epidemic. This is probably due, in part, to an effective vaccination program for domestic animals. More outbreaks will undoubtedly occur in the future though so, until scientists find a way to rid the world forever of this terrible disease, it is prudent to be wary of strange behavior in animals.

Crash Landing

The RCMP officers in Fort Resolution were easy to get along with, especially when there was no pressing work in the offing. Corporal Tom and I began building model airplanes in our leisure time; not the expensive gas-engined radio-controlled models of today, but stick and tissue crates powered by strands of rubber. We used to take the models down to the airstrip to fly them, much to the amusement of some of the local Natives who thought that we were reverting back to our childhood days. If the truth be known, we had never completely grown up.

We also visited back and forth during office hours for the purpose of discussing local affairs and consuming large quantities of coffee. One day, in the single men's quarters of the RCMP establishment, Constable Don and I were sitting in the kitchen waiting for our morning coffee to brew. At one end of the kitchen there was a small holding cell for the incarceration of anyone who might be serving a few days in jail after conviction of some relatively minor offence. The prisoner shared the kitchen facilities with the constable.

Don went to the cupboard to get some cookies to serve with our coffee. He had to open a new box. "Son of a gun," he exclaimed as he picked the box up, "some mice have been into my food supply!" Sure enough, a hole had been gnawed through one corner of the box of cookies. Then Don picked up a box of dried apricots. "Jeez, they've been into the fruit too." There was another hole in the corner and some fruit was missing. The RCMP provided most of the food supplies for their men in the North, shipped in on an annual basis. Much of Don's fruit for months to come was stored in the cupboard, and almost every box had been nibbled at. "How could the mouse problem get out of hand so quickly?" Don wondered.

I got up from the table to have a look. "Don," I said, "these tooth marks don't look like they were made by mice. And besides that, how could mice chew away at a corner of each package and them stack them neatly back on the shelf, box against box? I believe you should check with the juvenile that you were holding in the cell a few days ago." Don must have just gotten up after a late night or he would have thought of that explanation himself.

"Son of a gun," he said again, "I believe you're right. I thought he was harmless so I let him have the run of the kitchen without keeping an eye on him." The young offender had carefully bitten away the bottom rear corners of the dried fruit boxes, about two dozen in all, and extracted a bit of fruit from each one. Then he had stacked the boxes back on the shelf, arrayed in the same fashion as before, so no holes were visible. Presumably, he thought that he would be long gone before the act was discovered. He might have gotten away with it too, if he had left the cookies alone. They were used on a daily basis, whereas the fruit was used only infrequently. Actually, he did get away with it. What else could Don reasonably do except consider that he had been the victim of a practical joke?

When it was the Mounties' turn to drink the game warden's coffee, Mary usually did the making and the serving of it. She also made delicious cakes and cookies to accompany it. This attraction made the Mounties very forgetful; they kept insisting that it was their turn to come to my house when they had just been there the day before. Sometimes Mary was away Outside for long periods, and the chore of brewing the coffee fell to my lot. I couldn't be bothered using the percolator—too much trouble. I used to throw some coffee in the pot, put it on the stove to come to a boil, and then move it off to the side of the hot spot where it could simmer and stay warm. If the level of liquid got low in the pot, I just added some more coffee and water. I have to admit that the coffee was pretty thick. When the coffee grounds filled about one-third of the pot, I dumped them out and started over again.

I didn't realize that Don had a problem with this kind of coffee, although I did notice that he didn't come over to the house nearly as often when Mary was away. I thought it was just the absence of homemade goodies. One day he phoned me up on the rudimentary party line system that served the village. "Bill," he said, "come on over; I've got something for you." As I entered the RCMP office, Don shoved a pot of coffee at me. "Here, drink this," he growled. "I've been boiling the stuff for three days so it should be just the way you like it." I got the hint, and incorporated some minor improvements into my coffee-making technique.

❖

A plumber, down from Edmonton to do some repair work on the RCMP plumbing system, joined us for coffee one day. The Mounties and I were trying to outdo each other in boasting about the intelligence and stamina of our dog teams. The plumber listened for a while, then announced that he, too, had a very smart dog. The animal was a large male German shepherd, a good pet and watchdog. Each morning as the plumber left for work in his panel truck, the dog would run exuberantly after him for several blocks. Then, tiring of the chase, the dog would turn around and walk back to the plumber's house to resume its guard duties there. The dog always stayed on the sidewalk, never running out on the road, certainly suggesting an intelligent animal.

One morning, as the German shepherd was making its usual run along the sidewalk in pursuit of its owner's vehicle, a yappy little lap dog came charging out of a driveway, barking furiously in high-pitched indignation at the intrusion on its territory. The big dog—moving along at great speed—turned its head to see what all the commotion was about. Its attention thus diverted from its forward path, the unfortunate animal ran headlong into a telephone pole and was knocked unconscious for a few moments. The plumber, observing the action in his rearview mirror, pulled over to render assistance. However, the dog had regained its feet and was quickly retreating toward home, "ki-yi-ing" as it went.

The plumber maintained that his dog was so smart that it had considered the available evidence, namely that the little dog had been charging at him just before the lights went out, and had come to the only reasonable conclusion. That pooch had clobbered him! The German shepherd, not wishing to be deprived of its morning fun, still ran along the sidewalk each day as his owner departed for work but, ever afterwards, crossed to the opposite side of the street before it reached the point at which the attack had occurred. Once safely clear of the danger zone, it crossed back again. The Mounties and I agreed with the plumber—that was one smart dog. But we knew in our hearts that it was not in the same league as our own team leaders.

❖

On one memorable occasion in the middle of winter, I was having coffee in Tom's office when a stranger walked in. He had a big cut on his forehead and appeared to be greatly fatigued. It soon developed that he was the pilot of a light aircraft which he had crashed late the previous day while flying in the midst of a blinding snowstorm. The crash site was several miles to the west of Fort Resolution, out on the lake ice. The night had been cold, more than thirty below zero. The pilot, shaken and cut but otherwise not badly injured, had initially occupied his time by walking back and forth near his downed craft in an attempt to keep warm. When the blizzard stopped just before daybreak, he saw some lights off to the east and started walking toward them. The lights were those on the antenna towers at the Signal Corps establishment. Soon dawn arrived and, with it, enough daylight to make out the village off in the distance, spurring his weary steps onward. When he finally arrived at the settlement, someone directed him to the RCMP office.

The pilot quickly related his story. He was employed in picking up boxes of fish from various fishing sites out on the ice of Great Slave Lake and then flying the load back to Hay River for processing. He had only just left Hay River at the commencement of another round trip when the blizzard swept in from the north. By the time the pilot decided that he should turn around and fly home, it was too late. He was already lost. He headed in what he assumed was the appropriate direction. He thought that the airplane was in level flight several hundred feet above the surface of the lake, and was totally surprised when it flew into the snow-covered ice. He could remember none of the events relating to the actual contact of his craft with the ground.

It was necessary for the RCMP officers to examine the crash scene preparatory to reporting on the incident. They hooked up their dog team and headed west. I was invited along, so I hooked up three of my dogs to my sled and threw a full sack of dog meal into the carryall for ballast. (It will be noted that I was taking an earlier lesson to heart.) The temperature had warmed up to only twenty-below, but a gusty north wind prevented the weather from being described as balmy. We followed the pilot's footsteps in reverse and, in about thirty minutes, arrived at the wreckage of the aircraft.

The plane was a small high-winged single-engined Cessna. It was lying on its back with its tail pointing to the sky. One of the two aluminum skis used for the main landing gear was torn away. The cabin roof was crushed in and the top of the pilot's seat was jammed up close against it. The compass needle was stuck on a heading which would have taken the aircraft far into unpopulated territory had it not crashed when it did. The pilot was very fortunate not to have been hauling a load of fish in the rear of the fuselage at the time of the crash. Fish were normally carried in wooden crates behind the seat. The momentum of a loaded crate would have carried it forward with great force, to crush the pilot against the back of the engine compartment.

Close by the Cessna, we noticed an extremely hard-packed track through the snow. It seemed as though the craft must have ploughed its way along there on its nose, compacting the snow beneath it. Further investigation, though, revealed that the track was actually the path traced out by the pilot as he walked back and forth many hundreds of times during the night, stamping his cold feet as he moved along! From the evidence of the other marks in the snow, it was obvious that the plane had flown into the ground at a fairly shallow angle, hitting just hard enough to break one ski away from the fuselage. Then it bounced back into the air, traveling about 300 feet further before coming down again. This time, because of the missing landing gear on one side, the engine and propeller hit the ice and the aircraft flipped over on its back as it came to an abrupt halt. At this point, the pilot had apparently collided with the instrument panel, causing his head injury and knocking him unconscious for a while.

We returned to the village to find the pilot was not much the worse for wear. His friends from Hay River drove over in a bombardier and hauled him away on the following day. Definitely, he was one very lucky fellow. A few minor differences in the circumstances surrounding the crash—a little steeper angle of descent, a few minutes longer in the air, a load of fish in the fuselage, an injury to his legs—any one of these might have put an end to his days on earth.

I recalled several other crashes where the pilots had not been so fortunate. They hadn't made me waver from my early desire to be an aviator but they had brought a realization of the dangers inherent in flying. One incident still vivid in my memory was of a small biplane which stalled and dived into the ground at the old Calgary airport as my classmates and I were exiting the adjacent school building for recess. The plane crashed just outside of the school grounds, bursting into flames on impact. We ran excitedly toward the scene, separated from it by a tall wire fence. The wreckage was quickly consumed by the fire and we were left gawking at a pile of smoldering rubble.

Some years later, while employed for the summer at Williams Brothers General Store (a large emporium near downtown Calgary which catered to farmers), I was sitting in the open door of a boxcar about to begin eating my lunch after unloading heavy sacks of cattle salt all morning. Suddenly there was a horrendous sound in the sky above. Looking up, I saw that two aircraft had just collided several hundred feet directly overhead. I could see pieces falling away from them. I watched as one airplane, a single-engined military trainer called a Harvard, peeled off in a fast glide toward the west. Later, I learned that it had crashed at an intersection in a residential neighborhood, killing a horse which was pulling a milk wagon, and setting a nearby house on fire. The second airplane was a twin-engined navigational trainer. It dived steeply away after the collision and appeared to crash only a few blocks from the store. I hurriedly finished my sandwiches and climbed on my bicycle. Pieces of painted fabric and splinters of wood were falling around me as I pulled away from the boxcar. They were parts of the two aircraft, having taken several minutes to tumble and twirl down to ground level.

I rode toward a plume of black smoke off in the distance and soon found myself within the Calgary fairgrounds. I climbed a telephone pole so that I could peer over the tall fence which surrounded the Stampede race track and infield, where rodeo events were held every year. The crash site was just inside the fence. There was only a smoking hole in the ground, with a few pieces of twisted metal lying around the edges. The occupants had been killed on impact. Would-be rescuers were just arriving on the scene. I was so intent on the tragic spectacle that I didn't observe a policeman approaching the telephone pole. In a gruff voice, he ordered me down from my perch immediately. I came down in a startled rush, ripping the seat out of my pants in the process, and returned to my duties at the box car.

In the final year of the war, shortly before Victory in Europe, an air force bomber was touring Canada as part of a war bond drive. It was a twin-engined de Havilland Mosquito nicknamed "F for Freddie." During its visit to Calgary, it demonstrated some spectacular flying maneuvers. One afternoon, as I was moving some soil around at Whitburn's Nursery, I heard the distinctive sound of Freddie's engines. I scanned the skies for a sight of the bomber, to no avail. As the intensity of the sound increased, I couldn't understand why I was unable to locate the aircraft. Then I happened to glance toward the nearby tree-lined Elbow River. A wing tip flashed by, a few feet of wing showing above the tops of the poplar trees. The daring pilot was flying his craft in a vertical bank down the narrow, winding river! What confidence he must have had in his machine and his own ability. A few days later, while taking off from the Calgary Municipal airport, he struck the control tower and crashed, killing himself and a crew member.

Aurora

Attendance at the local movie theater might be classified as a rather mundane event but it led, in one instance, to a stirring experience. The theater was actually the small gymnasium of the Fort Resolution day school, movies being screened there occasionally through the courtesy of the local community association which had feature films flown in from Edmonton from time to time. One summer night the film was *Destination Moon*, a realistic representation of a voyage to our great natural satellite, predicated on science rather than fiction. This was years before man's age-old dream of visiting the moon was finally fulfilled, and even before the advent of manmade earth satellites. I don't recall the cast of characters, but I do remember that the roles they played were not far-fetched ones—none of this Flash Gordon or Buck Rogers stuff.

After the entertainment ended, the audience drifted out of the school into the warm night air. The sky was free of clouds. Stars sparkled faintly above our heads, seemingly less radiant than usual, diminished by the dazzling light of the nearly-full moon. One could almost believe that a rocket ship really would travel there some day. But the moon was not casting its usual amber illumination on the earth, a pallid reflection of the sun's brilliant yellow fire. Instead, everything the moonlight fell on seemed to fluoresce faintly with a ghostly blue glow, like a very weak aura of Saint Elmo's fire.

What was happening here? Were we still under the influence of the filmed illusions? Apparently not; the spectators were all in agreement about the curiosity confronting us. We were actually viewing that legendary celestial vision—a blue moon. Its light truly was blue in color, tinting our surroundings a pale azure blue. What a marvelous coincidence to sit through a film predicting the possibility of man's close encounter with the moon and then to be subjected to the once-in-a-lifetime sight of a blue moon. It was a stimulating experience, tempered only slightly by speculation that the blue color was the result of the moonlight being scattered preferentially from the many small particles present in the atmosphere, combustion products from the numerous forest fires burning across the North that summer.

❖

A much more frequent phenomenon in the night sky at Fort Resolution was the wonderful spectacle of the Northern Lights— the aurora borealis. Auroral displays can be exciting and awe-inspiring. For observers in the right location at the right time, the English language has a bare sufficiency of superlatives with which to describe the sight. Robert Service offered his impression of the aurora in "The Ballad of the Northern Lights."

And the skies of night were alive with light, with a throbbing, thrilling flame;
Amber and rose and violet, opal and gold it came.
It swept the sky like a giant scythe, it quivered back to a wedge;
Argently bright, it cleft the night with a wavy golden edge.
Pennants of silver waved and streamed, lazy banners unfurled;
Sudden splendors of sabres gleamed, lightning javelins were hurled.
There in our awe we crouched and saw with our wild, uplift-ed eyes
Charge and retire the hosts of fire in the battlefield of the skies.

Very dramatic, and as true as any other description. No wonder the sight was looked upon with superstitious dread by primitive people. Some Indian tribes believed that the dancing lights were the spirits of departed braves.

The aurora has been the subject of civilized speculation for centuries, and the advent of sounding rockets and satellites has allowed scientists to confirm what was long suspected—it is intimately related to solar activity. The sun experiences energetic "magnetic storms" which send out streams of charged particles, mostly protons and electrons, in all directions. This plasma

211

reaches out for millions of miles into space, forming the "solar wind" which interacts with any magnetic fields encountered along the way. The speed of the particles is tremendous, any change in solar activity being propagated to the earth in two or three days. Recall that the sun is approximately 93 million miles from earth, so the particles are not coming at the lowly pace of a dog team on a winter trail; they are traveling a million miles per hour, more or less. That's really moving!

Our earth is surrounded by a magnetic field which is generated by the earth's molten core—exactly how is still unknown— and which extends into space for a thousand miles and more. When the protons and electrons from the sun encounter the earth's magnetic field lines, they are constrained to spiral down into the ionosphere where they undergo collisions with the constituents of the atmosphere, principally atomic or molecular oxygen and nitrogen. In the collisions, energy is transferred to the atoms or molecules and subsequently released by them in the form of light, the spectacular light of the aurora. The basic process is akin to that which takes place in a television picture tube or in a neon sign.

The particle collisions occur in an annular band circumscribing the earth—centered on the magnetic pole—so there is therefore a preferred region on the earth's surface from which to observe the aurora. Churchill, Manitoba, and Barrow, Alaska, are two places lying within this region. The area around Great Slave Lake is another. The locations of the magnetic poles, unlike the geographic poles, drift around on the earth's surface, gradually changing their positions with time, but it doesn't make much difference to auroral viewing. The North Magnetic Pole is generally to be found somewhere in the Canadian Arctic Archipelago. When the solar activity becomes especially violent, then the resulting auroral displays may be seen very far south, even to the lower boundary of the United States.

Most people have seen pictures of auroral phenomena, with their vivid colors and their multitude of shapes. Colors range through the spectrum from red to violet, some tints—like green— much more prevalent than others. The color of the auroral light depends on the composition of the atmosphere at the altitude of the collisions with the charged particles and on the energy of motion of those particles. The average height of an aurora is 70 miles or so, but they range from about 50 miles to 200 miles. Some Arctic explorers were (mistakenly) convinced that auroral displays extended to within a few hundred feet of the ground, so vivid did they appear to them. According to the experts, oxygen at high altitudes (above 150 miles) produces a deep red light and, at lower altitudes (60 to 150 miles), a green light. Below 60 miles, the emissions are from nitrogen, usually red in color, but sometimes blue or violet.

The shapes of the auroral displays are as varied as one could wish for: horizontal bands and sweeping curved arcs with many kinds of striations; constantly shifting vertical bands; curtainlike draperies, folding and unfolding across the sky; pulsating filaments and rays and patches; even just a uniform sheet of color reaching from the zenith to the horizon.

I once saw an aurora in Vancouver, in the winter of 1957, that completely filled the sky—from zenith to horizon—with a ruby red glow. According to the papers the next morning, this same aurora was seen as far south as San Francisco. Presumably it was the result of a strong solar wind colliding with oxygen molecules high in the ionosphere.

I could travel by dog team with only the auroral light for illumination, especially if the trail was on lake ice or over open countryside. Most frequently the light would be green, sometimes tinged with yellow and—rarely—with blue. Occasionally pinks and mauves and reds would appear. I exulted in the more spectacular displays. Bands and curtains would shimmer in the night sky, moving torpidly at first, then more swiftly, rising to a dramatic crescendo of motion, slashing their way across the heavens, only to slow down again and repeat the whole performance in a slightly different way. One early explorer stated that his dogs howled in fear at bright displays, but mine never paid any attention to them.

An interesting question remains—does an aurora make an audible sound? This subject has been debated for centuries and still does not have a definitive answer. There is no known physical mechanism for the production of sound from an aurora, with the possible exception of some form of induced electrical discharge. Attempts to record sounds have not been fruitful. The great height of an aurora, and the low atmospheric density at which it occurs, means that there can be no direct transmission of sound from the region.

George Back, a captain in the British navy who studied the aurora during two winters at Fort Resolution between 1833 and 1835, stated that sound was never heard to accompany the auroral motions. Samuel Hearne, an employee of the HBC fur trade in the eighteenth century, thought he heard auroras "rustling and crackling" as he traveled to the Coppermine River with a band of Indians. David Thompson explored parts of Western Canada, also in the eighteenth century. Some of his men insisted that they could hear auroral sounds, so he blindfolded them in an attempt to see if they would claim to hear noises in coincidence with auroral activity. Thompson concluded that the men did not actually hear anything but only thought they did. Numerous other travelers, trappers and traders in the Arctic regions have also believed they could hear noises emanating from auroras.

More recently, Andy Russell, rancher and author, stated in print that anyone who can't hear auroral sounds has had his hearing abused by all the racket of modern civilization. (He's got a point there!) But Hank Stuck, a wilderness traveler and author from an earlier era, was a nonbeliever in such sounds, never having heard any himself, although he was unwilling to call anyone a liar for claiming to hear them. He did encounter many strange noises in the bush which, he thought, some people might mistakenly attribute to an auroral display.

I saw an occasional aurora in my youth in Calgary but don't recall hearing any auroral sounds even when remote from urban noise. By far my best opportunity for the possible observation of such a phenomenon was during night travel with my dog team over the frozen surface of Great Slave Lake. Even then there were many small noises vying for contention, however quiet the night might seem at first. When underway, there was the swish of the toboggan across the snow, the noise of my moccasins against the yielding surface of the trail, the padding sound of the dogs' feet as they trotted along, the slight rattle of the leather harness, and the occasional distant booming sound from the lake ice as it expanded or contracted in response to changing temperatures.

If a halt was called for a rest, quiet would descend on the team, so quiet that I could sometimes hear my heart beating if I wasn't jumping around to keep warm. Then I too may have thought that I could hear swishing sounds as the auroral curtains danced across the sky. Now, I believe that the physics of the aurora suggests otherwise. Robert Service said that the Northern Lights "rolled around with a soundless sound." Perhaps there is a psychological effect stemming from the motion of the light streaming across the sky. The brain may think that if something is moving, then it should make a noise. But the brain is oft times fooled by past conditioning. Let us just conclude that the case for auroral sounds remains unproven, so those who are incurable romantics may feel free to believe in them if they so wish.

Crime and Caribou

The arrival of the weekly DC-3 aircraft at the landing strip in Fort Resolution, weather permitting, was a big event in the life of most residents, for it carried the mail. Each week contact with the Outside would be renewed—letters from friends and relatives, daily newspapers from Edmonton, parcels from mail-order catalogs.

Fred Camsell was the local postmaster. He was getting on in years and his eyesight wasn't as good as it used to be, so, when the weekly mail sacks arrived with many letters and parcels to be sorted, he welcomed the assistance of the army personnel, the RCMP or the game warden to help with the chore. We were all only too willing to pitch in. It meant getting our mail on the day of its arrival, rather than having to wait impatiently until the following day. As well, there was always the possibility of an unintentional slip-up on the part of the postmaster, age having dulled his powers of observation. One day when I arrived at the post office to offer my assistance, I found Fred searching for a registered letter which he had misplaced. I pulled his battered old desk away from the wall, thinking that the letter might have fallen behind it. Not only did I find the missing registered letter, but also a number of old undelivered letters, some bearing postmarks which were several years old.

The Camsell name was famous throughout the North. Fred was one of several sons and daughters born to an adventurous Englishman who, after military service in Canada in the middle of the nineteenth century, joined the Hudson's Bay Company to serve as post manager, first at Fort Liard and then at Fort Simpson. One of Fred's brothers, Charles, became famous as an explorer and geologist, then served for years as Canada's deputy minister of mines. With various governmental reorganizations, other responsibilities were added to Charles' portfolio, including Indian affairs. The Charles Camsell Indian Hospital in Edmonton was named after him.

During the Klondike gold rush of 1898, Charles and Fred joined an expedition which was attempting to get to the gold fields overland from the Liard River—through the back door, so to speak—rather than using the more common approach from the Pacific Coast. In the process, they nearly starved to death, and never did make their objective.

Fred Camsell was a man of the country and had been, by all accounts, a very proficient bush traveler as well as a good hunter and trapper. Like his father before him, Fred joined the HBC staff, eventually to serve as post manager at Fort Simpson during the 1920s and 1930s. He never sought fame and fortune outside of the Northwest Territories. Now, in his waning years, he lived with his wife in a small log cabin in Fort Resolution. He no longer had the stamina to wrest a living from the land, but he did have the good fortune (or the good connections) to obtain several government appointments. He held the positions of postmaster and justice of the peace, and was also in charge of the government wharf. With so many irons in the fire, Fred overlooked paying taxes on some of his income. When the revenue department caught up to him, they threatened to garnishee his wages until the tax bill was paid. According to Fred, a note to brother Charles—who was then still serving in the government in Ottawa—resulted in an arrangement whereby he was able to pay off his debt at the rate of five dollars per month.

Since Fred was the justice of the peace, he sat in judgment on various minor infractions of the law which occurred locally. The post office building served as courthouse during trials. It was quite crowded when the justice of the peace, the prosecuting law officer, the defendant and, perhaps, a witness or two took their places. There was no room for spectators.

The first case that I presented before Fred was one Bill Day had investigated initially, but I had to tie up the loose ends after his departure to a new posting. Someone had left a campfire smoldering at a spot along the Slave River, resulting in a fire which burned over a small area of timber. That same someone had also left behind a piece of cutlery, a war surplus item bearing a distinctive design. Bill knew that only one person for many miles around possessed such an article, a logger from the Hay River area. On the man's next visit to Fort Resolution, I laid a charge of negligence against him, to which he pled guilty and was fined the sum of eight dollars.

One day I was hiking through the bush on a trail which ran close to the air strip and parallel to it. When a cross-trail appeared I followed it to the air strip and stepped out in the open. I looked around and, about a quarter of a mile away, I saw a Native carrying a gun. When he spotted me, he ran into the shelter of the bush. Suspecting some skulduggery I hurried toward the location and apprehended the man. At my request, he dumped out on the ground the contents of the pack on his back. There lay a dead mother duck and nine or ten recently-hatched little ducklings. All of them taken together wouldn't have made a meal. I charged the culprit with hunting out of season, contrary to the provisions of the Act for the Protection of Migratory Birds. At his court appearance the following afternoon, Fred levied a fine of five dollars against the man. On leaving the courthouse I met the local HBC manager, Herb Figgures, who asked me about the outcome of the trial. When I told him, he mused that the result showed a remarkable coincidence; just that morning the defendant had borrowed five dollars, to be charged to his account at the HBC store.

My biggest "bust" came as a result of a trip to the Consolidated Mining and Smelting Company camp, which was being established at Pine Point. My inquiries there seemed to confirm that the personnel were abiding by the game and timber regulations. I was invited to stay overnight at the camp and, in the evening, one of the engineers asked me if I would like to view some of the photographic slides he had taken to document the progress of construction. I was willing, so the projector and screen were set up and the room lights dimmed.

After a few scenes depicting the original primeval wilderness at the camp site, an image appeared on the screen showing a Native of Fort Resolution holding a rifle in his hands and standing beside the carcasses of a cow moose and its calf. At the time of the picture the moose season was closed. In addition, even when the season was open, the shooting of cows and calves was expressly prohibited. That was the end of the slide show! At my exclamation of surprise the engineer realized that he probably should have suppressed that particular picture. He was not sufficiently conversant with the game regulations to know that an infraction had occurred when the moose were shot. At least that was his claim, obviously supported by his naivety in showing the picture to the game warden.

My investigation into the affair resulted in the hunter admitting his guilt. What else could he do in view of the photographic evidence! I wanted to confiscate the meat and hides, but the meat was gone; that which his own family hadn't already consumed had been distributed among a multitude of relatives and friends. He had disposed of the hides in the lake, bundling them together with a big rock so that they would sink to the bottom. This action proved that the hunter knew he was in violation of the law. The killing had been done with a .22-caliber rifle. The game regulations banned the use of such a small-caliber weapon for hunting game animals. Generally speaking, it was completely inadequate for hunting anything bigger than a coyote, although a competent hunter—with luck—might down a large game animal. In this particular case, according to the engineer, the cow moose had required seventeen shots to kill it; the calf had only taken twelve!

I hauled the offender into court and presented my case to Justice of the Peace Camsell. There were three charges: illegally killing a cow moose, illegally killing a calf moose and using a prohibited weapon for hunting big game. In reverse order, Fred said that the last charge was not a serious one. A fine of five dollars was levied. For killing the calf, the fine was ten dollars. The slaughter of the cow was a little more important—it cost the culprit fifteen dollars.

I was prepared for the inadequate punishment levied by the court. The fines in total didn't begin to match the value of the meat obtained from the animals. However, the rifle used for the offenses was a Mossberg semi-match rifle with a telescopic sight, a relatively expensive gun in those days. So, before Fred could declare the case closed, I exercised my prerogative to register a complaint about the penalties assessed and recommended that the rifle be confiscated to the Crown. This suggestion was turned down with the comment that there was no valid reason for confiscation.

Two weeks later, as I was helping to sort the mail, I saw the rifle standing in a corner of the post office building, partly obscured by other items. I picked it up and examined it closely, confirming that it was the same rifle that had been used to kill the moose cow and calf. Then I asked Fred what it was doing in his possession. Fred's response was that it wasn't in his possession; the owner had just left it there for a while. I made some discreet inquiries around the village and an informant told me that the slayer of the moose had actually borrowed some money from Fred with which to pay his fines. Talk about conflict of interest! Was Fred holding the rifle as security for the loan? Did this influence his decision against confiscation? The informant was unwilling to appear in court and I was unable to obtain any other evidence. In the absence of sworn testimony, the chief warden told me to forget about proceeding further with the case.

To be fair to Fred, I have to admit that his outlook was the product of a lifetime spent in the North and his actions were no doubt based on his ideas of practicality, whereas I, an outsider and somewhat of an idealist, had a different view of things. Regardless of our confrontations on the legal front, Fred was friendly and we got along well on a personal level.

Occasionally, in my impatience with his often sluggardly ways, I relegated Fred to the status of "old fogey." At the time, I wasn't aware of many of his early experiences and didn't make any effort to inquire into his past, to my subsequent regret. Now, I realize what a wealth of historically interesting information he possessed, a loss to Canada from not having been properly recorded for posterity. But it is often the case that young men are mostly concerned with the present and not with the past, and I was no exception to the rule.

❖

Among the illegal acts which brought themselves to my attention, none were related to caribou. Probably this was due partly to the fact that the caribou herds were usually far from the settlements and partly because I couldn't be everywhere at once. In winter, scattered groups of caribou sometimes appeared just east of the Slave River, the numbers increasing as one traveled even further eastward. When caribou were reported within a distance from Fort Resolution of a few days' travel by dog sled, some ambitious local people would hitch up their teams and go on a legal hunting trip for the purpose of stocking their larders with wild meat.

Natives could shoot as many caribou as they desired during the open season, but other residents had to be satisfied with a permit allowing them to take just five of these animals a year. This might sound like a lot, but caribou are relatively small animals, generally weighing 150 to 200 pounds on the hoof and far less when dressed out; and northerners are big meat eaters. Any person who hadn't lived in the N.W.T. for at least two years was out of luck with regard to hunting caribou—he was not considered a resident under the game laws.

It was against the law to feed caribou meat to dogs, but I'm certain that it happened on occasion. For one thing, it had been legal in times past and some folks were reluctant to change their ways. For another, when trapping back of beyond, it was not always easy to keep up a supply of fish for dog food. And, as always, the game warden had to catch them at it, a difficult thing to do. It was also illegal to chase down caribou with vehicles such as bombardiers, but who would know. Certainly not the game warden, traveling slowly by dog team, unless he just happened to be in the right spot at the right time. But anyone likely to engage in such tactics would check on the warden's whereabouts before leaving the village. I, and other wardens, used to petition the powers-that-be in Ottawa to provide us with bombardiers, so we could make quick trips and appear unexpectedly in various parts of our districts, but it never happened while I was in the warden service.

❖

Once, while checking fur returns, George Pinsky showed me some caribou hides that he had obtained from Natives living at

Snowdrift, a small community far to the east of us on the south shore of Great Slave Lake. The hides, when tanned, were used to make items of clothing. Since caribou never arrived in the vicinity of Fort Resolution in large numbers even in the winter when they were trekking southwards, and since they were in the remote Barren Grounds in the late summer when their skins were at their best for clothing, the local Natives seldom got a chance to hunt for themselves without traveling far from home. Thus, George would buy excess hides from the Snowdrift Indians and resell them locally.

Caribou, like humans, are greatly annoyed by a variety of insects in the spring and summer months, including mosquitoes, black flies and bulldogs. They can sometimes be observed shaking, shivering, pawing at their muzzles, and just generally jumping around, all in an attempt to relieve themselves of their insect tormenters.

Caribou also endure attacks by some insects that don't trouble man in the same way. For example, the nostril fly lays its eggs inside the nose of a caribou. The eggs hatch into larvae which move into the inner passages of the nostrils, fasten themselves on, and feed on mucous. Perhaps a hundred of these predators will share a single host, irritating the nasal passages and making breathing both difficult and painful. After a month or so, they are ready for the next stage of their life cycle. For this, they move out of the nostrils and drop onto the ground, where they pupate. The following summer the pupae hatch into flies and they start the whole dastardly business over again.

Caribou face another insect foe, one which may cause even more torment than the nostril fly. This is the warble fly, sometimes known as the deer fly. (Caribou are often just called deer in the North.) The flies look a bit like a pale version of a bee. Around August, this pest lays its eggs in various locations on the exterior surfaces of the caribou—in the hair of the back, belly or upper legs. The eggs hatch into larvae which burrow beneath the skin of the animal, leaving a hole in the hide. During autumn, the larvae migrate through the body of the caribou to a location alongside the backbone. Here they chomp another aperture through the hide of the long-suffering animal, allowing themselves to breathe through the winter months while they are feeding off their host. When the weather warms up, they use this same opening as an exit from whence they leave the caribou and drop to the ground. Then they pupate, soon to emerge as another generation of misery-causing creatures.

The warble fly problem results in poor hide quality during the meat hunting season; therefore, the government had decreed a special season on caribou during the month of August. This was open only to Natives to allow them to hunt at a time when the caribou hides were at their best for making clothing. The hides had the fewest perforations then, new larvae holes not yet being made in large numbers and old punctures having had some opportunity to heal over. Of course, the Natives weren't supposed to sell the hides taken in August, but it was perfectly all right to traffic in those taken at other times of the year.

The tanned hides which George now showed me had holes aplenty, suggesting that they were a byproduct of the winter food hunt, but most could still be utilized for the manufacture of clothing. A few of them were completely worthless, bearing so many perforations that I couldn't put my hand anywhere on them without covering up one or more larvae-produced holes. On one very small hide, no puncture was farther away from any other than about three inches. Some were much closer. The holes themselves varied from an eighth to a quarter of an inch in diameter. Imagine the anguish of the animal that wore that skin. Why anyone would expend the energy to tan such poor-quality hides was a mystery to both George and myself.

On dog-team trips to Rocher River, I often saw caribou tracks and sometimes encountered four or five animals traveling together. If Harry was with me, he usually managed to get some meat for his family larder. While I didn't hunt myself, I liked to come across a few animals now and then to reinforce my team's Pavlovian speed-up response to the snick of a closing rifle bolt.

Caribou were usually plentiful near Snowdrift and at Fort Reliance at the eastern extremity of Great Slave Lake. The small

RCMP detachment at this latter location used to send me an occasional wireless message complaining about the great numbers of wolves harassing the caribou herds in their vicinity and suggesting that poison should be used to get rid of them. They were apparently unaware that poisoned baits had been tried for wolf population control in the N.W.T. in the previous two or three years, without much success; and in addition to wolves, the poison claimed many more victims—foxes, weasels, ravens and other scavengers—so the use of such baits was abandoned. From then on, it was a case of letting nature take its course.

Farewell N.W.T.

Spring breakup was always eagerly anticipated by the village inhabitants. The event was signaled by the arrival of more temperate weather, with the sun rising up higher in the sky, providing welcome relief from the dark dreary days of the long winter months and reducing the feelings of isolation and anxiety—cabin fever—from which some people suffered.

The dogs, too, seemed grateful for breakup; it gave them a rest from travel, their winter enthusiasm having worn a bit thin with the advent of higher temperatures. Their frozen fish were thawing under the warming sun, getting ripe around the edges, and the supply was almost depleted. A spawning run of jackfish, when the ice was breaking out of one of the nearby channels in the Slave River delta, provided an opportunity to obtain enough fresh fish to tide the dogs over until the bay was also free of ice. Then our nets could be set again in the normal way for summer fishing.

The jackfish channel was so narrow that a person with a fishing rod could cast his line completely across it. I just used some old cord wound up on a tin can. At the end of the cord was a lead weight which I could heave out for some distance into the channel, with the line unspooling automatically from the can. A fishhook was attached a few feet above the weight. This was as productive as a proper fishing rig. No bait was required—the jackfish grabbed for the bare hook as it went whizzing by them. In fact, these voracious creatures grabbed at anything that went by them, including the line weight. Every cast returned a hooked fish, usually between one and two feet in length. Within the space of an hour a persistent angler could easily fill several water buckets with fresh fish. This state of plenty continued only for a few days, but it was fun while it lasted.

❖

One day in 1953, after the ice had cleared out of the lake, Max Ward (of subsequent Wardair fame) flew in to Fort Resolution with a beautiful new single-engined aircraft on floats. It was a de Havilland Otter—the latest development in bush planes, its design based on lessons learned from past experience and with an eye to the future.

Originally, Max had toured the northern skies with an old Fox Moth biplane. That crate was an aircraft capable of containing two or three passengers in an enclosed cabin between the wings, the pilot carrying out his flying duties from a cockpit on top of the fuselage. There was a little glass window in the pilot's instrument panel through which he could keep an eye on the welfare of the people in the cabin. In the first model of the Fox Moth, the cockpit was wide open to the weather, exposing the pilot to the wind and the cold, with the concomitant threat of freezing to death. Max's Fox Moth was a little different. It had a plastic canopy covering the cockpit to help keep him warm. The trouble was that the canopy frosted up in cold weather, so he had to keep it open in order to see where he was going. Max had dreamed of better days ahead.

Now, with the magnificent Otter, those days were coming. To begin with, the pilot's seat was inside with the passengers, out of the weather. Also, the plane could carry a much greater load than the old Fox Moth—fourteen people or a ton of freight. These were the official manufacturer's ratings; all such numbers were usually considered by bush pilots to be minimums, and they sometimes exceeded them in the name of expediency. Even the pilots of the RCMP air division turned a blind eye to overloads on their own aircraft. I have seen their Noorduyn Norseman aircraft piled to the cabin roof with freight, almost certainly over the legal weight limit, but necessarily so to avoid an extra flight of many hours duration. Their long takeoff run was confirmation of the overloaded condition. But the Norseman, a legendary aircraft, was conservatively rated with regard to its capacity, so it's unlikely that the pilot had any qualms about carrying the extra weight. Proper load distribution was more important than weight alone, and good judgement was the key to safe operations.

The Otter was in a different category from the Norseman, their respective conceptions being separated by a period of about two decades—a lifetime in aviation. Both were leaders in their own generations. The Otter's performance was spectacular, even when fully loaded, with a long range, commendable cruise speed and rate of climb, and a low landing speed. I was greatly impressed as Max Ward rattled off the numbers while he showed me over his new pride and joy.

I thought he might be exaggerating slightly when he described how quickly the aircraft could get off the water in its present empty state. I soon changed my mind, though. As Max left to continue on to Yellowknife, he taxied a few hundred feet out from the wharf where I was standing. Then he pointed the nose of his shiny blue and red aircraft toward me and opened the throttle. I was certain that he was just having a little fun with me, but no...he was off the water almost immediately and passed well above my head, the geared-down propeller barely ticking over—an impressive demonstration.

Max Ward went on from there to acquire an assortment of larger airplanes, flying on routes around the world, but I doubt that he was any more thrilled with them than he was with his first de Havilland Otter.

Another visitor to Fort Resolution at this time was a man who had been tracking down lost treasures. Not the legendary kind like the glittering nuggets of the Lost Dutchman Mine or Blackbeard's trove of doubloons, but well-documented valuables which he stood a good chance of finding and recovering at a profit. His loot had included such things as wartime heavy equipment—bulldozers and big trucks—left in the bush at war's end when work came to a halt on the Canol Pipeline which ran from Norman Wells on the Mackenzie River to Alaska. Once, he had recovered cases of expensive whiskey from a sunken ship. In the present instance, he knew that a bargeload of valuable drill pipe had been lost during a violent storm in the bay at Fort Resolution. He brought in a team of divers who found the pipe after a few days of searching. Then it was a relatively simple operation to anchor a barge at the site, set up some hoisting tackle, and salvage the pipe. Two weeks later, he was gone—off to search for some more modern-day treasures.

As the forestry officer for the district, everyone expected me to assume the mantle of village fire chief, there apparently being a link in the minds of some people between forest fires and house fires. In this capacity, my main responsibility seemed to be to maintain several small foam fire extinguishers. In the event of a house fire, George Pinsky drove his truck over to my warehouse and picked up the extinguishers. Most fires resulted from the ignition of creosote residues in chimneys, people being neglectful about cleaning them frequently. When a chimney caught fire and overheated, part of the adjacent wooden structure would often start burning, threatening to destroy the whole building. So another of my duties as fire chief was that of lecturer, trying to make people more aware of fire hazards and fire prevention methods.

When a fire did start, prompt action was necessary to suppress it. At such times it seemed to me that everyone in the immediate vicinity suddenly became a fire chief, each shouting out what they thought should be done, sometimes acting at cross-purposes. One time a building on the mission property caught fire from an overheated chimney. George and I arrived with the fire extinguishers to find that a hole had been burnt through the roof, destroying a small portion of it. Several men had already assembled at the scene and had successfully used buckets of water to stop the spread of the fire. The roof materials were still smoldering, so I passed out our foam extinguishers to the men for the *coup de grâce*.

In the meantime, Dr. Lyshak—the local physician—arrived with a small Pyrene extinguisher. From a perch on a ladder overlooking the hole in the roof, he carelessly sprayed the extinguisher fluid in the direction of the chimney, most of it falling on the men below. Apparently his training had not extended to a study of hazardous chemicals. The Pyrene liquid was primarily carbon tetrachloride, a noxious substance now banned, but even then known for its deleterious effects on some of the body's internal organs if the fumes were inhaled. I had to shout at him several times before convincing him to discontinue the harmful spray.

❖

It was probably unfair to expect the doctor to have much knowledge of the harmful chemicals in common use in North America. He was a recent refugee from Hungary, and was sent to the North by the federal government to gain experience in Canadian medical procedures before being licensed to practice in more lucrative areas Outside.

Our first contact with Dr. Lyshak had come when our son Billy was suffering from inflamed tonsils, a condition which eventually required their removal. The doctor performed the surgery at the mission hospital and all went well. So well that, bright and early the following morning, Billy—not quite four years old and anxious to get back home—found his clothes in a closet in his hospital room, dressed himself, and walked out into the minus twenty-degree weather. Fortunately, his absence was noticed almost immediately by a nurse. He was soon recaptured and returned to the hospital, much to his disgust.

The next experience with the doctor came a short time later, in the middle of a brutally cold winter night. We were awakened by Dick—then about six months old—struggling for breath in his crib. He was also running a very high fever. We sponged him down and took him into our bed in order to more closely monitor his progress, but his body was so inflamed that we couldn't stand the heat. We contacted Dr. Lyshak and the army signals establishment, where someone was on duty around the clock. One of the army men managed to start their truck—a difficult task in the extreme cold—and drove Mary and Dick to the mission hospital. I stayed home to watch over the other two children. The doctor spent the remainder of the night doing whatever he could to reduce the fever. The nurses claimed later that Dick's temperature had reached an unbelievable one hundred and eight degrees, and they had not expected him to live. However, survive he did, thanks to the doctor's ministrations.

Sometime after this event, when Mary was suddenly stricken with appendicitis, we had no qualms about allowing Dr. Lyshak to perform an appendectomy using the facilities of the mission hospital. The operation took place one afternoon. In the evening I went to the hospital to see how Mary was feeling but she still hadn't recovered from the anaesthetic. This didn't seem too unreasonable considering the relatively primitive anaesthetics in use at the time. However, when I returned the following morning, I was met in the hospital corridor by the doctor. He rushed up to me, waving his arms excitedly and rolling his eyes. "Mr. Bell," he said, "I didn't know that your wife neither smoked nor drank, so I gave her too much anaesthetic." He had mistakenly assumed that everyone in the Northwest Territories used tobacco and alcohol and were thereby made less sensitive to other drugs. After we both calmed down, the doctor assured me that no harm had resulted from the overdose, although Mary was still groggy. Even so, we were grateful for the doctor's treatment—the alternative might have been a ruptured appendix while awaiting the weekly airline flight out to Edmonton.

Once, when entering the hospital to visit Mary, I observed the Catholic priest engaging in a strenuous argument with Howard Peever, the Pentecostal preacher, about religious dogma. The priest kept shouting that his religion was the only true religion and Peever was going to end up in Hell, and the preacher was shouting back in a similar vein. At one point I thought they would come to blows. Fortunately it just ended in a final exchange of sarcastic comments. I was reminded of a more peaceful clash between religious beliefs when my father and I were busy replacing a derelict fence in the backyard of one of the several homes in which we lived when I was a youth. I was digging post holes and Dad was engaged in the disagreeable job of creosoting the wooden posts. Creosote is a preservative used to inhibit rot in the portion of the post in contact with the soil. It works well, but is messy and has a strong odor. He was at a point where his hands were covered with the stuff when a local preacher walked into the backyard. He went up to Dad and extended his hand for a handshake, saying, "I don't believe I've seen you in church." Dad thought about it for a fraction of a second, took the proffered hand in his and replied, somewhat caustically, "No, and I don't believe you will, either." The flustered preacher detached his hand from my father's sticky grip and hurriedly excused himself from our presence.

❖

We were again thankful for Dr. Lyshak's presence in Fort Resolution when our middle son, Ron, developed a lump on his forehead. The diagnosis suggested one of two possibilities, the first a malignant cancer and the second a more benign form of tumor. The doctor said the latter was the more likely of the two, but he prepared us for the worst case. Mary and Ron flew out to the University of Alberta Hospital at Edmonton, where tests showed that Ron had a granuloma, a nonmalignant growth resulting from the breakdown of adjacent bone due to some rare disease whose cause, and cure, were unknown. It was known that the disintegration could be stopped with radiation although, at the time, there was little information available concerning the dosages required.

The prognosis was encouraging following the treatment, and Mary and Ron returned home. Unfortunately, other lumps continued to show up in different locations on Ron's body, necessitating more trips to Edmonton for further radiation. One of these trips, when Mary took all the children with her, occurred as the Christmas season approached. Feeling very lonely, I obtained a Christmas tree from among some nearby conifers and decorated it by myself. I mounted the tree in a bucket of water, trying to keep it green for some delayed Christmas festivities on the return of my family at some indefinite time in the future. After a month the needles suddenly dried up and fell off.

I typed some tender notes to Mary, including quotes from lovelorn poets, and hid them around the kitchen where she would find them from time to time on her return. Some went in the back of utensil drawers, some in the flour bin, some in the tea and coffee canisters, some in with the tea towels, some wherever I thought they would eventually come to light after Mary's return and give a lift to her spirits. They worked too, turning up at unex-

231

pected moments. A few even delighted Mary's friends who, having come over for a cup of tea and some chatter, found the notes while they were helping out in the kitchen.

Two long months passed before my family was together again in Fort Resolution. At first Ron couldn't remember me and shoved me away. I think he mistook me for just another doctor, and his reaction made me wonder what kind of unavoidable pain he had been subjected to in the hospital. We had our Christmas celebration in February and hoped that no more trips Outside would be required for at least a little while.

The cost of the flights to Edmonton was being born by the federal government under regulations concerning medical care for employees in the North. The regulations stated that, if a medical examination showed the employee to be in good health at the time he was hired, the government would assume the costs of transporting the employee or his family to the closest suitable place for any subsequent medical treatment. No mention was made of a prior medical exam for anyone but the employee. After three flights by Mary and Ron some bureaucrats in Ottawa discovered this little oversight and had the regulations changed to require medical examinations for the whole family. That seemed reasonable—for future employees. However, the new legislation was declared to be effective retroactively so, not only did the government refuse to pay for any future flights, but they also demanded repayment for the cost of past flights.

Ron's doctors in Edmonton were of the opinion that a medical examination, probably even at the time of his arrival in the Northwest Territories and certainly at the time I was hired on, would have given him a clean bill of health. Thus it was our misfortune that the regulations had originally ignored family medical examinations. Now, the doctors' opinions made no difference to the bureaucracy. My supervisors in Fort Smith petitioned the powers-that-be in Ottawa to make an exemption to the retroactivity clause for my case. They wrote glowing letters about my performance in the job and the need to retain my services as a warden in the Northwest Territories. But the Ottawa mandarins wouldn't relent. We had to pay up. The cost of each return trip exceeded my monthly salary so it took some time to settle the account.

My first reaction to this new situation is best left unstated in a tome meant for family consumption. It was followed by an application for transfer to a national park on the Outside, where transportation costs to Edmonton would be less expensive than they were from Fort Resolution. Then we settled down to await results.

❖

The government, acting more quickly than usual, soon arranged the transfer. A telegram from Ottawa advised us to pack up immediately in order to get our household effects out on the first riverboat of the season. Our new location would be in Waterton Lakes National Park. This was welcome news, Waterton being at the top of our list of preferences.

I made some wooden crates out of old lumber which was lying around the warehouse, packed our belongings in them, nailed down the lids, and painted our new address on the outside. In a few more days, the sturdy crates would be loaded on a barge for shipment upriver, and my family and I would be winging our way out to Edmonton and points south.

Then came another message. "Hold everything," it said. Someone had just stumbled onto the fact that I was a married man with a family. The position in Waterton Park was for a single man. The accommodation was a small one-roomed cabin out in the hinterlands, miles from nowhere. What a lack of communication in the bureaucracy! Hadn't they read the stated reason for the transfer requirement? I grudgingly unpacked our gear.

Ten days later, yet another telegram: "Pack up immediately." Now a spot had been found for us in Prince Albert National Park in Saskatchewan, and we had to get there before the fire season started in about three weeks. More frantic packing and more painting of addresses on crates, and then we were all set. The community association held a farewell party for us, complete with embarrassing speeches concerning our contributions to village life. Some friends gave us a more informal leave-taking, including the presentation to me of a cowboy hat because they had heard that I would henceforth be dealing with horses for transportation instead of dogs.

The hearsay was true to some degree. Dogs weren't used for patrolling in the more southerly national parks. I would no longer need my hard-won knowledge concerning the care and handling of a sled dog team. There would be no more canine companionship out on the solitude of the winter trail, miles from another human being; no more breakneck dashes with the dogs in the chill air of early dawn, wondering if this was the day when I might have the front torn out of my parka again. I would miss my team more than they could ever know. However, we did take a link to the past with us when we left Fort Resolution. Billy's bitch had recently presented us with a pack of future sled dogs. We picked the best pup from the litter, crated it up, and shipped it out with our hand luggage aboard the aircraft which took us away on the first stage of the journey to our new home.

Boundary Cabin

The southern entrance to Prince Albert National Park is about thirty miles north of the town of Prince Albert, the gateway city for much of northern Saskatchewan. The park comprises approximately 1,500 square miles, mostly cloaked in typical boreal forest—mixed spruce, birch, aspen, jack pine and tamarack—and watered by several large lakes, in particular, Kingsmere, Crean and Waskesiu Lakes. Many species of mammals and birds can be found there to entertain the observant visitor.

One of the park's claims to fame is that it once sheltered the naturalist, Grey Owl, and his beaver companions. Grey Owl, supposedly an Indian, was actually an Englishman named Archie Belaney. The exposure, after his death in 1938, of this relatively innocuous deception did not detract from the good work which he had accomplished.

The main tourist center is the town of Waskesiu, located on Waskesiu Lake near the eastern boundary of the park. I was thankful that we were headed for the much more isolated western boundary.

We arrived at the town of Prince Albert by train to find a park employee waiting at the railway station to present us with a vehicle and some sparse directions about the route to be followed to our new home. The vehicle was an old Fargo pickup truck of three-quarter ton capacity. It was to be our main mode of transportation so long as the roads were in passable condition. We headed north on a paved highway leading to Gatehouse Cabin on the southern boundary of the park. From there we turned onto a gravel road which, except for slight deviations due to the vagaries of the topography, was directed more or less up the western boundary of the park. Along this route, at intervals of fifteen to twenty miles, we encountered three other warden stations before arriving at our destination. We disembarked at each of these

235

establishments to introduce ourselves and confirm that we were still heading in the right direction.

Warden Ed Sipes was in charge of the first station. Although surrounded by large aspen trees, it was perversely called Spruce Grove Cabin. At this point the gravel road was replaced by a dirt trail. The second station was designated Rabbit Cabin, for reasons unknown to me. Here we met Warden Emmett Millard and his wife Signe, a very friendly and accommodating couple, long-time residents in the park. The last of the three stations went by the name of Sturgeon Crossing because there was a wooden bridge nearby which spanned the diminutive Sturgeon River. This bridge gave access to a trail leading westward to the settlement of Park Valley.

The warden at Sturgeon Crossing was Cliff Millard, a nephew of Emmett Millard. Cliff, his wife Ethel, and their two young daughters were our next-door neighbors within the park boundaries—if a separation of sixteen miles can be considered as next door. Cliff advised us that we couldn't get lost from there on—the road only went to Boundary Cabin, our new home. We also learned that Park Valley, our nearest post office, consisted primarily of a general store which served a community of small farms carved out of the surrounding bush.

Proceeding onward, we passed through several miles of prairie meadowland, much like my old stomping grounds around Calgary. Then we came to a small region once heavily forested with green timber but now left only with blackened tree trunks, the result of some long-ago fire. Many dead trunks pointed starkly to the sky, their roots not yet rotted sufficiently for the wind to blow them down. Shortly thereafter the trail turned down a hill, to a wooden bridge crossing the Sturgeon River. This stream drains the swamps and muskegs of the dank interior recesses of the park, heading first west and then south, eventually to join the North Saskatchewan River whose great discharge mingles, in the end, with the waters of Hudson's Bay. Just here, at the bridge, the Sturgeon River turned southward, meandering along to form about twenty miles of the western boundary of the park. We

236

drove across the bridge and were now in the district for which I was to be responsible. Only eight more miles to Boundary Cabin.

❖

Finally we were there. A lovelier setting could not be found within the northern forest than the one that presented itself to our view. The house sat on a bit of a hill looking out to the west over a small lake of dark water created by a beaver-dammed creek. To the south were groves of sparsely spaced poplars, with a host of wood lilies growing among them, displaying their beautiful bell-shaped orange flowers in a dappled mixture of sunshine and shadow. The siding on the house, stained golden brown with linseed oil, was milled to look like real logs. Some outbuildings stood in a clearing to the north of the house—a stable, a storage shed and a log garage. The latter had once been the first warden cabin on the site.

Beyond the outbuildings the creek materialized briefly in its original form. It was narrow enough to be bridged by a few planks, giving access to a trail leading off eastwards into the woods. This was the so-called 57 Trail, sometimes passable to vehicles, and sometimes not. A little distance to the rear of the cabin was that essential structure, the outhouse. Close behind it was another lake, this one of substantial size, with a large beaver lodge protruding above the surface of the water.

As we climbed down from the truck and stretched our legs, a loon yodeled from the lake in front of the cabin. Several cheeky Canada jays, better known as whiskey jacks, moved in close to us to see what they could scrounge. A belted kingfisher, blue feathers sparkling in the sunlight, flitted about in a tree near the little bridge. High overhead, pelicans were soaring on the rising air currents of a warm spring day. What a great welcoming committee!

We entered the house for a quick tour before unloading our belongings from the truck. There was a kitchen, a living room and two bedrooms, all rather small for a family of five, especially when compared to the relatively large domicile we had become used to in Fort Resolution. Another comparison was also obvious—no electrical power and no running water. It was back to using gas lamps and pumping water by hand. Once again the

237

Saturday night bath would have to be effected in a washtub, using water heated in buckets on the wood stove. The same tub, along with a corrugated scrub board and a bar of soap, would serve to do the laundry. It was all reminiscent of the days when we were first married, living in the little shack above the CPR irrigation ditch.

There was one major difference from past circumstances. At Boundary Cabin I couldn't just arrange a contract with someone to haul in several loads of firewood to meet our fuel needs for heating and cooking. I had to go out with an ax and a saw and harvest the wood myself. I didn't mind it—it was healthy exercise and part of the outdoor life—but it consumed a lot of time. How a small chain saw would have helped, but the advent of that labor-saving device was still somewhere in the future. The other west side wardens also had to gather their own wood supply, so, when each had his quota of logs ready for the winter, we ganged together for a sawing bee. A large gas-powered circular saw was towed to each warden's woodpile, where we all cooperated in sawing the logs into stove-sized lengths.

The water from the well offered some compensation for the other rustic attributes of our new home. It was the sweetest drinking water we had ever tasted. It had been obtained at a terrible price, though. Two workmen were employed in the excavation process, one to dig away at the dirt in the bottom of the well and shovel it into a bucket, the other to haul the loaded bucket to the surface and dump it off to the side. While the hole was being dug, a pump driven by a gas engine was used to keep the groundwater at bay. On one sad day, the workman in the well was overcome by carbon monoxide fumes from the engine exhaust. The fumes, being heavier than air, fell to the bottom of the hole and caused his death by suffocation. His fellow worker, in a rescue attempt, also succumbed to the fumes.

In our isolation, we did have a telephone of sorts. It was a single-wire tree line with a ground return. Which meant, first, that it was a weak communication link, voices sometimes being heard only faintly if at all. And, second, the wire merely being strung from tree to tree, it was prone to breakages from falling trunks and limbs, especially during windstorms or snowstorms. The line could be connected into the regular telephone going to the park headquarters at Waskesiu, so that Chief Warden George Davis was able to pester me at will. The biggest problem with the line was that a switch had been installed at Sturgeon Crossing Cabin. This allowed the occupants of that cabin to switch our part of the line out of the circuit when they wanted to call a cabin to the south of them, improving their reception by the reduction in line length. Occasionally, though, they would forget to switch us back in again, leaving us incommunicado until such time as they discovered their oversight.

After checking out the house, we went to investigate the stable. Empty! Where were the horses that, according to rumor, were to be part of our life at Boundary Cabin? Upon inquiring, I learned that all of the wardens' horses were idling the summer away in pastures on the southern fringe of the park. Late in the autumn they would be shipped out to the various cabins. For most of the year I could travel the local trails with the old Fargo truck. To penetrate the bush beyond these byways I had to go on foot. In the winter months, though, the roads would often be snowed in for days at a time, preventing travel by motor vehicle. And, when the frosts of winter were being forced from the ground by warm weather, all of the routes became quagmires. At such times I would have to use horses for moving around my district. They would be returned to pasture in the spring after the roads dried out.

The current absence of horses notwithstanding, this might be a suitable point to introduce the two which I eventually received. I had no problem with the idea of using horses. In fact, I was looking forward to it. During my first days at grade school I had been introduced to what was then the principal recreational activity of young males, Cowboys and Indians, and horses—even imaginary ones—were definitely part of the scenario. Since I didn't possess the appropriate regalia of the cowboy—a cap pistol (which fired a tiny encapsulated charge of powder, making a satisfying bang) and a red bandana as a minimum, ranging up to a fancy belt, holsters, chaps and shirt for the inordinately affluent—I was

239

usually relegated to the role of Indian. The Indians always lost. My father made me a primitive gun from the end of a wooden apple box, but this didn't command much respect in our Wild West community.

Eventually I acquired a single-shot cap pistol, and was able to borrow one of Dad's big red handkerchiefs for a bandana, so I was promoted to cowboy status on occasion. But, by then, repeating pistols were in vogue. These accepted a whole role of caps at once, producing a bang with every pull of the trigger. When I finally did become the proud owner of a repeater, the technology had advanced to true six-shooters with revolving cylinders that took flat paper disks bearing several caps on each one. I badly wanted one of these state-of-the-art weapons, but no amount of wheedling and whining persuaded my parents to put one in my possession.

Naturally, horses were of great interest to young cowboys, but the prospect of actually owning one was an impossible dream. We did have daily contact with these animals, though, because various commercial activities depended on them, even in the urban scene. In particular, they were extensively involved in the delivery of goods and services, not to be replaced completely by trucks and vans until after the end of World War II. Horse-drawn wagons were used by bakeries and dairies to deliver bread and milk, by market gardeners to distribute their produce, by junkmen who loaded up their carts with discarded items from back alleys, by jacks-of-all-trades who could sharpen scissors or knives and supply needles and notions or pots and pans, and by icemen bringing blocks of ice for the ubiquitous iceboxes; there was even a small one-horse snowplow used by the city in the winter to clear residential sidewalks.

On a hot summer day, when the ice wagon hove into view, a gang of children would materialize from nowhere to pick up the chips left behind when the iceman chopped a large block of ice down into smaller icebox-sized chunks. A mean-spirited driver would chase us away from his wagon, but a kindhearted one would chop a few extra chips just for us. To keep the ice from melting rapidly in our hands, we twisted our handkerchiefs around the chips and sucked at them through the cloth. Chasing the ice wagon was one of the minor delights of my childhood.

The horses pulling these various rigs knew the routes at least as well as the drivers. When a delivery man left his wagon to carry his particular product up to a residence, his horse, on its own initiative, would move ahead until it was in front of the house belonging to the next customer. This performance, coupled with my admiration for the tricks performed by the mounts of some of my cowboy heroes—Buck Jones, Tom Mix and Gene Autry—made me think that all horses were clever. So, as I said, I was looking forward to using horses in my new job at Boundary Cabin.

I was, that is, until Jolly and Dolly arrived. First, they were big, fat, lazy plow horses, so big and fat that I couldn't use them as saddle horses, something I had been anticipating with relish, something that might have taken me back to my childhood days of Cowboys and Indians. Instead I had to settle for hitching them up to a two-wheeled cart when I needed their services. Second, I've no doubt that horses are like people—among the general population there are some bright ones and there are some stupid ones. Dolly and, especially, Jolly were probably among the most stupid horses on the face of the earth. Anyone acquainted with this pair would never use the term "horse sense" in a complimentary manner.

Individually or as a team, those two horses would shy at everything, even familiar objects. I could lead them by the same thing for days on end with no reaction until, suddenly, they would take exception to its presence. Pretending to be startled out of their wits, they would rear up and try to stampede. If the item was something unfamiliar, they no longer just pretended to be startled. They became so nervous and frightened that I could hardly hold them in check. Once or twice, under such circumstances, I lost control of the team and had to let them run with the cart. They never ran far because their lazy dispositions quickly slowed them down.

I had hoped that the equine pair would smarten up as they became more familiar with me, or I with them, but it never happened. I lavished extra attention on them, naively believing that, in their gratitude, they might respond by paying more attention to the task at hand. Instead, they just found more opportunities to nip me when I wasn't looking. I used the team when I had to, but we never did become close friends. Give me a dog team every time!

Our three boys were delighted with their new home. I cut down a few trees and used the logs to construct swings, a teeter-totter and a sandbox for their use. Also, the surrounding woods and water provided lots of scope for imaginative play, and they had their new puppy—rapidly growing into a full-sized dog—to help keep them from harm. We had a contest to name the pup and finally settled on Dusty because of the gray tips on his black fur. He also looked like his namesake, the tough old sled dog from my team in the Northwest Territories.

Beaver Dams
(or Damn Beavers!)

After we settled in at Boundary Cabin, I had some time to scout around and become acquainted with my district before the tourist season arrived. Not that it made much difference to me. Any tourists arriving in my district were almost certainly lost and I had only to direct them back down the road they had just traversed. I found it necessary to put up a "Road Closed" sign at the little bridge which gave access to the 57 Trail because some of the lost travelers were unwise enough to drive right past our cabin without stopping to inquire as to their location. I guess they figured that the trail would lead them to civilization eventually. Most of the time this was an incorrect assumption.

The 57 Trail was a bush road about twenty-five miles long that headed east across the park and eventually connected to a gravel road leading to Waskesiu. Where its name came from is uncertain. Some people maintained that the trail had fifty-seven turns per mile, which was slightly on the high side of the correct count. Occasionally, I had to drive a crew of workmen across it and, from their position bouncing around in the open box of the Fargo, they usually swore that it was just one continuous winding curve, which was close to the truth. Some of them also swore that they would never make the trip with me again. A few of them just swore. I tried to reassure them that it was not the driver but the rough road conditions that made it such a thrilling trip. Most seemed unconvinced. My own guess about the name is that it came from the location of the road, which pretty much followed along the latitude of 53°57′ N.

The first time I headed out on the 57 Trail, I had only driven about a mile when I came to a culvert that had been washed out by the runoff from melting winter snow. I got a shovel from the back of my truck and shoveled enough dirt from the surrounding trail to make the culvert passable. Continuing on, I soon came to another washout. This time it was a small log bridge with a big ditch where the western approach used to be. I chopped up some trees into short lengths to fill up the gap, shoveled some dirt on top to smooth things out and carefully drove across to the other side. Half a mile on, I rounded a bend in the trail to find a log bridge standing well out in the middle of a creek, minus the approaches to either side. There was no way that I could fix it in short order. I left the truck there, waded the creek, and continued to investigate the trail on foot.

After finding several more washouts of various sizes in the next couple of miles, I had seen enough to know that the road was definitely not in very good shape. I returned home and relayed a description of the condition to the chief warden in Waskesiu. He had already checked his end of the trail and had a crew out making repairs. After about two weeks, they had fixed all the washouts right through to Boundary Cabin, so it was in good shape for the summer. Or so it seemed.

A few more small washouts occurred after heavy rains but I was able to keep those repaired myself. The biggest cause of road maintenance problems in my district turned out to be that creature revered by Grey Owl—the beaver. These animals just love to plug up culverts and bridges to make new dams. The dams back up the water into the trees, enlarging their foraging grounds. Beavers like to cut down aspen and poplar trees to eat the bark and use the branches for building houses and dams. They don't like to travel far from water, though, because this exposes them to attack by predators such as coyotes. So, instead of bringing the food to the water, they try to bring the water to the food.

After the beavers are through with their construction work, the water that used to run through a culvert or under a bridge now backs up until it fills the whole depression to the level of the road surface. Then it starts running over the road, gradually carrying away the roadbed. Soon there is a big washout into which the industrious beavers keep shoving more branches in a determined effort to maintain the new water level. If left alone, the whole process stabilizes when the dam is just long enough so that the seepage through it equals the amount of water flowing down the creek, while the water surface is maintained nearly up to the road surface.

Of course, the beavers couldn't be left alone to build their dams indiscriminately and unhindered. Park roads had to be maintained in a usable condition, especially during the fire-danger season. Every day I would patrol the roads and pull out all the wooden trash from the culverts and bridges. Every night the beavers would return and plug them up again. Sometimes they wouldn't wait until nightfall. On occasion, I would park my truck down the road from a bridge newly freed of brush and carefully stalk back toward the creek. Watching quietly, I would often observe a beaver swim silently up to the bridge, its path through the water traced out by a few V-shaped ripples on the surface, a branch from a tree in its mouth. Then the animal would fuss around under the bridge until the branch was firmly wedged into place. As it left for more material, another beaver would approach and carry out the same procedure.

I was amazed at the tough, tenacious networks that beavers could weave out of branches and mud. When it came to tearing their work apart, there was no keystone, no single piece of wood that, when pulled out, would cause the dam to start collapsing. Every piece of material that went into the dam, entangled with all of the surrounding pieces, was very difficult to extract. So difficult, in fact, that I couldn't compete against the work of the many beaver colonies thriving in my district. They gradually got ahead of me and were able to take a bit of a holiday. I just could not clear the dams out faster than the beavers could rebuild them. I finally had to ignore the problem along the 57 Trail and concentrate solely on the main road along the park boundary.

❖

After a while some relief arrived in the form of a request to the park headquarters—from Scotland, no less—for a number of live beaver pairs. Apparently Scotland wished to reestablish a beaver population. The chief warden sent some live traps out to me and told me to get busy with them. I was only too happy to oblige because it would help solve my road maintenance problems if I could get rid of some of the beavers. The traps were like big suitcases, made out of heavy wire mesh, and completely harmless to the animals except for the shock of being caught. I would make a small break in a main dam where there was room for a trap to function properly. Then I would open the two sides of the suitcase out flat, set the trigger, and carefully position the trap just under the water surface on the upstream side of the dam at the location I had damaged. When the trigger was released by an animal moving into the trap, the two sides snapped together, hemming the beaver in above the water so that it wouldn't drown.

The noise of the water trickling through the breach, or the change in the nature of the flow, would usually alert the beavers to the fact that they had a repair job on their hands. If not, no matter. The beavers made regular patrols around their territory and would soon discover the damage in any case. Sometimes one of them would come empty-handed to survey the problem. Then it might swim right up to the break and trigger the trap. At other times, though, an animal would swim up with an extra-large piece of repair material in his jaws. Then there was a chance that the material would trigger the trap before the beaver was into it. Occasionally, a beaver kit would swim into the trap but it didn't have enough weight to activate the trigger. I observed all of these happenings at various times by dousing myself with mosquito repellent and hiding quietly nearby.

I checked the traps each morning and, if any beavers had been captured, I took them, still in the traps, to Sturgeon Crossing Cabin where I released them into a temporary holding pen. From there they were taken to better facilities in Waskesiu, awaiting the day when we had trapped the total number of animals required. I trapped about fifteen beavers from the major trouble spots along the main road in my district, to a slight extent alleviating the problems with clogged culverts and road washouts. These beavers, together with a number trapped elsewhere, were shipped over to Scotland. I never did learn if the transplant was successful. I suspect not, since I read in a newspaper article in 1992 (almost forty years later) that Scottish biologists were still trying to establish beaver colonies in their country using Canadian stock.

❖

Whether the beavers that were transported to Scotland prospered or not was of little concern to me, for the animals continued to thrive in my part of the park. I monitored their activities constantly, not just along the main road and the 57 Trail, but also well back into the forest. The colonies out in the backwoods acted as sources for new immigrants, the young beavers eventually spreading out to establish their own domains. By the time autumn arrived, in that first year of our stay at Boundary Cabin, it was obvious that we had a population explosion on our hands.

Plans were laid at the park headquarters to employ a number of Indians from a nearby reserve to bring the beaver population down to manageable proportions through trapping. A deal was struck with the Department of Indian Affairs whereby the Indian agent from the reserve would bring some proficient Native trappers to the park in the early spring, when beaver pelts were in prime condition. The Indians were to get the money realized from the sale of the pelts.

They started trapping at the beginning of the spring breakup. The roads were impassable to motor vehicles during the day, but were still freezing solidly enough at night to distribute the Natives around to the chosen locations. About a dozen men were allotted to my district. Shortly afterwards, the temperature began staying above the freezing mark all the time, so I had to hitch Jolly and Dolly to the cart in order to distribute supplies and monitor the progress of the trapping.

Two weeks into the program there was a severe snowstorm. Heavy, wet, white flakes dropped from the sky for more than six hours, piling up to a depth of sixteen inches on level ground. The snow clinging to the trees quickly turned them into amorphous bundles of gelid slush. Strained to the breaking point, the tree trunks began snapping off several feet above the ground, emitting a noise like a loud gun shot.

As more and more trees toppled, the cracking and booming sounds occurred with greater frequency and became louder and more invasive. I was harbored snugly at home during the storm and was amazed at the intensity of the noise, even inside the house. The sounds, some close at hand, others more distant, soon formed a continuous cannonade. It would have been a dangerous barrage for anyone outside. I worried about the Indian trappers camping out in the bush with only canvas tents in which to shelter. There was nothing I could do for them at the moment. It was very risky to venture outdoors while the trees were still falling at random. Our telephone was out of action, the line having been broken in many places. Also, the road was littered with downed trees, some portions completely blocked off to anything but foot traffic.

The morning following the storm dawned clear and chill. I began removing the trees from the road, using my ax and buck saw. How much easier the job would have been with a portable chain saw. The road for the first half-mile south from the cabin turned out to be the worst section for blockages. It took all of that day to make it passable to vehicles.

The following day I started clearing the trail east toward the trappers' camp. The weather was now warm and the snow was disappearing rapidly, leaving a very mucky road behind. About midmorning the Indian agent's vehicle appeared, chains on its tires, churning up the mud as it slithered around in the ruts. The agent, too, had been worried about the men in the bush, and was making every effort to get to them.

We reached the campsite at noon, to the relief of the trappers who had been anxiously awaiting our arrival. Their original campsite was crisscrossed with fallen trees. Shortly after the storm started, fearing for their own safety, they had wisely retreated to a swampy area where they had huddled together beyond reach of any tall trees which might tumble down. Several miserable hours later, after most of the dangerous trees had already fallen, they were able to recover their gear and reestablish their camp on solid ground at an open spot near the trail. Here we found them on the second day after the storm, in good spirits for the most part, but also somewhat shell-shocked. Since they had finished their trapping efforts in that particular location, we moved them to a new area.

The trappers continued working at their task until spring had truly arrived. The peak time for prime beaver pelts had just passed and the fire season was fast approaching. The Indian agent gathered up his charges and returned them to their reserve. The trapping program had been very successful. In the space of a few weeks, a dozen trappers procured approximately 1,000 prime beaver pelts from my district alone. A lesser number were taken in several other districts where some reduction in beaver numbers had also been desirable.

Even so, in the months that followed, I still observed many beavers about the countryside, evidence that the cull had been most timely in terms of preventing an overabundance of the animals, with a consequent increase in their mortality rate from starvation and disease. The cull also eased the road maintenance chores, at least for a while. As for the forest, it would take many years before Nature could erase all signs of the destruction caused by the storm.

Feathered Friends

Returning to the morning after our arrival at Boundary Cabin, we were all awakened at dawn by a loud metallic clamor echoing and re-echoing around the house. I threw on my clothes and hurried outside, wondering just what could be making so much racket.

I quickly located the source of the noise. It was not some crazed human drummer flailing away with a sledge hammer against a forty-five-gallon drum—my first wild guess—but a common woodpecker; not even the large pileated woodpecker with the big red topknot, but the smaller ubiquitous red-shafted flicker. It was performing an avian version of a paradiddle, a drum roll, repeated over and over. The foolish bird was using its beak to pound away at the galvanized metal flashing of the chimney on the roof of the garage, accounting for the volume of the sound.

What the 'pecker hoped to accomplish by this action is uncertain. Probably it was advertising for a mate—this being spring—and striking at the metal sent the strident message over a larger territory than would have been the case by merely pounding away at a dead tree. Or, who knows, maybe the bird just liked cacophonous music. I watched for a while until it got tired of performing and flew away.

The next morning the same thing happened. Our family wasn't getting its full quota of sleep when it was awakened by a metallic rat-a-tat-tatting each morning at dawn. The woodpecker seemed determined to make music every single day. Something had to be done. On the third morning I was ready for that dratted bird. With the first rattle on the drum I dashed outside carrying my .22-caliber rifle. No, I wasn't about to shoot the woodpecker. After all, this was a national park and I was there to protect the wildlife, all of it, no matter how wilful its behavior. I stood alongside the garage and fired a shot into the air. The sudden noise startled the bird and it flew away, hopefully for good.

It was not to be. The first rat-a-tat-tat on the following morning found me outside by the garage again. Once more the bird flew away at the sound of a shot. Would this second try be successful? Twenty-four hours later, in the dawn's early light, the woodpecker gave the answer. Rat-a-tat-tat. I knew now that a really big scare was required. I raised my rifle and took careful aim. Slowly, I squeezed the trigger. Boinggg! The bullet impacted the flashing an inch away from the feathered fiend, making a very loud noise and probably generating a bone-jarring shock wave in the metal. The bird leaped into the air, squawking, and fluttering its wings. It landed back on the garage roof, pausing just long enough to get its bearings. Then away it flew, shaken but otherwise unharmed, this time never to return for another jive session. At last we could sleep until breakfast time. I assume that the woodpecker went back to banging away in more conventional places—like dead trees—along with the rest of his relatives.

A pair of loons that had set up housekeeping on the lake in front of our cabin enjoyed greater favor with us. They probably arrived a couple of weeks before we did, just after the lake was clear of ice, and had already selected a secure nesting spot along the lakeshore. Being clumsy on land, however graceful on the water or in the air, they like to nest near the water's edge. Loons mate for life and generally inhabit the same body of water year after year. If the location is lacking in sufficient food, they may fly out daily for a repast at a more productive location.

No doubt our loons found the lake to their liking. It seemed to me to be somewhat deficient in flavorsome fish and frogs for the birds to feed on, but who am I to say. The male used to fly away every day, so no doubt he was obtaining some nourishment elsewhere. Initially, the female remained hidden from view, occupied with the task of incubating her eggs, but she responded to the calls of her mate as he swam around the perimeter of their domain.

Loons have several different songs, made up of various combinations of tones which ornithologists term wails, yodels, hoots and tremolos. The resulting euphony has been variously described as achingly beautiful, electrifying, enigmatic, enthralling, haunting, lonely, maniacal, melancholy, mournful, mysterious, plaintive, spine-tingling, unearthly and weird. Their vocalizations are all of that and more. They suggest the thrill of adventure and the lure of remote places. In that sweet music resides the quintessence of the wilderness. Would that I could have recorded all of those echoing notes. How I would love to hear them again.

The male loon soon found himself faced with what seemed, at first, to be an insurmountable problem. Before the beavers had constructed the dam which caused the little lake to form, a line of tall willows grew across the center of the area. Even after the dammed-up water flooded their roots, the bushes continued to thrive. During the previous winter, in order to enlarge the field of view along the lake, my predecessor at Boundary Cabin had gone out on the ice and chopped the willows off level with the frozen surface. When the loons first arrived in the spring the willow-bush stubs were covered with perhaps a foot of water, the high water level being a result of the runoff from the snow still melting back in the bush. This provided the heavy birds with a suitable length of runway when they wished to return to the sky. A few weeks later, when most of the snow melt had departed on its long journey downstream to the sea, the level of the water on the lake began to fall. Now the willow stubs poked their jagged ends above the surface, forming obstacles right in the middle of the loons' airport.

One morning as I was doing some chores near the cabin, I looked out at the lake and observed the male loon attempting a takeoff. He got close to the near shore, pointed his bill toward the far shore, and then paddled furiously away, wings flapping, slowly gaining momentum. But he couldn't break free of the water surface before he reached the hazardous stubs, so he had to slam on his brakes to avoid a crash. Once again, the loon idled up to the starting line, revved his engine, threw in the clutch and peeled rubber down the runway. Then it was a brake-squealing stop to avoid running into the barrier at the end of the strip.

Time after time the loon repeated the performance. Then he gave up and began swimming slowly in circles, perhaps gathering his strength for more attempts or, maybe, pondering some new strategy. I wondered if he might be waiting for a headwind to develop down the lake. This would help to get him airborne, but the odds on sufficient wind appearing in the right direction over the sheltered lake were not great. After a while the bird pulled up to the starting line again, and began accelerating toward the willow stubs.

This time it was different. Instead of slamming on the brakes he flapped his wings harder than ever, hard enough to just barely lift his bulk out of the water and over the barrier. Then he settled back onto the surface of the lake. Now he had momentum though, lots of it. He kept going, paddling and flapping furiously, and soon lifted into the air with space to spare. Water dripped from his body, dropping back to make small splashes in the lake below. Who says that loons are crazy! He gave a triumphant call to his mate on the ground, then flew away on some unknown errand.

I saw the loon perform again on numerous occasions. At first he often needed more than one attempt but each time he became more adept at skipping over the willows. He had to keep increasing his proficiency because the water level continued to drop for a few more days and a few more inches. Soon, he was completely confident about his ability to cope with the barrier and his take-offs became smooth and trouble-free.

Sometime thereafter, the female loon appeared cruising around the lake with two young birds following in her wake. Whereas the male loon had come to ignore my presence, the new mother was much more wary. As soon as she spotted me, she would lead her chicks into the shadows of the grass along the shore. Or, if caught out in open water, the chicks would climb onto her back and the trio would sink silently below the surface, disappearing into the depths. A short time later, three heads would pop back into view, the young now separated very slightly from their mother. Once, as I awaited their reappearance, the

253

female loon suddenly shot out of the water like a missile fired from a submerged submarine, emitting a loud squawk as she broke through the surface. Then the chicks bobbed up in her wake. It looked for all the world as though the mother had been the recipient of an underwater "goose," speared in her posterior by the beak of one of her offspring.

The loon family thrived, and provided us with quiet thrills and wonderful melodies until the autumn, when it came time for them to depart for warmer climes.

Unlike the loons, the saucy whiskey jacks hung around all year long. They were always entertaining. While I was building the children's playground, I also put in a clothesline for Mary's convenience. It was one with stranded galvanized wire running over large pulleys, so the clothes could be pegged out and retrieved from one location by moving the line back and forth. As Mary came out of the house, laundry basket in hand, to baptize the system with its first load of wet clothes, she noticed that two whiskey jacks were clinging to the far end of the clothesline. She pinned up a shirt and thrust the line out to make space for the next garment. As she did so, the birds fluttered comically up in the air for a foot or two, then settled back down again. After several repeat performances, the birds no longer jumped when the line moved but just stayed cool and enjoyed the ride. Soon Mary was ignoring the job at hand, moving the line back and forth just to provide a ride for the whiskey jacks. I believe they would have been happy to have her keep at it all day long.

There were always a dozen or more whiskey jacks hovering about our establishment. The name "whiskey jack" is applied to the Canada Jay throughout the North. It is supposedly derived from a Cree Indian word. In the Rocky Mountains this cheeky extrovert sometimes goes by the appellation of Camp Robber. Dusty, our dog, considered the latter name to be appropriate since the birds got part of their sustenance from the leftovers in his dish. Whenever Dusty wasn't actively feeding from his dish there would be two or three whiskey jacks perched on its rim, pecking at the contents. Dusty didn't appreciate sharing his food with anyone, so he would charge the freeloading birds and chase them away. But there were always others ready to sneak in for their turn at the trough. Sometimes, taking turn about, they ran the dog ragged. Then Dusty would return to his dog house and lie in the doorway, watching the birds with a jaundiced eye, resting up for the next round.

On one occasion, the whiskey jacks got what I'm certain they considered to be a most delightful treat. Mary's father, who lived on Vancouver Island, sent us a crate of fresh, home-grown plums. Before doing so he inquired of his local post office as to the likely transit time to our location and was advised that it would be two or three days. All well and good, he thought, they'll get the fruit while it's still in prime condition. He forgot to multiply any post office delivery estimate by a factor of four or five. Several weeks after mailing, the crate of plums arrived at our post office in Park Valley. We learned about it when the postmaster sent us a message, via the warden at Sturgeon Crossing, to please come and pick up our parcel as soon as possible because it was leaking badly and he didn't have suitable storage facilities.

I drove to the post office in the Fargo and retrieved the crate. There was a powerful alcoholic smell about it, and fermented plum juice was draining from all the cracks. I probably should have jettisoned its contents somewhere along the road, but I brought it home intact thinking that some of the fruit might still be salvageable. This was not the case, however, so I dumped the disagreeable mess out in the bush a little distance from the cabin.

Soon all the whiskey jacks in the neighborhood had sniffed out the pile and were gorging themselves on the rotten brew. Most of them quickly became inebriated from the alcoholic content, bickering among themselves, staggering around haphazardly, making comical attempts to fly and usually ending in a ground loop. Was this anthropomorphic behavior or wasn't it? The amusing spectacle was certainly reminiscent of some human parties I had observed. Fortunately for the birds, the effects seemed to wear off quite rapidly, but they probably suffered bad hangovers.

❖

Other feathered friends, birds of passage, entertained us briefly from time to time. There were mallard ducks and a few pintail and teal on the lake behind the house. A bittern resided there also, occasionally booming out its distinctive call in the late afternoon. The clamor of a bittern, like the cry of a loon, once heard is never forgotten. I usually refer to it as being like the sound of an old-fashioned hand-powered cistern pump, but this description draws blank looks from city folks who have never had the experience of using such a device at their kitchen sink. Despite its excellent camouflage, I was able to observe the bird calling on a number of occasions. With its beak pointing straight up to the sky, it moves its head and neck up and down in excellent imitation of a pump handle at work. The bittern sometimes goes by the common name of Thunder Pump, which suggests that others besides myself have recognized the similarity of its call to the sound of a laboring pump.

Any little sandy beach areas were usually occupied by a killdeer or a sandpiper peeping out a claim to ownership, sometimes with fuzzy-coated young ones scurrying about on toothpick legs. On too close an approach, the killdeer hen would go into its famous broken-wing act, designed to lure interlopers away.

A brightly colored kingfisher made his abode in a tree near the stable, close to the water where he could catch his fill of tadpoles and aquatic insects.

Pelicans—from a colony on a large lake to the west of our cabin—soared high overhead in the summer, their white wings glinting brightly in the sunlit sky. They circled lazily around in thermal air currents for hours at a time, seemingly just for the pure enjoyment of flight. Why else would they do it? Unlike hawks and eagles, the pelicans weren't doing it in pursuit of food. I know that crows will fly for the fun of it. I once observed two crows taking turns flying into the turbulent air stream generated by high winds blowing over the edge of a building. A strong vortex, like a miniature tornado lying on its side, was formed near a corner of the roof. When one of the playful birds entered this whirlwind, it would be tossed about like a rag doll, unable to control its own motions until the gusty air smoothed out a few yards downstream. Then it would cackle in delight, as if to say to its companion, "Your turn next. It's lots of fun!"

In the spring, the ruffed grouse, having lurked quiet and unseen in the nearby forest for most of the year, began their noisy quest for mates. The males, beating their wings together, would produce a staccato drumroll of sorts, sounding very much like a farm tractor starting up on a cool morning. At first the tractor's engine just barely turned over—putt-putt, putt-putt-putt. Then it got faster and faster—chug-chug-chug-chug-chug, terminating with a roar as the throttle was advanced to the maximum.

Many varieties of song birds flitted melodiously about our home grounds, often sending us dashing for our field guide for identification purposes. All of our feathered friends were welcome. We even forgave the perverted woodpecker once it gave up its habit of playing reveille on the chimney flashing.

Wild Hazards

In addition to the birds that lived around Boundary Cabin, we also had some animal friends. The most frequent visitors were squirrels. Like the whiskey jacks, they too indulged in the game of irritating Dusty by stealing food from his dish. In the winter, I would stick a bamboo ski pole, top end down, in the snow by our kitchen window and put some food on the pointed end, just above the attached ring which encircled the pole. On the warmer days one or two squirrels would put in an appearance and scamper up the pole. They would sit on the ring while nibbling at the bait. We could watch out of the window as they stuffed their cheek pouches and then scampered away, soon to return for another load.

In the summer, muskrats and beavers swam in the lake behind the cabin, most easily observable at dusk, and then only if one could remain still among the myriad mosquitoes. The beavers, working in the dark of night, helped to supply us with firewood by cutting down some of the large poplar trees on the fringes of our clearing. On occasion, a beaver would paddle silently up to the shore near the outhouse, to startle any unsuspecting resident of that peaceful little edifice with a loud smack of its tail against the surface of the water.

Just down the road, a short distance from the cabin, was an area much favored by porcupines. Two species of trees grew there in the marshy ground, tamarack and black spruce. The tamarack bark seemed to appeal to the palate of slow-moving "porky" more than did the bark of nearby poplars. The twisty-grained tamaracks dropped their needles in the fall, covering the ground with a yellow blanket. The stunted spruce grew so closely together that it was difficult for a person to walk through them, but the smaller animals had no such trouble. Dusty encountered a stray porcupine or two wandering around there, much to his subsequent discomfort.

For larger game, it was necessary to go farther afield. The presence of the dog warned most animals away from our immediate vicinity. There were black bears in the area but they kept their distance. I never packed a rifle when hiking through the bush, relying on the noise of my passage to avoid surprising bruin. If a bear should happen to take exception to my presence in the woods, I had a plan of attack ready, providing that the animal gave me time to climb a tree. Now black bears can climb trees too, so one might ask what is the good of seeking safety there? Many years before, I had read about a man treed by a bear in a forest in the United States. The bear started to climb the tree after him. As the bear got closer to his intended meal, the man showed great presence of mind. He removed his shirt, took his cigarette lighter from his pants pocket, and used it to set the shirt on fire. Then he dropped this flaming missive on the bear's head. In less time than it takes to tell about it, that bear was down the tree and heading for the next county. I was very impressed by the tactic—anything goes in such a situation.

Moose, elk and deer were abundant in different parts of my district. I used to like listening to the peculiar high-pitched call, or bugle, of the elk during rutting season, but I was careful to steer clear of them at that time because they were not usually in a friendly frame of mind. The Cree word for elk is *waskesiu* (just like the park headquarters' name). One winter, when the snow was very deep—up to five feet in places—and foraging in the woods was difficult for all the ungulates (hoofed mammals), a big bull elk started visiting the hay pile beside our stable. This was hay that I used to feed Jolly and Dolly. At first the elk moved off as I approached, but later on it just kept chewing, seemingly not wary at all.

After a few days I found the elk lying dead. It had a wadded-up ball of hay in its gullet which may have prevented it from feeding properly. The winter kill of ungulates was very high that year, especially for deer. Some estimates placed the deer kill at more than 50 percent. The great depth of snow prevented them from moving very far without the expenditure of much valuable energy. This energy could only be replaced by finding sufficient nourishing food, a difficult task in a limited area. So it was a vicious circle, spiraling downward to end in death by starvation.

I always expected to see moose when I traveled the 57 Trail and was never disappointed. The middle portion of the trail was replete with good moose pasture. Most of my sightings were short ones because the roar of the truck as I rounded one of the many curves in the road would send the big animals scattering. I kept a rough score sheet of the number of moose observed on a single trip through the trail. My record was eighteen. Usually I would see from three to ten moose, depending on the wind and the weather, with up to three animals grouped together in any one swamp.

I never encountered any moose actually standing on the 57 Trail, in a position to challenge for the right-of-way. This would have been bad business during the rutting season. I did once meet an ornery bull moose on the road along the park boundary, blocking further progress. I stopped the truck, wondering what might happen next. Visions of a similar situation flashed through my mind, when Billy McNeil was attacked by a buffalo on a road in Wood Buffalo National Park. I especially thought about it when the moose lowered its heavily antlered head to the charge position. Next it tossed its head skyward and wandered a few feet away where it began thrashing the roadside bushes, telling the world that it was ready to do battle. Then it came back into the center of the road again, glaring angrily at me or, rather, at the truck. Normally, I would have put the vehicle in reverse gear and backed away from the confrontation, but this day I had an engagement down the road which I had to keep. Fortunately, the animal was not feeling sufficiently antagonistic to charge the truck. I wanted it to stay that way so I didn't follow my inclination to honk the horn and rev the motor. After about twenty minutes the moose got tired of the game and disappeared into the bush.

I learned to be cautious in certain locations along the park roads where elk and deer habitually crossed. They were always wary about exposing themselves in open areas. The deer, especially, would congregate unseen in the bush at the side of the trail, gathering courage before making the attempt. Then they would suddenly leap out—one by one at brief intervals until they were all across—and dash into the bush on the other side of the road. If I saw a deer cross ahead of me, I would slow to a crawl, because the odds were that another one would be jumping out a few seconds later.

Miles away, on the main highway leading to Waskesiu, a man was killed when he hit a deer with his car. The animal was thrown through the windshield, almost decapitating the driver. When a vehicle is traveling at highway speeds, a struck animal will nearly always be tossed into the windshield. I once read the 1991 statistics concerning wild animal species responsible for fatalities among the human population in that year. The animal that topped the list was not the grizzly bear, the wolf, the crocodile or various poisonous snakes. It was the deer. Running into deer on highways killed 135 people in North America in 1991. So, to keep your name out of the obituary column of your local newspaper, always be on guard when driving in deer country. Bees were second on the list—about forty people died from bee stings.

With all the wolf food in the park, running around fresh on the hoof, one might have expected a problem with these predators. Strangely enough, I never encountered any wolf kills or even any wolf sign in the bush. Nor did I hear from the other wardens of any wolf populations in their districts except in the far northern section of the park. A few wolves howling at the moon would have complemented the wild music of the loons, but I never heard any such sounds. Coyotes could often be heard yipping and yapping in the meadowlands near the Sturgeon River, but they posed no threat to the ungulates.

The thought of an elk steak seemed to attract the occasional poacher across the western boundary of the park, where the elk population was especially large. I never found any evidence of poaching in my district, but I was quite far removed from the local centers of population outside of the park. Most of the poachers seemed to hit the area around Rabbit Cabin, and the warden there caught several culprits over the years.

261

On one occasion I did briefly think that I had a poacher to deal with. It was during the spring breakup. I was returning from a hike along the park boundary in the hills north of our cabin. There was no trail, just an old cut line through the trees, now partially reclaimed by nature. Suddenly a shot rang out, very close by judging from the loudness of the sound. I felt a great pain in my right foot. My leg buckled under me and I fell to the ground. I crawled behind a tree for protection against what I thought might be a sniper or, at least, a careless hunter—perhaps a rustle shooter, so-called because of a proclivity to fire at any noise in the bush. I looked carefully around. Nothing to be seen. Nothing to be heard, either, except some bird song. It was strange that they should still be singing if someone was skulking around out there.

After a short while, I turned my attention to my foot. It was causing me considerable pain so I assumed that it had been hit by a bullet. Carefully removing my moccasin, I looked for a wound. There was none. But there was an angry red swelling on top of the foot and in the instep. Some gentle probing made me wince aloud. Then I realized what had happened. I had twisted my foot on a root, not an unusual occurrence for me. But this time a small bone had snapped, making the sound which I had mistaken for a gun shot. It had certainly seemed loud enough to be one. Putting my moccasin back on, I used the tree to pull myself back to my feet and broke off a branch to use for support. Then I hobbled painfully back to the nearby cabin, thankful that the accident hadn't happened when I had been much further back in the hills.

Since it was spring breakup, I couldn't go for proper medical attention because the roads were impassable. Mary taped my foot to provide it with a little support. Then I sat around the cabin, doing nothing but reading. After a few days, I was able to cautiously put some weight on the foot. Finally, by the time the roads had dried out enough for a trip to the nearest doctor, I decided that I didn't need one any more. So ended the case of the phantom poacher.

❖

As well as the apparent absence of illegal interlopers in my district, good fortune held in other aspects of park preservation.

In particular, no fires broke out. There were several reasons for this. First, my sector of the park was quite remote—relatively far away from tourists and other people—so the fire risk due to the human element was much reduced. Also, trapping was not allowed in the park (discounting the beaver cull), thus removing that from the list of possible causes. And, if there were occasional poachers, they would be especially careful with fires to avoid detection. Second, I was just plain lucky that none of the summer electrical storms started a conflagration in my sector. During times of high fire hazard, when the bush was tinder dry or after a violent storm, I always had a sharp-eyed towerman on duty—looking for smoke—in a lofty lookout tower perched near the top of a hill.

Another reason for the lack of bush fire problems involved good management. The wardens in all districts sought to make settlers and other users of park roads very much aware of fire hazards. We had a good sign campaign in place, so that no one could travel far along any road or trail without the need for caution being brought to his attention. We also went to considerable effort to destroy any old dried grass in the vicinity of the roads so that there would be no ready fuel available in case of a carelessly discarded match or cigarette butt. We did this by burning the grass in the early spring when it was just dry enough to set ablaze, but the bush itself was still protected by unmelted snow and ice lying on the ground.

When I judged the situation was suitable for the spring burn, I hitched Jolly and Dolly to the two-wheeled cart, climbed in with a box of wooden matches on my lap and set out for the grassy areas. Once there, I began lighting the matches as we traveled along, throwing them out to right and left—a pyromaniac's delight. If conditions were just right, the grass would quite readily catch fire and burn sedately over a small area. These small patches, each the result of ignition from a single match, soon united with one another and, the fuel being exhausted, that was the end of it.

If conditions were unsuitable, the grass being a little on the damp side, it might be necessary to gather handfuls of dead grass together, kindle them, and hope they would burn hotly enough to get the rest of the grass combusting. This sometimes had to be done at frequent intervals over the whole area and was very time-consuming.

Cliff Millard at Sturgeon Crossing once encountered just such difficult conditions. He had much grass to burn off in his district and, on this occasion, spent all day laboriously igniting small parcels of it. He started early in the morning at the boundary between our two districts and worked toward his cabin, where he arrived about supper-time, dog-tired and smelling strongly of smoke. "Thank God," he said to his wife as he slumped into his easy chair, "I've got that chore over with for another year."

It so happened that this was the period when I had the Indians in my district, trapping the beavers. The same day that my colleague was trying to fire his grass was a day that the Indian agent was returning from a visit to his charges. Shortly after Cliff had gotten himself comfortably ensconced in his easy chair, a knock came at his door. He opened it to find the Indian agent standing there, a look of accomplishment on his face. "Mister," he said to the warden, "you sure are lucky. Some nut started dozens of fires out there alongside the road. But don't worry, I put them all out for you." Well, at least the message of our sign campaign had gotten across.

❖

The lookout tower was built on a hillside about a mile from Boundary Cabin. It consisted of a small window-filled hut perched atop an eighty-foot-high, very flexible, steel framework. I know just how flexible it was because I endured a few sessions up there myself, watching over the countryside with a pair of binoculars, looking for columns of smoke that shouldn't be there. Any movement on my part, or any gentle breeze blowing by, would set the whole structure swaying and rotating. It was definitely a hazard for those susceptible to seasickness. A single-wire telephone linked the tower to Boundary Cabin and beyond to facilitate the reporting of any signs of smoke.

Each summer when the fire hazard was high, the tower was occupied from sunup to sundown by a locally hired towerman.

This person, besides keeping his eyes open for smoke, was expected to maintain a short diary describing the weather and other appropriate observations. The diary was sent to the chief warden in Waskesiu at the end of every month. It was generally assumed that such diaries were never read, the chief being too busy with other work and, in any case, who wants to read about the weather of days already past. However, on at least one occasion he did peruse the information contained therein and discovered that the wind speed at the tower on a certain day had been written down as 100 miles per hour. He phoned the towerman to ask, somewhat facetiously, if the wind speed had really been that high. Came the reply, "You would have thought so if you'd been up here!"—further confirmation of the flexibility of the tower.

Dusty

Our dog Dusty was such a character that he deserves a chapter of his own. He was one of a litter that I had planned to raise as a new dog team at Fort Resolution. When we were transferred to Saskatchewan, I selected one of the pups to accompany us. Dusty's mother was half wolf and half husky, and he inherited genes that gave him a wolfish countenance and many wolf-like traits.

Dusty was wary and nervous by nature, yet he enjoyed company. He would beg to be allowed into the house to join the family in the evening and, when the kitchen door was opened to him, he would cautiously creep in and lie down under the table. Every time anyone moved a muscle, though, he would leap to his feet, his back raising the table an inch or two in the air. We finally stopped letting him in—his behavior was making us nervous. Then he took to climbing a pile of firewood, stacked high against the side of the house, where he could peer in through a small living room window. One evening we had a visitor who was not acquainted with our dog. The man turned around from his seat in our lamp-lit room and saw behind him, clearly illuminated by the light escaping through the window, a wolf staring in with a ravenous look on its face. We thought for a moment that we would have a heart-attack victim on our hands.

The response of lost tourists when they first met Dusty was also amusing. The tourists, two or three groups per summer, would encounter the "Road Closed" sign that I had installed at the little bridge signifying the start of the 57 Trail. They would stop their vehicle at the bridge and start walking back to the nearby cabin, which they had just passed. Invariably, Dusty would run enthusiastically out to meet them and, just as invariably, the people would flee back to their cars, certain that they were being pursued by a wolf. Then some member of our family would have to walk over and convince them otherwise.

Because Dusty was such a friendly dog we didn't, at first, keep him chained up unless the whole family was going off somewhere in the truck. I never saw him chasing deer or elk, although he may have tried it unbeknownst to me. Dusty loved to romp with the children and was very gentle with them. Just as much, but less gently, Dusty liked to engage in a wrestling match with me. He nearly matched me for weight and height so it was quite an even struggle. Whenever I wanted to wrestle, I had only to call the dog and he would come running up, anxious for combat. However, if I wanted to chain him up, I could call in what I thought was exactly the same manner and he would not respond. Somehow, Dusty sensed the difference in the two situations. I had to get Billy to call the dog and grasp his collar. Then I could walk up and attach the chain without any further objections from Dusty.

Dick was about two and a half years old at the beginning of his first winter at Boundary Cabin. When dressed up in his winter togs for some outdoor play, he would waddle around like an overstuffed duck, arms sticking out at an angle from his sides. At the ends of those arms were a pair of woolen mitts. Dusty used to start running—building up a good head of steam—and then charge past Dick from behind. At the critical moment he would swing his head sideways and grab a mitt from the child's hand. He did it with no lost motion and without so much as grazing Dick's skin with his teeth. That part of the game was all well and good, but then, instead of dropping the mitt at his master's feet like any good dog should, Dusty swallowed the thing. Later on, as I walked around the yard, I would find the remnants of the mitt, regurgitated after being partly digested. Dick went through three or four pairs of mitts before the winter ended.

Dick wasn't the only one to suffer the indignity of having his mitts swallowed. One day a fisherman drove into our yard. He had been fishing through the ice on a lake just to the west of the park boundary. His catch was in a wooden box on the back of the truck, out of Dusty's reach. But his gloves were lying just on the edge of the truck bed. The dog snuck carefully up to them. Then, as quick as you can say "Gulp! Gulp!" the gloves were in the dog's stomach. The fisherman could only stare in wide-eyed amazement.

Dusty had another trick which he reserved for Mary. He didn't get to try it very often because Mary wasn't outside playing in the snow all that much. If the dog thought that he could catch her unawares, he would charge from behind, bunting her just at knee level as he continued on past. The usual result was that Mary took a tumble in the snow, much to everyone's amusement. Dusty never tried that stunt on me. I guess I was one rung higher in his perception of the hierarchy of our family group.

Soon after we arrived at Boundary Cabin, Dusty met that nemesis of all dogs, a porcupine. After the encounter he came howling back to the cabin, looking for some relief. I got out my pliers and tried to pull the quills, first cutting off the ends to expel the enclosed air, but Dusty took violent exception to the treatment. Since he had only a few of the spiny objects sticking out of his face, I decided to let him carry on, knowing that the wounds would fester a bit and the quills would probably then come out when the dog pawed at them. The first lesson wasn't sufficient, though, so Dusty went looking for a return match with Mr. Porky. This time he came back with his face looking like a well-stocked pincushion. Now I had to do something.

I fashioned a padded restraint collar from some wood scraps and some old blanket material. It was designed to fasten very tightly about the dog's neck, tight enough to greatly restrict his fore and aft movement but not quite tight enough to choke him. With Billy's help, I got the collar in place on Dusty. Then we backed him into his dog house and nailed the wooden ends of the collar to each side of the dog house entrance. I was certain that he couldn't budge while I attempted to remove the quills. My assumption held while I yanked out the first one. I had taken Dusty by surprise. As the second, third and fourth quills were removed, he yelped and tried unsuccessfully to back out of the collar. About all he could do was wiggle his head from side to side. However, as I was trying to grab another quill, the dog developed a new tactic. He began to rotate his whole body. I couldn't hold on to his head at all, let alone snag any more quills. Finally, I admitted defeat. Dusty was turned loose once more to fend for himself. He was completely off his feed for a few days and just moped around the yard, not at all inclined to wrestle or engage in any of his usual activities, not even chasing birds away from his food dish. Every so often he would paw at some of the quills around his mouth and either dislodge them or break them off where they entered his hide. After a while, only a few bumps remained on his snout, indicating festered locations where pieces of quills were still lodged in his flesh. Eventually, even the bumps disappeared and the dog was back to his old playful self, never to bother another porcupine.

Dusty was tendered a special treat when the Indian trappers left their camp in the bush at the end of the beaver cull project. The trappers assembled at Boundary Cabin before being taken back to their reservation in the Indian agent's truck. While trapping, they had been saving the beaver tails to take home to their families. Cooked properly, beaver tails were considered a delicacy. Fancy restaurants in the big cities used to charge fancy prices for a plate of beaver tail. They probably had a fancy name for it, too. Now, as the Indians repacked their gear, they discovered that many of the beaver tails had spoiled, becoming unfit for human consumption. Stacking the tails up in a pile, they invited Dusty to help himself. This the dog proceeded to do, warily at first, but soon with abandon. He would extract a tail from the pile and dash off into the bush to bury it. Quickly, he would return for another tail and dash off in a different direction to dig another shallow hole. This procedure was repeated until all of the several dozen beaver tails had been secreted in spots known only to Dusty.

The dog was hiding his newly acquired groceries for future meals, but I never did observe him actually eating any of the tails. He was too busy guarding his hoard to think about consuming any part of it. For the rest of the summer, whenever anyone walked toward the bush fringing our yard, Dusty assumed that some of his property was about to be stolen. He would dash ahead to one of his caches and dig up a beaver tail. Then he would take it to some other location and rebury it. The task of protecting his treasures kept him quite busy. In the end, I suspect that the little creatures of the forest consumed more of the meat than did the dog.

Dusty, having been removed from the bosom of his canine family at a very tender age and apparently having no recollection of them, probably thought that he was the only dog in the world. He had never seen another of his own kind during the first year of his life in Prince Albert National Park. Then, one day in the middle of the spring breakup, a trapper came out of the bush from his trap line outside of the park somewhere to the northwest of Boundary Cabin. As a courtesy, he came up to the house to advise me that he would be traveling south on the park road. He was driving a team of horses pulling a wagon. Trailing behind the wagon, and attached to it by a long rope leash, was a dog—another dog!

Dusty came to attention. His ears pricked up and his hackles raised, not in anger but in excitement. He couldn't believe his senses. Here was another one of the canine clan! He was no longer the only dog in the world! In celebration, he zipped around the house at a tremendous speed, slowing a bit as he skidded at the corners. After several rounds, he changed gears and began prancing and dancing around the yard like an antelope, four stiff legs acting somehow as springs, rebounding him straight back into the air after each successive landing. Then he engaged in other, most undogly, acrobatics too weird to be described, almost like somersaults or cartwheels. This was followed by a session of mighty leaps, back and forth over the wagon and over the trapper's dog. The latter stood there with a puzzled look on its face, trying to figure out what all of the commotion was about. What an exhibition! Mary and I, and the trapper, had never witnessed anything like it. Finally, before Dusty wore himself to a frazzle, I called Billy to catch him and chain him up. That objective, usually no problem at all, was this time only achieved with difficulty.

After taking on a load of Mary's coffee and cake the trapper climbed aboard his wagon, jiggled the reins at the horses to get them moving again, and continued on his southward journey. Dusty made a big fuss as the group disappeared down the road. He didn't want to lose touch with his new-found relative. He began leaping to the length of his chain. After more than an hour of this treatment, the chain yielded from the stress and away went the dog, speeding down the road in the wake of the trapper. I couldn't hop in my vehicle to go after him because of the condition of the road—passable to a team and wagon but not to a truck. There was no point in attempting pursuit with Dolly and Jolly, my slow old plow horses. I just hoped that the trapper would catch Dusty when he arrived at the wagon, and keep him tied up until I could reclaim him at some later date.

In fact, that is more or less what happened, but not until Dusty added an undesirable flourish to his escapade. He caught up to the trapper several miles down the road. The trapper tried to make him head back home by shouting and throwing rocks at him, but finally gave it up as a bad job, allowing Dusty to trail along behind his outfit while they continued on their way. Now, about eight miles along from our cabin and just west of the park boundary, a homesteader maintained a small flock of sheep. Several of these animals happened to be near the road as the trapper and his entourage passed by. Once again, Dusty's ears pricked up and he dashed over to the sheep to see what they might be. Apparently the dog decided that what they might be was prey—and he was the predator. The trapper said that Dusty grabbed the first sheep by the neck and crunched his jaws together, killing it with one bite.

The trapper managed to capture Dusty before he had time to go after the next sheep in line. He chained the dog up to his wagon and then examined the dead sheep. There were no obvious marks on it to indicate that it had been killed by the dog. There was no love lost between the trapper and the homesteader, so he had no qualms about what he did next. He shoved the carcass into the nearby Sturgeon River to make it appear that the animal had drowned, thus relieving Dusty (and his owner) of the possibility of being blamed for the death. Then he took Dusty home with him, to return the dog to us after the condition of the roads improved sufficiently for the use of motor vehicles.

When Dusty got back home, I decided that he would have to be permanently restrained somehow. I couldn't just keep him chained up with his short chain because he wouldn't get any exercise. Besides, if he broke the chain again, he could get down the trail faster than I could drive my truck over it, even at the best of times. There weren't sufficient materials lying around to build a proper fenced-in run for him so I decided on the next best thing. I strung some old telephone wire of very heavy gauge between two trees about seventy feet apart and hooked Dusty's chain to it in such a manner that he could chase freely back and forth along the length of the wire.

This telephone wire run seemed to work well, at least for a while, but the dog was developing an escape plan. One day Dusty began to race full speed ahead from one end of the run to the other. When his chain came to an abrupt halt at either end of the wire his momentum would carry him off his feet. For a brief instant Dusty would be suspended in the air, straight out from the end of his chain, like a scene from some comic strip. There was enough elasticity in the system to absorb the sudden shocks so that neither the dog's neck, nor his chain, were broken by this action. For several days he got his exercise this way. Then suddenly he was gone again. The constant stress on the wire had gradually stretched it slightly at one spot, reducing its diameter until it became thin enough to yield after one final hard jolt.

I got in my truck and roared off down the trail to the sheep farm. Too late! Dusty had struck again. I met the exceedingly irate farmer at the gate to his property. The dog had gotten in among his sheep but had not managed to kill any on this occasion. Two of the sheep had been bitten slightly before the farmer was able to capture the outlaw. Had a gun been handy, the farmer said, he would have shot the dog on the spot. And, I had to agree, he would have been within his rights to do so. I thanked my lucky stars that the damage assessment was so slight, swallowed my pride and begged forgiveness for the dog (and owner). It took a while, but the farmer eventually agreed to return the dog on the promise that he would be kept securely tied from then on.

We tried our best to keep Dusty happy at home, but he'd had a taste of a wider world and its offerings and wasn't willing to pass them by. He was too much of a free spirit to keep chained or penned. We looked for ways, unsuccessfully, to somehow break him of the habit of traveling away from home. We tried to find another home for him with settlers living outside the park, but no one wanted a renegade with a predilection for chasing sheep and other farm animals. Eventually, to everyone's great regret, Dusty had to be destroyed. It was a sad day for the whole family.

End of an Epoch

L ife in Prince Albert National Park was always interesting, and occasionally exciting, but it had its problems too. Not the least of these was the fact that the road south from Boundary Cabin was sometimes impassable. It was actually a trail through the bush in those days, but we called it a road, often prefaced by a few choice adjectives.

Not only were we isolated for nearly a month during the spring breakup, but also for several days at a time in the summer when heavy rains made parts of the road as slippery as a skating rink. On a few occasions we started out for the "big city"—Prince Albert—for our monthly grocery shopping excursion, only to end up stuck in a ditch or a mudhole before arriving at the paved road outside of the park boundary. Then it was out with the shovel, the ax, the jack, the tire chains and whatever else it took to attack the problem. Usually it required an hours-long struggle to get the truck back on solid ground, making it too late to do anything but turn homeward again. To add insult to injury, much of the road surface had often dried out by the time the truck was extricated from its predicament.

Our road was often impassable in winter, too, when heavy snowfalls or blowing winds clogged the road with deep drifts. Snowplows, usually traveling in pairs for safety, made several trips each winter to our cabin, throwing up hard banks of snow on each side of the road, freeing us temporarily from our isolation. The snow banks became higher with each passage of the plows and the trough between them became narrower. To negotiate a few tight curves in the road, it was sometimes necessary to carom my truck off the banks, like a ball bouncing off a cushion on a billiard table.

On one memorable winter day, the day before Christmas, I started out early on a drive to our post office at Park Valley to pick up the mail-order parcels that we hoped had arrived there. If they hadn't then we were in trouble—they contained the children's gifts from Santa Claus. The distance from our cabin to the post office was about twenty-five miles, mostly along bush trails but partly across a windswept prairie.

I left home in my truck shortly after seven o'clock in the morning. The road was in good shape to begin with, at least for a winter road, and I reached the Sturgeon Crossing warden station by nine o'clock, having had to shovel my way through a few snow drifts on the open prairie. Cliff Millard then informed me that the road to Park Valley was impassable to motor vehicles. However, a settler just across the river was hitching his horses to a sleigh to undertake the trip and I was invited to go along.

It looked like a good day for a journey behind the horses. The sun was shining brightly in a tranquil blue sky so I accepted the invitation. Aside from the slow mode of travel, no problems were encountered along the way. Thankfully, all our expected parcels had made it to the post office. Now nothing was lacking for a joyous Christmas morning.

By late afternoon, with the weather deteriorating, I was back at Sturgeon Crossing with the booty. The wind was rising and the sky was turning gray. Small frosty flakes were dashing erratically about, precursors of another fall of snow. After thanking the settler for his assistance, I loaded the parcels into the back of my vehicle and covered them with a canvas tarpaulin. Ethel Millard had an early supper ready and invited me to partake of it before starting on the return trip to Boundary Cabin.

It was six o'clock, and dark and cold and windy, as I pointed my truck north. The weather had changed drastically in the past hour. A howling blizzard was underway. I had difficulty seeing out of the windshield against the glare of the headlights reflected back from the swirling snow. I drove partly by the feel of the truck traveling in the old ruts left over from my passage south earlier in the day. With the aid of chains on the tires, I plowed my way through the new accumulations of snow. It was slow going and I was glad that I'd had supper with the Millards instead of waiting until I got back home.

275

Soon I began to encounter large drifts, some of them with a surface already packed hard by the wind. I floored the gas pedal and charged at these barriers, hoping for sufficient momentum to crash through to the other side. Often the truck ended up high-centered on frozen crusts, wheels no longer in contact with the road, spinning uselessly in the air. Then it was a matter of shoveling the mound from under the truck until the tires made contact with solid ground again, backing up for several yards, and taking another run at the obstacle. Usually the whole process had to be repeated several times in succession. Some drifts were so wide that I despaired of an end to them.

Eventually, though, I found myself crossing the bridge which marked the beginning of my district. Now I was back among tall trees which sheltered the road from the wind, where I had only to drive carefully through deep soft snow. No more hard charging at drifts and no more shoveling. After a time I spotted the welcome light from the windows of Boundary Cabin. It lacked a few minutes of midnight as I climbed wearily from the truck cab and hauled the parcels into the house. Mary was waiting up for me but the children were sound asleep in their beds.

I would have liked to have fallen into bed too, but first some of Santa's gifts had to be assembled into their final form. Where were the elves when they were needed? Fortunately none of the toys required batteries—I wasn't inclined to make another trip to the store for quite a while. Early the next morning, the children awoke to find that Daddy had come safely home and that Santa Claus had been able to make his annual visit despite the stormy weather.

Worrisome times sometimes coincided with impassable roads. Once, when no vehicles could come to our assistance, we had a chimney fire which threatened to burn the house down. As a safety measure, I made a practice of cleaning our chimney frequently to rid it of flammable creosote and other products of combustion, the inevitable consequence of burning wood. Obviously, in the present instance, the flue should have been cleaned a little sooner, but that wasn't the main problem.

Someone had incorrectly installed the insulating collar through which the kitchen stovepipe was attached to the main chimney, allowing any large flames in the chimney to come into contact with combustible material in the kitchen wall.

The first sign of trouble was a great roaring noise. After puzzling over the sound for a moment, I realized what it was. The creosote in the chimney was burning. Immediately, I dashed down to our dugout basement, where we had a floor furnace made of two forty-five-gallon drums welded together, and threw some baking soda on the flames in the firebox. This produced a gas which robbed the burning residue in the chimney of oxygen, extinguishing that part of the fire. Then I dashed outside to make certain that no hot particles had ignited the roof.

While I was doing this, Mary was on the telephone to Sturgeon Crossing Cabin, advising them of the problem and indicating that we would phone back within fifteen minutes. If there was no word from us by then, they were requested to get a rescue party started in our direction because we would be without food and shelter—not to mention the lack of heat after the ashes of the house cooled down.

Everything seemed under control until I reentered the kitchen. Then I could hear a crackling sound coming from within the wall by the chimney. In desperation, I ripped the wallboard from the studs and found the source of the noise. The interior framework was on fire! The contents of our water bucket, thrown carefully at the blaze with a dipper, soon extinguished the flames. Exposing the interior of the wall also revealed the faulty installation of the collar. Feeling safe once again, Mary phoned to call off the alert. From then on I cleaned the chimney more often than necessary, but it gave us peace of mind.

Another exciting moment occurred just after the road had been cleared of snow. The plow operators had stopped in for some coffee and some of Mary's famous cake and cookies. In fact, they ate the last of the cookies so, later that day, Mary started washing out the large glass cookie jar. Suddenly a crack propagated around the side of the vessel near the bottom and the lower portion fell into the dishpan. In a startled move to withdraw her arm from within the jar, Mary accidentally slashed her wrist on one of the jagged glass sides. She called the children from their play in the living room and sent them outside to find me.

Luckily, I was doing some work around the yard and not off hiking through the bush. I rushed in to find Mary bleeding profusely from the cut. We stemmed the flow of blood with difficulty and bandaged the wound. By now, we assumed, the snowplows would have the road opened all the way to the park boundary, but it was too late in the day to find any medical assistance within a reasonable traveling distance. We decided to wait for morning before leaving home, and spent a wakeful night from worry that the bleeding might begin anew.

All went well, fortunately, and the next day we set off for Prince Albert to get Mary stitched up. Along the way, we had one of the wardens phone in to the medical clinic to alert them for our arrival. What transpired during the phone call I don't know but, when we got to the clinic, Mary was ushered promptly into a doctor's office. The doctor began by asking some leading questions about Mary's feelings concerning life in the bush. It soon developed that he thought he had a stressed-out patient with suicidal tendencies. When the mix-up was straightened out, Mary got her wound stitched up and bandaged properly, ending our worries. For a while she had to endure joking remarks about people going "bushed" and slashing their wrists to get away from it all.

The summer before we left Boundary Cabin, a complete reconstruction of the road was begun, including rebuilding the roadbed, installing proper ditches and bridges, and graveling the surface. This turned it into an all-weather road for most of the year. The only remaining problem was caused by the drifting snows of winter, so the plows still had to make their sporadic rounds.

Years after we departed the park the wardens were moved into Waskesiu. They then had to patrol their districts by daily traveling out from this central point, a relatively inefficient operation allowing greater scope for illegal activities to go undetected on the remote west side of the park. The relocation of the wardens also meant that they could no longer indulge in that time-honored practice known as an "armchair" patrol. This requires a word of explanation. Wardens were required to submit a diary each month, showing in some detail exactly what they had done each day. Wardens also had no fixed working hours then, being required to put in whatever time was necessary for the job at hand, without any recompense in the way of extra pay or days off. Sometimes in the summer we worked twelve- or fourteen-hour days and seven-day weeks.

Thus, to get a little respite from time to time—on a rainy day, perhaps—a warden might sit in his easy chair at home and imagine, as he wrote in his diary, that he was making a patrol into the dense bush in the interior of the park, on the lookout for poachers. Or he might conjure up an image of himself giving all the fire-warning signs in his district an extra coat of paint. No one ever had a twinge of conscience about this practice, because every warden always did much more work than that represented by the wages he was paid.

Our son Ronald was still beset with medical problems and, on occasion, had to go to the hospital in Edmonton for further treatment. This required a trip to Prince Albert by truck, with the remainder of the journey made by rail, much less costly for us than the airline flight from Fort Resolution. Happily, the trips were never hindered by road problems, although once Mary and the children had to walk over an impassible section and transfer to another vehicle on the other side of the bad stretch. We were fortunate to have a very knowledgeable physician, Dr. Grisdale, handling the case. He was also sympathetic and understanding and, in more than one instance, declined to present bills for his services when he thought that they would stretch our financial resources. (Government-financed medical care was still in the future.)

As the children approached school age, another difficulty loomed on the horizon. They had to be taught at home through the medium of correspondence courses. Mary needed to find time to be a school teacher in addition to all of her other chores. The first candidate to be inducted into Grade One was Billy. He didn't enter

279

the educational arena willingly. Why should he have to sit at the kitchen table, surrounded by paper and pencil and books, when his younger brothers were still playing outside in the yard? No amount of explanation sufficed, and many battles ensued. The thought of two more classmates joining the fray in the coming years didn't thrill Mary, especially since the students would all be in different grades.

I was happy in my own work but, perhaps, out of consideration for the other family members, a return to city living might have to be contemplated. The prospect of finding a new occupation didn't appeal to me in the least, and it could mean the end of the outdoor life. After much reflection I enrolled in a correspondence course in aeronautical engineering and settled down to some hard studying. I had always been interested in aviation but, before I could get to the good stuff about airplane design, I had to endure months, and even years, of learning calculus, strength of materials, physics and related subjects. I began churning through the lessons, mailing each completed one to Toronto to be marked and returned.

I was engaged in these studies one evening when a car pulled up to our cabin. It contained a young itinerant preacher who had taken a wrong turn in the road, and was now uncertain as to his exact whereabouts. He was invited in for coffee and cake while we provided directions to his destination. After noting that I was working on a correspondence course in engineering, he made the casual suggestion that I should consider going to university.

The idea took me by surprise. Me go to university? Me, who didn't have the least idea about what was entailed in attending a so-called institute of higher learning? Then, "Why not?" I thought. Attendance at a university would shorten the learning period compared to the home-study lessons, and the credentials obtained would be more respectable. But what about money, and a lot of other things? My head was whirling in excitement. Was the preacher's visit going to be our salvation, or was it the work of the devil?

We gave much thought, over the next few days, to the suggestion of university attendance and how it might be managed.

We could sell off some of our belongings to raise funds—our furniture, our lovely moosehide jackets, my guns and fishing tackle and books. We could move to Vancouver Island again, where Mary might get some part-time employment in her sister's store. I wrote to the University of British Columbia to determine their admission requirements and received a very encouraging letter from the registrar indicating that I could be admitted as a mature student.

I resigned my position as park warden, effective in the spring of the approaching new year. We sold most of our household effects and personal belongings, realizing almost enough money to pay for a year at university. Then we left Saskatchewan and headed for British Columbia. The saga of *Snowshoes and Sledges* was at an end and another adventure was beginning. There were new worlds to conquer.

Epilogue

Rather abruptly, with our departure from Prince Albert National Park, my career as a warden was over and done with. It had seemed more like a vacation than a vocation. A different goal challenged me now, with a new pinnacle of personal achievement awaiting.

Returning to Vancouver Island, we first turned our attention to the rehabilitation of our children. Having been raised in the bosom of Nature, they now had to be instructed in the conventions of civilization—they were introduced into the school system, a jurisdiction they accepted in vast preference to being taught at home by Mother; they were informed about crossing roads and about avoiding strange dogs and people; finally, they were taught that it was not fashionable to relieve themselves on the street wherever and whenever the need arose, as they had done when living in the bush.

I thought the boys had assimilated the lessons well. Then one day I took them shopping at a department store in downtown Nanaimo. A need to find a toilet being indicated, I led the way to the men's restroom with the boys in trail behind me. Just as I put a hand on the restroom door to push it open, I heard a faint voice in the distance calling, "Hey, Dad, here it is." I turned around to find that Dick, the youngest, was missing.

Immediately I realized what had happened. Walking in single file through the crowd, we had passed through a replica bathroom display. I dashed quickly back. Sure enough, there was Dick in the mock-up bathroom, standing in front of the shiny new toilet bowl. The lid was raised and his zipper was lowered. His hands were fumbling around in the front of his pants. Shoppers were standing around the display in amused anticipation. The delight on their features turned to disappointment as I snatched the lad away just in the nick of time!

❖

I registered for the fall session of the engineering physics program at the University of British Columbia in Vancouver and then, to fill in the intervening months, found employment as a surveyor with BC Engineering (the technical arm of BC Electric—the predecessor of BC Hydro).

How quickly the summer passed. I was nervous at the prospect of becoming a full-time student and had some second thoughts about the whole endeavor. What if I flunked out some-where along the way? Was it fair to my family to deprive them of the things they could have if I stayed on with BC Engineering as a permanent employee? But I knew that the survey work would once again keep me away from home for long periods and none of us wanted that to go on forever. The decision was inescapable. Buckle down to the books for four long years. Then a new phase of our life would begin.

It was a tough struggle but I stuck with it. I have always believed that the more one learns, the more interesting the world becomes, and this conviction was reinforced during my time at UBC. Unlike my high school days, I now had the motivation to study. In fact, my grades in the first year were high enough to place me on the Dean's Honor List, an accomplishment which made it easier to obtain scholarships, bursaries and student loans in succeeding years. Eventually the studies—and the worrisome examinations—were over and done with, and Mary and the chil-dren were able to look on proudly as I went through the gradua-tion ceremony. Together we had reached our goal.

There still remained the long process of clearing off our accumulated financial obligations. Mary and I didn't wait to be out of debt, however, before deciding that we would like to have a daughter or two in our family along with our three sons. The boys were amenable to the suggestion so, through adoption, Nancy Dianne came to us at the age of seven months, followed three years later by six-week-old Rosanne Louise. Now, all of the children are grown and gone from home, making their own way in life and eventually, perhaps, having their own story to tell.

❖

My days in the North are long past and much has happened in the interim, and yet...it was only yesterday. I still experience the *Snowshoes and Sledges* syndrome from time to time. But I have come to realize that the strains and exertions of such a life are beyond me now. My spirit might be willing but my worn-out body parts would exercise their veto power. On the other hand, were I a warden today, life would be somewhat easier than it used to be. I would certainly be driving a speedy snowmobile of some description instead of a comparatively slow dog team. I don't think I would care much for it, though. The companionship of the dogs on the trail would be lacking, a benefit which no machine can replace.

I remember my dog-sledding days with great fondness and can still conjure up in my mind the image of past trips along the lake marge, my way illuminated by the auroral glow. The soft huffing of the dogs as they pull in the traces mingles with the swishing of the toboggan moving over the hard-packed snow. I can hear the rhythmic padding of my own footfalls as I trot along behind. The only other sounds are the occasional creaks of toboggan joints and, once in a long while, a low complaining rumble from the lake ice, perhaps more felt than heard, as the frozen bulk accommodates itself to unseen forces.

I have a feeling of euphoria, of being able to run on forever. But the dogs have traveled far today and there is some distance yet to go before we reach our destination. I stop them for a welcome rest. The aurora borealis provides a magnificent display to entertain us as we wait, shimmering and sweeping from horizon to zenith, an ever-changing awesome spectacle. Soon we are on our way again, putting more miles behind us on a trip that both the dogs and I have greatly enjoyed. Such are the good memories of a challenging way of life. I hope my dogs are running yet, somewhere in the mists beyond the Northern Lights.

MORE GREAT HANCOCK HOUSE TITLES

History

Cariboo Gold Rush Story
Donald Waite
ISBN 0-88839-202-8

The Craigmont Story
Murphy Shewchuck
ISBN 0-88839-980-4

Curse of Gold
Elizabeth Hawkins
ISBN 0-88839-281-8

Early History of Port Moody
Dorathea M. Norton
ISBN 0-88839-197-8

End of Custer
Dale T. Schoenberger
ISBN 0-88839-288-5

Exploring the Outdoors
Eberts & Grass
ISBN 0-88839-989-8

Guide to Gold Panning
Bill Barlee
ISBN 0-88839-986-3

Guide to Similkameen Treasure
Bill Barlee
ISBN 0-88839-990-1

Gold Creeks & Ghost Towns
Bill Barlee
ISBN 0-88839-988-X

Gold! Gold!
Joseph Petralia
ISBN 0-88839-118-8

Logging in B.C.
Ed Gould
ISBN 0-919654-44-4

Lost Mines and Historic Treasures
Bill Barlee
ISBN 0-88839-992-8

The Mackenzie Yesterday
Alfred Aquilina
ISBN 0-88839-083-1

Pacific Northwest History
Edward Nuffield
ISBN 0-88839-271-0

Pioneering Aviation of the West
Lloyd M. Bungey
ISBN 0-88839-271-0

Yukon Places & Names
R. Coutts
ISBN 0-88839-082-2

Northern Biographies

Alaska Calls
Virginia Neely
ISBN 0-88839-970-7

Bootlegger's Lady
Sager & Frye
ISBN 0-88839-976-6

Bush Flying
Robert Grant
ISBN 0-88839-350-4

Chilcotin Diary
Will D. Jenkins Sr.
ISBN 0-88839-409-8

Crazy Cooks and Gold Miners
Joyce Yardley
ISBN 0-88839-294-X

MORE GREAT HANCOCK HOUSE TITLES

Descent into Madness
Vernon Frolick
ISBN 0-88839-300-8

Fogswamp: Life with Swans
Turner & McVeigh
ISBN 0-88839-104-8

Gang Ranch: Real Story
Judy Alsager
ISBN 0-88839-275-3

Journal of Country Lawyer
Ted Burton
ISBN 0-88839-364-4

Lady Rancher
Gertrude Roger
ISBN 0-88839-099-8

Ralph Edwards
Ed Gould
ISBN 0-88839-100-5

Ruffles on my Longjohns
Isabel Edwards
ISBN 0-88839-102-1

Where Mountains Touch Heaven
Ena Kingsnorth Powell
ISBN 0-88839-365-2

Wings of the North
Dick Turner
ISBN 0-88839-060-2

Yukon Lady
Hugh McLean
ISBN 0-88839-186-2

Yukoners
Harry Gordon-Cooper
ISBN 0-88839-232-X

Outdoor Titles

12 Basic Skills of Flyfishing
Ted Peck & Ed Rychkun
ISBN 0-88839-392-X

Adventure with Eagles
David Hancock
ISBN 0-88839-217-6

Alpine Wildflowers
Ted Underhill
ISBN 0-88839-975-8

Birds of North America
David Hancock
ISBN 0-88839-220-6

Eastern Mushrooms
Barrie Kavasch
ISBN 0-88839-091-2

Guide to Collecting Wild Herbs
Julie Gomez
ISBN 0-88839-390-3

Northeastern Wild Edibles
Barrie Kavasch
ISBN 0-88839-090-4

Orchids of North America
Dr. William Petrie
ISBN 0-88839-089-0

Roadside Wildflowers NW
Ted Underhill
ISBN 0-88839-108-0

Sagebrush Wildflowers
Ted Underhill
ISBN 0-88839-171-4

Tidepool & Reef
Rick Harbo
ISBN 0-88839-039-4

MORE GREAT HANCOCK HOUSE TITLES

Native Titles

Ah Mo
Tren J. Griffin
ISBN 0-88839-244-3

American Indian Pottery
Sharon Wirt
ISBN 0-88839-134-X

Argillite
Drew & Wilson
ISBN 0-88839-037-8

Art of the Totem
Marius Barbeau
ISBN 0-88839-168-4

Coast Salish
Reg Ashwell
ISBN 0-88839-009-2

End of Custer
Dale Schoenberger
ISBN 0-88839-288-5

Haida: Their Art and Culture
Leslie Drew
ISBN 0-88839-132-3

Hunters of the Buffalo
R. Stephen Irwin
ISBN 0-88839-176-5

Hunters of the Forest
R. Stephen Irwin
ISBN 0-88839-175-7

Hunters of the Ice
R. Stephen Irwin
ISBN 0-88839-179-X

Hunters of the Sea
R. Stephen Irwin
ISBN 0-88839-177-3

Indian Artifacts of the N.E.
Roger Moeller
ISBN 0-88839-127-7

Indian Art & Culture
Kew & Goddard
ISBN 0-919654-13-4

Indian Healing
Wolfgang G. Jilek, M.D.
ISBN 0-88839-120-X

Indian Herbs
Dr. Raymond Stark
ISBN 0-88839-077-7

Indian Tribes of N.W.
Reg Ashwell
ISBN 0-919654-53-3

Indians of the N.W. Coast
D. Allen
ISBN 0-919654-82-7

Iroquois: Their Art & Crafts
Carrie A. Lyford
ISBN 0-88839-135-8

Kwakiutl Art & Culture
Reg Ashwell
ISBN 0-88839-325-3

My Heart Soars
Chief Dan George
ISBN 0-88839-231-1

My Spirit Soars
Chief Dan George
ISBN 0-88839-233-8

Tlingit: Art, Culture & Legends
Dan & Nan Kaiper
ISBN 0-88839-010-6